The National Purple Heart Hall
New Windsor Cantonment State Historic Site
P.O. Box 207
Vails Gate, NY 12584-0207

SUNFLOWER WILD

by

George Joseph Brooks

George J Brooks

Dedicated to all Purple Heart women and men

FIRST EDITION

Copyright 1993, by George Joseph Brooks
Library of Congress Catalog Card No: 93-93783
ISBN: 1-56002-318-X

AEGINA PRESS, Inc.
59 Oak Lane, Spring Valley
Huntington, West Virginia 25704

Copyright 1993, by George Joseph Brooks
Library of Congress Catalog Card No: 93-93783
ISBN: 1-56002-318-X

Dedication

I dedicate this book to all the men and gals, friend and foe, who took a fighter aircraft into the skies for combat and especially those who fell and did not rise again.

Chapter One

Childhood

My place of birth was Salina, Kansas, February 14, 1924, at home, a product of the union of Samuel Remington Brooks and Agnes Veronica Spacek. My Dad was of English, Scotch, and Irish decent, Mom is of Czech decent. Dad's occupation was with the Union Pacific railroad as a section foreman. My first remembrance of early life was at New Cambria, Kansas, a few miles east of Salina, Kansas. I was three at the time, the boy next door was about six and had an unusual wagon, instead of the tongue that one pulled the wagon with and folded same back over the front end of the wagon box to guide with when one put a bent leg into the wagon and pushed with the other leg, this boy had a bent rod that came up through the wagon bottom and was affixed to the front wheels that he steered with the bent rod, an innovation even by today's standards. Next town was Belvue, Kansas, about a hundred miles west of Kansas City, Kansas, a population of perhaps 100 people. Our first home was the yellow railroad house provided for the section foreman. I was five at this time with a little sister by the name of Dorothy Mae, a year younger than I. Our next door neighbors were the John Cook family of about six kids. John had worked on Dad's section gang, but was bumped off by another man with more seniority, no job and that big family. I remember one time I was over at their house at dusk after I had finished my supper at home, all they had for supper was bread and gravy, but they made do and Mrs. Cook was always cheerful and jovial. John picked up odd jobs and caught cat fish somewhat illegally for sale. Their oldest kid was named William, but was nick-named Buddy, he was a couple years older than I, but was mentally deficient. I sort of looked out for him when we started school because he needed help badly, school was a waste of time for him. Buddy had a little sister a year younger than I by the name of Alberta. Alberta and Dorothy played together a lot. One evening after supper in the summer time I went over to the Cook's front gate to pass a little time with them and there was Alberta with a new pair of anklet stockings, she was very proud of them and showed them to me, I allowed they were nice and promptly whipped out my peter and pissed all over them, the dust puffing up between her ankles as I hosed from one anklet to the other. Alberta was so dismayed at my gross act that she didn't react until I had buttoned up and damn well fled for home. No sooner had I gotten home, here come Alberta and her mother. I was made to apologize and when they left I had a new ass built for me. The trains came by within a hundred feet of our front door. One train every day stopped at the station while west-bound, the depot station was a block east of our house and the train didn't have too much speed by the time it reached our front yard and I would race it as far as my yard ran. Most times I would beat it and sometimes the engineer would give me a little shot of steam as he passed me. Before we moved to Belvue, I remember living in Wamego, five miles west of Belvue. We lived on a hill two blocks north of the railroad, it was here that I was given a tricycle. On nice days, Mom would let me go to meet Dad after work. At first I would descend the hill with back pressure on the trike pedals so as to not pick up too much speed, as the days went by, I became more proficient and went down a little faster. One day at the top of the hill, I lifted my feet clear of the pedals and headed down the hill, one helluva ride until I hit some uneven sidewalk and collided with a telephone or light pole. I remember seeing stars then a long sleep. Dad picked me up on his way home from work and carried me home, I woke up none worse for the wear. I never rode a tricycle after that or owned one. My Uncle Joe Spacek, a dwarf, used to come visit us every now and then at Wamego. At this time we owned a Model-T-Ford and Uncle Joe could drive it. I used to sit in the front seat with him and was amazed at how he could reach the three pedals on the floor boards and work the spark and gas levers on the steering post. One day, Dad loaned the Model-T to Uncle Joe to go down-town Wamego with Dorothy and I as company. He gave Dorothy and I a nickel for candy, Uncle Joe went in the beer joint, he came out half an hour or so later damn well inebriated. He had one helluva time cranking that Model-T, but start it he did and headed up the three or four blocks from home. Uncle Joe wasn't going too fast, but he was very erratic, one side of the street to the other and those short legs working the hell out of those floor-board pedals. We approached our house where Uncle Joe skidded into our driveway and braked to a shuddering stop, Dad was home from work and allowed Uncle Joe wouldn't drive that car again. Another time at Wamego while we were all at the breakfast table Dad asked Uncle Joe if he would go to the basement during the day and sprout some potatoes. Uncle Joe indicated a willingness to help and that afternoon after dinner went to the potato bin in the basement to sprout potatoes. When Dad arrived home from work, he inquired of Mom as to where Uncle Joe was, Mom replied, "in the basement." Dad descended the basement stairs rather fast and found Uncle Joe lying under the spigot of the wine barrel, he couldn't get up, but he could raise that short arm and small hand to manipulate the spigot a fraction to allow a trickle of wine to enter his mouth. Dad got him up the stairs and with some supper and a lot of coffee in him, he was in decent shape by bed-time. While at Belvue living in the yellow rail-road house, Dad raised two pigs that were butchered during early winter, I remember him feeding them coal to prevent them from getting intestinal worms. Before they attained one-third of their maturity, they were to be castrated, John Cook, our neighbor to the west came over to assist Dad. I watched from the top of the hog shed as Dad and John cut their testicles out and poured kerosene in the cut to prevent infection. John Cook felt fortunate to have those hog nuts for supper for his family. We moved from the rail-road house to a small house a block away to the west end of town along the highway. Here I entered my formal education, first grade, I pissed my pants the first day, but readily fell into the routine after this incident. I made a good friend by the name of Eddie Weeks, who lived across the street south of the school- yard. Eddie's Dad was the post-master of Belvue and did some farming also to support a large family. Eddie's job was to feed the livestock and harness the horses for the field when his Dad needed them, at times I used to help him when I was visiting him, perhaps you can imagine two six year old boys harnessing a team of big horses, the harnesses were heavy and had to be slung over the horse so that all the various straps could be snapped to their correct places, Eddie had it down pat. Eddie and I were a pair to behold, he in his coveralls with his tousled curly hair, I in overalls with wire-brush hair straight down my fore-head. We were of the opinion that the world was our oyster. At the post office Eddie and I put on wrestling matches of short duration for his Dad and the two rural mail carriers, our wins were even and a couple of nickels were given to us, at the instant one of us showed signs of losing our temper, the match was halted. At this time my little sister Marcia was born into our family, a nice even tempered little girl. Our Grandpa and Grandma Brooks lived next door east of our home, we were always welcome there. Grandma baked their bread and made jelly and preserves on her wood burning kitchen range. Grandma was also hearing impaired, but used no aid as they weren't available in the early thirties. Grandpa ran a second-hand store, I spent many an afternoon there looking at things I couldn't identify then, but now days I know them as antiques. He also purchased cream from the farmers. A small lot between Grandpa's store and the barber- shop next door provided the horse-shoe pits where many a good match was played, if I remember correctly Grandpa lost to Mr. Ramsey more than he won. Our first summer at our new home was a bad one for me for two or three weeks. I caught the whooping cough, when I could eat, I would start coughing and lose my meal. The attacks were so violent I would hang on the front yard fence and whoop it up. Folks told me later they thought they were going to lose me, they had lost three kids already. Later that summer a paving crew came by our front yard paving the highway, I remember the men, with their shovels moving the wet cement around, damned hard work and I doubt if they were making two-bits an hour. We lived on the north side of the highway and west of our home was a large alfalfa field with a lot of gophers. Dad asked me if I would like to trap them and make a little money, I was eager so he purchased five gopher traps and proceeded to show me how to dig into their burrow, set the trap and cover the burrow with a large tuft of grass and cover it with a little dirt. I caught a dozen or so, Dad cut them around the neck and pulled the skin off from the neck, salted them and strung them on a wire and hung them on a rafter in the garage. Damned if some damn cat didn't get in the garage and eat all of my gopher skins, there was a bounty of 10¢ a skin. There was one day I was running my trap line when I heard a two-winger airplane circling me with his engine missing badly. I watched and damned if he didn't disappear into a field across the tracks at the west end of my alfalfa field. I was told not to leave the alfalfa field, but that airplane had to be found and search I did, he had made an emergency landing a good half mile from me. There that bird was with the engine running smoothly now and one of the pilots looking at something in front of the airplane, he finally got in the front open cockpit, buckled up and took off to the west. This was the first airplane I had ever seen on the ground and up close, someday I would fly like those guys. I soon realized that Dad was a line Sergeant in W.W.I. with four or five major battles he went over the top with his squad. I asked him once if he seen many airplanes, he said, "Son, I was too busy to look for airplanes." He just didn't relate many of his experiences to me except the bad food and living conditions. There was one time he had went over the top and was well into no-man's-land when an enemy machine gun opened up on him, he immediately ran for a near-by shell hole and threw himself into it full tilt and hit another soldier already in it, the other soldier was knocked unconscious, but revived after some minutes. Dad told me he thought he had killed him. Another time his company had advanced into a forest and were ordered to dig in for the night, the next day, the Germans took them under artillery fire for two or three hours, Dad told me after the barrage was lifted he raised up, there was no more forest around them, just shattered trees lying on the ground. While going to school, I also met the Casto boys who lived a quarter mile east of Belvue, I used to go out there and jack around with them, they had a couple of good-looking older sisters that I enjoyed looking at. There was a drainage ditch near their house with water in it, we secured four or five railroad ties, laid them side by side, hammered some 2x4 boards across them and had a raft. We pushed it out into a large pool and slipped into the water while holding onto the raft, the water was well over our heads and no one knew how to swim. We managed to get close to the bank by kicking our feet, the two Casto boys were nearest the bank and jumped into the shallow water to pull the raft onto the bank while I was on the rear-end of the raft kicking my feet to assist them. They got a good hold of the raft and both gave a mighty pull and jerked the raft form my grasp, I immediately sank, all I could see was water, but my feet were on the bottom, so I merely used my hands like a fish uses his flippers and worked my way up from the bottom to where I could get my head out of the water. I immediately vowed to learn the act of swimming the first chance I got. Our grade school was two blocks east of our home, about mid-way was George Swank's automobile garage, Mr. Swank ran for the political office of County Sheriff and won and bought an airplane soon after. He was doing mechanical work on it at the garage, this was a must stop for me on my way home from school. I would pat it and was amazed that it was covered with fabric. Once a month on a Sunday we would get in the Model-T-Ford and travel to Emmett, Kansas to visit my Grandpa and Grandma Spacek and Uncle Joe, Emmett was eight miles north-east of Belvue by country roads. The Model-T had what you call a cut-out on the muffler, the cut-out was operated by a small handle on the floor-board between the driver and the front seat passenger. When the handle was down the engine was muffled, handle up and one could hear all the wonderful engine firing away. As we neared the edge of town I would ask Dad, "Can I pull her up, Dad?" Dad would reply, "Pull her up, George." Grandpa and Grandma Spacek were from Czechoslovakia, Grandpa from near the Austrian border and Grandma from near Prague, neither spoke English. Grandpa was a soldier in the Austrian army and saw combat action against the Turks during the late 1800's. He was a tall man of 6 foot and two or three inches, Grandma was an even five foot tall and both devout Catholics. They raised a family of thirteen kids. Grandma counseled me when I was a teenager by telling me, "You no lose one baby." Often times we would visit them and it would rain, the trip back to Belvue was an adventure, the roads were of a hard red clay and with a little shower were like driving on grease, I think to this day that Dad thoroughly enjoyed the challenge, as for myself, I damn near came unglued as he would slide from one side of the road to the other, the ditches looked six feet deep to me. If I yelled and cussed enough he would stop and put on the chains. The depression was bad in the early thirties and Dad was bumped from one section to another in the Kansas division. Fostoria, Marysville, Onaga and Natoma all in one year. We stayed at Natoma for one year, Natoma was located in western Kansas, well isolated and surrounded by hills and prairie. Our first home was a little white house on a hill next to the town water tower on the northern part of town. Our next door neighbors east was the Hoover family with two boys my age, we became good friends. Melvin, the oldest boy had a full sized bicycle and could ride it quite well. I had my own wagon of oak construction with side-boards, a beautiful toy to be sure, but I thought I was ready for a bicycle, hell, I was ten years old. Dad purchased a second hand one for me, full size, no fenders, wooden wheel rims, and a seat covered with a thick patent-leather material. Dad sent off for some new spokes plus a key to tighten or loosen the spokes to align the wooden wheels. It was a pretty good bike except the brakes were suspect, one had to put one's full weight on the pedal when reversing for decent breakage, also when going up a hill, one slid forward off the seat to apply more pressure and weight on the pedals, sometimes the mechanism in the rear axle would slip and wham, down on that damn bar my crotch would hit, after a few hits like that I christened the bike the 1934 NUT CRACKER. One trip to the store for Mom after a rain would put a helluva wobble in the wheels, rain and wooden rims weren't too compatible. Dad straightened them out for me a couple of times, after that it was up to me to do so. The wheels always wobbled, but they didn't quite hit the frame. A ten year old boy riding a full size bicycle will play havoc with over-alls, while cruising one sat on the seat and slid back and forth as you pedaled. First the seat bottom of the overalls turned a lighter color then to thinness and eventually you ass was hanging out. Mom patched many an overall seat for me, I looked like a baboon going down the street. A neighbor lady gave Mom a pair of knickers for me to wear, I hated those damn knickers that bloused just below your knees, sissy as hell, but riding my good ol' bike took care of them in short order and Mom with no like material to patch them. About this time my little brother Sammy made his appearance, I finally had a brother at last. I went to bed one night and the next morning I had a little brother. Dad and Mom's bedroom was next to mine and I didn't hear a thing, at ten years of age I knew how the keel was laid and where we came from, but Mom was an expert by now and was very quiet about it. For some time Mom wanted me to study the violin and there being a young lady music teacher available, a three-quarter size violin was ordered for me plus the bow and case with a handle from Montgomery Wards. I wasn't interested in music at that time, but my red-headed Mom prevailed with Dad's backing, so I reported to the music teacher once a week. Of course the instruction required the technique of holding the instrument, the grasping of the bow and the correct stroke across the strings. After a few lessons I could play a tune or two of the simple variety, an hour's practice a day was required or no biking nor play with my friends next door. While attending a lesson one week the teacher announced I would play for the high school assembly this week, Mom dressed me up in new waist pants, clean shirt and polished shoes and off I went. My teacher and I ascended the stage stairs to perform, she had to

10

tune my violin for me, I began to play from my sheet music and she accompanied on the piano with counter melodies and arpeggios, she made me sound great just playing that simple melody. She was much more than accomplished on the piano. Some of my friends got a hold of the fact that I was playing the violin, they were forever teasing me about catching cats so that I could use their guts for the violin strings. I couldn't let this teasing go on so I let go of the violin case one day while riding my bike home from a lesson, I told Mom what had happened and opened up the violin case, the violin had a damned nice crack in it. Mom prevailed again, the instrument was glued up by some one down town and lessons continued. I dropped the case again from my bicycle but Dad realized what I was doing, had the fractured violin repaired again and told me in stern council to cease and desist, you will study the violin as your Mother says. Half a block south of our home down the hill was the black smith shop run by Sy Miller, Sy had a Curtiss-Pusher airplane, a different bird than what I had previously seen, I stopped by everyday on the way home from school to gaze at it. The engine (radial) was aft of the high wing, the propeller swung just behind the rear cockpit. It had two open tandem cockpits, and was painted silver. A student pilot by the name of McFadden flew it a lot, but no one ever offered me a ride. During the time we lived in the house on the hill winter came around and a good snow storm rolled in. A block south of our home was a forty degree down slope hill that crossed another street. Dad purchased a second hand sled for me and to the hill I went, I laid belly down on the sled and proceeded down the hill, my first sled ride. As I approached the bottom of the hill and attempted to turn the sled onto the street situated ninety degrees to the sled route street, I got no response so I rolled off and let the sled go. The sled would go like hell but one couldn't guide it. I learned before the season was over to tip the sled to the left and effect a skidding controlled turn to the left and therefore going down the street at the bottom instead of across it. We moved to the south part of town four blocks away to a better house, when summer came so did the dust storms. As a matter of fact, the storms started before school was out for the summer. The dust would drift just like snow so Dad had to install snow fences along the railroad track in places susceptible to drifting. Dad came home from work one day with a dust mask issued by the Union Pacific Railroad, naturally I went out in the back yard, put it on, found a dust drift, stirred it up and the fifteen mile an hour wind did the rest The dust mask worked effectively, but my complexion was a bit darker than usual. I remember a few days later while playing in my front yard on a beautiful day with a clear azure blue sky above and a slight breeze from the north-west. For some reason I looked to the north-west and viewed a black-brown cloud against the sky rolling towards me. I went in the front door to tell Mom and then the day turned as like a moon-lit night with the moon obscured by a cloud. The dust would sift under and around the doors and windows, dust everywhere, even the food prepared by Mom was gritty with dust. Sammy was a small baby so Mom moved his crib into the kitchen, the smaller room, then hung wet sheets across the windows and doors, we even stuffed wet rags under the doors. All these sheets, towels, etc. had to be washed every day as they were literally black after a days use, these storms lasted three to four days. We visited both sets of Grandparents one week-end at Emmett and Belvue although Grandpa Spacek had died while we lived on the hill, quite an extensive trip even today with the good roads. We returned to Natoma Sunday evening and entering our home we discovered it had been violated, some one had used the bathroom stool without flushing it, urinated in the bath tub, but had done little else. It had been a neighbor boy who had been released from the reform school, I knew him slightly, he didn't seem to have a full deck. This really bugged Mom, so we moved to the west end of town five blocks away, the neighbor boy went back to the reform school. The flying of kites was an avid interest to me at this time. Dad purchased the first one for me at the cost of a nickel, but the cross sticks are easily broken and I had Dad saw some new ones almost every day for a while then I was told to do it myself. I soon became accomplished at sawing the very thin cross-sticks, notching the ends, tie the sticks in a cross, frame with string and cover with paper and flour glue. Our grocer was very helpful with wrapping paper. I got very adept at the flying and making of kites, the wind had to be just the right velocity. I got the idea of tying a small parachute about six or seven feet down the string below the kite by forming a small loop in the string, tying it off and hooking it to the small parachute which had a small wire hook attached to the middle of the canopy. I would get the kite well aloft, tie the string to a post, put my hand over the string and trot towards the kite, forcing it down, when I came to the loop I would hook the parachute on and release the string. The kite would soar aloft again, then back to the post where the string was tied, a small pull on the string then released and the parachute would fall free and float to the earth. A high school boy living in the east end of town five blocks away had made a box kite about six feet high, a small clothes line rope was used to fly it. He let me hold the rope for a while, I had to lean backwards so as not to be pulled off across the field. A Sunday afternoon's entertainment was cruising the country roads shooting jack-rabbits with a twenty-two caliber rifle from the car. Dad, the depot agent and I did this quite often, I became a good rifle shot. The jack-rabbits were not a nuisance, but a menace because they were so numerous, they ate all the green wheat in the spring time that the farmers had planted the previous fall. I attended many a jack-rabbit hunt with Dad, hundreds of people would report to some farm, from there we were dispersed around a section of land by truck, roughly a large square ringed by men and kids. No guns were allowed, only clubs, preferably a club one could throw. Everyone would start walking towards the other side of the square. After three or four hours of walking, killing the jack-rabbits that tried to get through the line a large circle was discernible, the middle was lousy with jack-rabbits. The circle was ever tightened killing rabbits with your club as you went, I was a bit squeamish about killing these wild animals with a club. The ground was literally covered with dead rabbits, the farmers loaded them in trucks, took them home and fed them to their hogs. Dad used to go uptown once in awhile to visit with the druggist, one night a dust storm rolled in while he was there, he started driving home, the visibility was so bad he took a chance, pulled over the curb in to a house's front yard, knocked on the front door and damned if it wasn't his home. I managed to acquire the mumps while at Natoma, I didn't feel too bad although I was swelled up on both sides of my throat, looked like a toad. The neighbor boy had a cave in his backyard, that is where Dad found me one evening after coming home from work, he told me about his experience with mumps back in 1917 when he was inducted into the army, the swelling went from his throat glands to his testicles. I stayed in until I was healed from the mumps after that council. Natoma became almost untenable by this time, so Dad bid a job at Linwood, Kansas, thirty-five miles west of Kansas City. This job called for maintenance of twelve miles of double track, trains were always coming and going. We rented a small crowded house north across the street from the grade school for a couple of months, then Dad purchased a large square house a block south of school south east of town. We had about four acres of land, all bottom soil in the Kaw Valley. The home stood on a bluff sloped down at a forty-five degree angle. The first thing Dad did was fence all the property in, half an acre garden north of the house, a triangle half acre at the foot of the bluff east of the house, another two and one half acres on east to a north south road, the other half acre the house set on plus a small amount of land south of us. When Dad put up a barbed wire fence of three strands it was put up to stay awhile as he was raised on a farm and worked on farms until he went into the army. The inside of the house was unfinished, no finish flooring and just lathing on the wall partitions, wood stove for cooking and heating, no water, but we did have electricity and an outside toilet plus the Sears and Roebuck catalogue. The pump well was at the foot of the bluff, I was the water boy. Dad also purchased a holstein cow, with four kids and my little brother Larry making his appearance. I didn't realize how much water it required to keep a baby in diapers, I quickly dubbed him as my shittin-assed brother. I remarked to my Aunt Dora Spacek who came down from north of Belvue to help Mom for a couple of weeks that I wished Mom and Dad wouldn't have so many kids. I even went so far as to ask Dad why so many kids, he replied that he and Mom didn't know how not to. I asked him about rubbers and he replied that was like washing your feet with your socks on. They did go see the town physician where Mom secured a diaphragm and that was the end to any new sisters and brothers. Bessie the cow had to have shelter so Dad built a small barn for her. There was a partial foundation for a small barn half way up the bluff, Dad fixed and built up this foundation and erected a barn on that, he milked her every morning and evening, my job was to keep her in water by pumping the water into an old washing machine tub of wood slat construction, Bessie could empty that barrel faster than I could pump, but I had orders to keep the barrel full at all times. I entered the sixth grade at Linwood where I met many new friends. The Ellard boys, Tom, Buck, and Skeeter, Red and Archie Chance, and the Silkey boys named Ed and Don. The Silkey boys lived on Stranger Creek just east of town, the other two families lived in town north of me. Buck Ellard was in my class as was Red Chance, Archie Chance and Tom Ellard were a year or two older than me, Skeeter was a couple years younger than I. Skeeter and I used to do a lot of swimming and fishing in Stranger Creek and sometimes fish on the Kaw River half a mile south of town where Stranger Creek flowed into it. Dad's council was no swimming in the river. My sixth grade wasn't too memorable except for the teacher Miss Anderson, much more of a figure than a teacher. One day I went up to the pencil sharpener, as I walked by her desk she said, "I'm not going to tell you again," later I was going by her desk again on my way to the three shelf library when she jumped up and slapped the hell out of me and said, "I'm not going to tell you again to take those marbles out of your pocket." She had never told me about the marbles in my pocket and the rattle they made when one walked, as a teacher, she was much too high strung. The following spring and summer was one period of Tom Sawyer days as all my three years at Linwood. Dad completed the inside of the house, all the partitions were lathed, Grandpa Brooks came down from Belvue for a few days to plaster and finish the entire interior, I was amazed how that old man could trowel that plaster onto the lathing and do such a smooth job, his finishing plaster job was as smooth as wall-board is today. I got to do some of the lathing and also learned how to put down oak flooring and the finishing of it. During this time a floor gas furnace was installed, plus the wall thermostat. Dad built a back porch and by the porch dug a cistern with a shovel, walled it up with red brick, finishing it up with a conical tip and left an access hole covered with a sturdy board weighed down with a heavy rock. The spring and summer after my sixth grade was gardening time and a big garden it was. Dad and Mom did most of the planting to insure proper placing of seeds, but the cultivation was up to me with Mom's company to make damn sure I did it right. Mom canned the garden produce and needed a place to store it so Dad got his shovel, went to the south side of the house and started digging, he dug under the foundation and on his knees and stomach, hollowed out a room under the house that you could stand up in, walked it up, installed shelves, and finished up with the steps down and a cellar door. He excavated all this soil with a shovel and carried it away with two old buckets and a home-made wheel barrow. When we moved to Linwood I thought my study of the violin would come to a joyous end but to no avail, Mom lined me up with a violin student at the University of Kansas by the name of Robert Sedore, during the summer months a trip was made to Lawrence every Saturday evening, I caught a bus up the hill to the campus while Mom and Dad shopped. Upon my return from my lesson with Robert a visit to the ice cream parlor was made. One could get a double-dip cone for a dime of the flavor you desired. The violin lessons cost seventy-five cents, Dad had to work two to three hours for that money. I had grown, so a full sized violin was purchased for me, Robert accompanied us to the Jenkins music store in Lawrence and played several violins to compare tone and value. I selected one which cost forty dollars plus a ten dollar bow. The folks also purchased a piano for Dorothy. During the winter, Dorothy and I would catch the Marysville motor train to Lawrence for my violin lesson and return on same Saturday evening. I did practice faithfully and played before audiences with a good accompanist by the name of Beverly Harbaugh, she was much better on the piano than I on the violin. I often went down to the creek to visit the Silkey boys, Ed and I usually played around and Don would follow. One day after our swim we were up on the steel creek bridge looking south towards the steel girder railroad bridge when a man and a woman came up the creek from the river in a boat, he standing up pushing the boat along with a long pole and she seated. They pulled up to the west bank between the bridges, got out and pulled the boat up on the bank aways, then walked towards Linwood. We hadn't seen them before. We watched that boat for four or five days and no one came back for it, it was somewhat worse for wear and leaked quite a bit, but we were tickled to death to utilize it. We built four sets of paddles by nailing flat boards about nine inches square on to dead tree limbs that fit our hands about a yard long. A hand full of mud placed over the leaks worked fairly well but a couple of coffee cans were put in the boat for bailing purposes. We had a helluva time with that boat for about a week, going up and down the creek, fishing from it, pulling over to the bank while at our favorite swimming hole. The Silkey boys mentioned one day the fact that their Grandpa Silkey had a watermelon patch about two blocks south of the bridge and allowed that he was picking some for market and surely he wouldn't miss a few if we were careful. We paddled the boat down the creek very quietly, paddled to the west bank pulled partially on to the bank, eased up over the bank and crept into the immense watermelon patch of six or seven acre size. I never seen so many big ol' striped melons, hell if we each took a nice one it wouldn't be missed. We each made our selection quickly and retreated down the bank to the boat, paddled to our swimming hole, placed our watermelons in the shade along the bank half in the water and mud, and went on with our swimming for an hour or so. By then the melons were reasonably cool and ready to eat by merely dropping them on a solid part of the bank, digging the heart of the melon out and enjoy, it was bad taste to eat the meat around the seeds. I might add that we always swam in the nude and never after eating. We pulled this little caper three or four times until one afternoon we were about fifty yards out into the patch when out of the earth an old gray haired man with a kaiser Mustache sprang weilding a corn knife and shouting guttural German. It scared hell out of me and I fled on the heels of the Silkey boys, we literally jumped down that creek bank, launched the boat and paddled like hell up the creek, looking over our shoulders at the creek bank in case the old man was running along the bank to intercept us at our docking site. He wasn't, much to our relief. I asked the Silkey boys who the old man was and they replied, "that was our Grandpa Silkey." I thought he moved pretty damn good for an old Grandpa. That was the abrupt end of my watermelon stealing career. During these days of my life, overalls and a blue denim shirt was the vogue of apparel, no shoes or hat unless working in the fields. During the winter the wearing of long underwear was a must until spring was well on it's way. The river rose one day from rains probably sixty or seventy miles west of Linwood, there wasn't a cloud around our area for a month or so. The creek was backed up and swimming was good all along our part of the creek, this condition lasted only a couple of days. We were swimming between the two bridges one day with passenger trains going over the railroad bridge, one came over very slow with all the passengers looking out the windows at us. We gave them the old weanie on a platter and the bottoms up. We were lucky the sheriff didn't come for us. The summer of 1937 saw my first job in the potato fields, I picked enough of them to earn twelve dollars, five cents a hundred picked pounds of potatoes was the pay and the potato crop was bad that dry year. My old 1934

NUT CRACKER bicycle was almost un-rideable of late, one summer evening after my violin lesson at K.U. in Lawrence, Dad and I visited a Firestone store to select a new one, damn but I picked a beautiful red one with balloon tires, fenders, new departure brakes, and steel chrome rims on the wheels. The price was eighteen dollars, and I still owe the additional six dollars to Dad. I have never to this day enjoyed a new automobile as much as I enjoyed that first new bicycle. Once in a while, the Silkey boys and I ventured down Stranger Creek to the Kaw River. This particular day, the Wright boys went with us. Martin Wright was a year older than I and Jack two years younger. We were exploring the bank of the river and admonishing little Jack to stay close to us as he couldn't swim. Sure enough he ran a few feet ahead along the sandy bank which caved off with him and into the strong current which was carrying him away. He was just starting to go under when I got to him, after this scare, everything his brother Martin said to him registered. During these days the forked stick sling shot was your weapon carried on the creek, it would project a marble size piece of railroad gravel at good velocity. I never hit or killed anything with it but I could come close. My typical appearance during those days was my right overall leg rolled up so as not to get it caught in the bicycle chain, left front pocket well full of sling-shot rocks and the sling-shot in right rear pocket, handle first. Sometimes I wore a shirt. We arose early Thanksgiving morning and journeyed to Grandma's Spacek's farm three miles west of Emmett, kansas. Uncle Joe came in from his trap line about nine o'clock that morning, I'll never forget that moment. He was on his pony, Topsy, his bag for that morning was a coyote tied to the rear of the saddle. Uncle Joe untied the coyote, let it drop to the ground and dismounted himself by grasping the saddle horn and letting himself down to arm's length and dropping the remainder of the way to the ground. He could almost walk under the pony without bowing his head. A day or two before this Thanksgiving day, Dad had purchased a gallon of moon-shine whiskey at a farm. My Uncle Vince Spacek dropped in for awhile to visit, he, Dad, and Uncle Joe were sitting around the table sipping the whiskey and talking when my Uncle Phillip Spacek dropped in also. He had a couple of small drinks then allowed he would show us how to drink like a man. He put his right index finger into the finger hole handle, lifted the jug while bending the wrist and elbow, lifting the jug to his mouth by elevating his elbow. He chug-a-lugged a good half pint or more before he set the jug back on the table. In a couple of minutes he went to the kitchen door, leaned against it and announced he had better be getting home as Edna was preparing Thanksgiving dinner for the family. He abruptly slid down the door as if a bucket of water had been thrown against it, out cold. I had never seen such a thing before,

I was afraid Uncle Phil was dead. Dad and Uncle Vince carried Uncle Phil to our 1936 Dodge to take him home on a farm two miles east of Emmett, Dad and Uncle Joe in the front seat and Uncle Phil in the back seat. Uncle Vince and I followed in Uncle Phil's Model-T Ford pick-up with side curtains. Aunt Edna wasn't too surprised when we carried Uncle Phil in the door and laid him on a couch in the front room. Dad asked Aunt Edna for a large glass of warm salt water which was forced down Uncle Phil, eventually his stomach rebelled as his breakfast and the whiskey came up and was caught in a wash basin by Aunt Edna. Uncle Phil gave a big sigh, rolled over and was snoring loudly as we left to return to Grandma Spacek's. I thought to myself that this was one helluva Thanksgiving for Uncle Phil and his family. During that winter about three inches of sleet fell, then the weather warmed above freezing during the next day and immediately froze again. One could skate everywhere, my clamp on skates weren't too effective as my shoe soles were too thin to hold them. This also presented a problem for our cow Bessie, it was too slick for her to walk down the bluff from the barn to her water barrel. I carried her water up the bluff for a couple of days, two buckets at a time, three trips in the morning and three trips after school in the evening. On Saturday morning, I went against Dad's council and opened the barn so she could walk down and get her own water, hell, I could walk up and down that bluff, why couldn't she? She hesitated a bit before starting down the bluff, but eventually started down and immediately lost her footing, didn't panic, simply sat on her ass, fore feet extended to the ice and slid forty yards to the bottom of the bluff, hit the fence with a twang and richochetted off to stop near her water barrel. She attempted to rise to her feet once, slipped badly, then sat down again. My ass was in a sling and I knew it with Mom asking me, "what are you going to do now, George?" and "wait till your Dad gets home." My ass was hurting already. I got a couple pitch-forks of straw from the manure pile thinking it would melt the ice for footage and eventually I could get her back up the bluff to the barn. I scattered this in front of her, immediately she slipped as she stepped upon this concoction and refused to take another step. This wouldn't work, so what to do now? Very fortunately Tom Ellard came by collecting for our daily paper, he saw my predicament and suggested we try wood ashes from Mom's wood-burning cook stove, I would try anything as I was about to get Dad's pick axe from the garage and chip Bessie a path up to the barn. There was a nice pile of these ashes at the top of the bluff and shovel after shovel was spread eighteen inches wide in front of Bessie in a path to the barn, Bessie would immediately step upon the ashes as Tom and I spread them in front of her but no more until the next bucket full was carried down the bluff.

Upon getting her into her stall in the barn I inspected her and found a few small cuts on her fore legs and chest where she had hit the barbed wire fence, I carried her water up to her which she drank thirstily and again during the afternoon. I then awaited Dad's arrival, Mom told him the story, I was confronted and gave him my thoughts on my screw-up. He inspected Bessie that evening after he milked her, which she readily gave down, a good sign of no injury, salved her cuts and asked me if I had learned anything today, my answer was very positive. When we first moved to Linwood, Uncle Vince and Aunt Dora gave me another puppy, I had always had a dog since pre-school. While we were living in Belvue, I went with my wagon to haul two home dead that were hit and killed on the highway. All were named Tony as my latest dog. He was quite a dog, rather small, short haired and carried his tail curled up over his back. He loved to fight other dogs, kill cats and was my constant companion during my Tom Sawyer days. In our yard were several large elm trees which squirrels inhabited frequently. Tony and a black squirrel had a chase often when Tony would spot him on the ground, the black squirrel would leap on to the nearest tree trunk, retreat up the trunk just out of Tony's reach, a barking battle would ensue. Out south by the garage was a large elm tree which Dad had topped, the bark was drying and cracking, often fell to the ground and ending up in Mom's cook stove. One day Tony had this black squirrel boxed off from the live trees so the squirrel had no alternative but to take the dead tree, up the tree he went and as he turned to bark back at Tony, the piece of bark he was on gave way, both hit the ground from twenty-five feet up, right at Tony's feet. All Tony had to do was reach out and grab the squirrel, kill it and have fresh squirrel for that day, for five seconds the squirrel lay there then attained its feet and dashed off to a green tree where the barking back and forth continued. When Dad and his gang worked close to town, Tony would often go out to see him. One day Tony was coming down the track on a fresh scent next to a rail outside of the track, his concentration was so great that he didn't see the train coming and was hit by the journal box of the engine, Tony lay next to the rail, feet extended into the air until the entire train passed, then all four feet fell over on the rail. Dad and his gang witnessed the entire episode and thought sure he was near death, Dad was going to finish Tony off with a pick-axe handle, but one of his men thought he might live, Dad carried him home from work and forced a tablespoon of lard down him to keep his bowels loose. For three for four days all Tony could do was arise from his bed in the garage, do a few tight walking circles and lie down again. He eventually recovered but one could see an indentation on the left side of his skull. We often swam in Stranger Creek when it was up from recent rains, fool-hardy as hell, but to swim across it when it was up and flowing fast was a dare. We usually did this a hundred yards or so up the creek from the bridges as there were no trees to impede us when we arrived to the far bank. When we swam at times like this we would be carried fifty to sixty yards down the creek before arriving on the far bank dodging logs while crossing. We would then walk along the bank up the creek opposite where we had left our clothes going another fifty or sixty yards further, jump in and swim to where our clothes were. I was very adept at the Austrialian crawl by then and could knife through the swift current very well indeed. My seventh and eights grades at Linwood were memorable, our teacher was Miss Coffin, she was gray haired and I judge to be about fifty years of age. In my opinion she was a teacher not just a figure head, easy to get along with as long as you paid attention and behaved yourself. Two incidents occurred during my eighth grade concerning Buck Ellard, whom Miss Coffin called James, his given name. All the Ellard boys smoked roll-your-owns except Skeeter. One day Buck jumped out from behind his desk an started pounding the hell out of his left front overall pocket, I thought he was maybe possessed by something until I noticed the smoke and smelled the fabric burning, the wooden kitchen matches had somehow caught on fire. Miss Coffin told Buck to not carry kitchen matches to school again. Another incident occurred concerning Buck again who was very opinionated and stubborn. I forgot how it started, but it ended up to be quite a bout as Buck didn't get his nickname for nothing. Buck told Miss Coffin he wasn't going to do it and Miss Coffin said you will this very instant and proceeded to his desk where she jerked him up-right, then Buck hit Miss Coffin a couple of times. She laid her glasses on a desk, grabbed Buck by the front of his shirt, held him out at arms length with her left arm and swung her right extended arm with clenched fist to the side of his head, after taking a couple of wallups like that, Buck would grab that swinging arm and hold on, Miss Coffin would then change hands on the neck of his shirt and come around with the left clenched fist to the side of Buck's head, after three or four of these shots, Buck was subdued to the correct class discipline. Miss Coffin put her glasses back on, smoothed her hair a bit, caught her breath in a minute, returned behind her desk and class went on as usual. Miss Coffin was a true educator and was later superintendent of schools for the county. During our last summer at Linwood, I was delivering a gallon of milk on my bicycle to a customer four blocks away at the north end of town, I had a wire mesh basket by then attached forward of the handle bars for such errands. When I left home, it was starting to storm, the wind came up to a high velocity, damn near dumped the bike, me and the milk, but I completed that delivery. When I arrived home Dad was in the kitchen holding his right hand over the wash basin, palm up cupped, his palm was full of blood. As Mom washed his hand up I could see it was badly mangled and suggested he go see Dr. Brown, he said he would wait a couple of days to see if anything was broken. Dad was in the garage when the wind storm came up, he was going out the east door and the west door was blown open by the wind, forcing the east door shut completely, closing with his hand caught in it. Mom redressed his hand before he went to work the next morning, it was one helluva looking member, but it healed completely and he never missed a day's work. Dad loved to eat fried cat-fish, about all I could catch was carp in Stranger Creek. There was a six or seven acre natural lake west of Linwood a mile or so and south of the railroad, it was located on the Browning farm. The old timers said it was formed during the 1903 flood and had an underground tunnel to the river south. The water was clear and green and very deep, not many people would swim in it, conscious of that underground tunnel going to the river. Another kid and I swam in it just to say we did, big cotton-wood trees surrounded it close to the bank and afforded good diving. On the east bank was a small patch of graded sandy bank from which we fished, one could throw his line in with two baited hooks and catch two bull-head cat-fish at the same time. They were only seven or eight inches long, but a long stringer of them would make a good meal for the family. The first stringer of these was a tedious job to clean, so the next batch I caught, I boiled a large pan of water, dumped the bull-heads in, it was easier to pull the skin off with the fingers than the pliers. Scalding the fish pre-cooked them somewhat, but with a stack of these fried golden brown, stacked up on a platter with fried potatoes, butter and bread with hot coffee, Dad thoroughly enjoyed his meal.

Chapter Two

Childhood Continued—High School

During my year in the eighth grade at Linwood, the whole class went to Lawrence to view Tchaikovsky's Swan Lake on film. It was the first time I had seen a ballet and a complete orchestra, I enjoyed it to no end and being in technicolor was a first for me. All the violin lessons and exposure to good music by my teachers had taken affect upon me.

Dad finally won a bid on the Silver Lake section forty miles west of Linwood, half as much track to maintain and less traffic. I hated to leave Linwood as I was established with friends, had a couple of girl friends, one was a girl named Juanita Culp with a little brother by the name of Bobby Culp. I often wonder if he is the actor Robert Culp. We moved to Silver Lake from Linwood in mid-summer 1938, all our belongings were packed into a medium sized cattle truck with side boards. In those days the expense of moving was paid by the one moving. At that time Silver Lake's population was about two hundred people with many farm families in the surrounding country-side. The area was three blocks square, bordered north by the railroad and south by the dry lake bed. The lake bed was shaped like a sprung horse-shoe, one end starting from the south west progressing east south of town and bending on south, even during dry weather one could dig a hole eighteen inches deep and find water.

My Grandma Spacek first settled at Silver Lake after she arrived from the old country. She stated to my mother that the lake was full of clear, cool water, one could see the fish swimming in it. At one time the Kaw River had run it's normal course here, but floods over the years had changed it's course one mile south of Silver Lake. Every time it rained to excess the Kaw River would rise, fill the lake with water, then recede, leaving water in the lake plus carp fish and a subsequent breeding place for mosquitoes. Highway 24 entered Silver Lake from the south, did a ninety degree turn west in the middle of town then proceeded on west. Our first home was a two bed room stucco house south of the ninety degree curve on the east side just south of a Phillips 66 gas station run by an old bachelor by the name of Grant Sickles. We lived near the curve for a year, during icy weather many a motorist and trucker had a thrill. Old Grant was almost wiped out twice. I used to visit Grant at his small one room filling station, it was his office, bedroom, and living quarters. He also owned a violin which he played a little and imparted no little philosophy to me about life in general. He was a damn smart old man and most people didn't have that knowledge of him. Grant Sickles was a person well worth knowing.

During the summer of 1938 I went to visit my Uncle Vince and Aunt Dora Spacek's farm twenty miles west north west of Silver Lake. I was getting big enough to help around the farm by then. They had two daughters, one named Georgiann, who was my age and another named Ella Marie who was three years older. One Sunday morning Uncle Vince backed the Old Model A Ford out of the garage, also a chicken roost, knocked the chicken manure off it, filled the radiator with water, gas tank with tractor gas and we all headed for the Onaga fair ten miles north of the farm. Times were difficult then and the entertainment of the fair was greatly looked forward to. After we arrived Aunt Dora and my girl cousins went off to look at things women enjoy, Uncle Vince and I looked at the livestock and new farm machinery. About mid-afternoon, Uncle Vince and I went to the lemon-ade stand where there was a small crowd watching a man with a black snake whip show his expertise with the weapon. His show partner was a young woman who would stand off ten or twelve feet away side-ways holding up a rolled up piece of paper in her teeth. The whip man would cut it off up to her lips, I feared for her as she was damn good looking. After a bit, Uncle Vince sidled up to the lemon-ade stand manager and asked him if he would cash a seventy-five cent check for him, the man did so, Uncle Vince gave me fifteen cents which I promptly spent a nickel of for a glass of lemon-ade as did Uncle Vince. We arrived back at the farm late that night happy and tired. I slept on the front porch for coolness, the last thing I heard Aunt Dora say before I dropped off to sleep was, "Vince, we have to get up early and get around to catch some chickens so that we can sell them to cover that check you wrote at the fair." I was up early the next morning catching chickens while they were still on the roost, then had a nice trip to Wamego seven miles west of the farm where the bank was located. This is what you call hard times, but it didn't take much to enjoy one's self during those times.

On top of the square farm house a wind-charger was installed, with it's two-bladed propeller and generator it charged the car battery behind the radio in the dining room. The radio was not played all week so that we could listen to it on Sunday, after one hour the battery was dead, but one hour was one hour of music.

Uncle Vince always made home-brew, whenever we would visit them, I can remember him lifting a board over the pump well, pulling on a long strand of bailing wire attached to a gunny sack, full of bottles of home-brew. The sack was cold dripping wet and so were the bottles of beer. Dad and Uncle Vince took their time drinking the brew as it was very potent, even red-headed Mom and Aunt Dora took a glass.

During this stay at the farm a young colt got out of the pasture one night and wandered onto the road where it was hit by a car, it was badly injured sustaining a broken fore-leg. The next morning Uncle Vince took his axe and hit the colt in the fore-head, putting the animal out of it's misery. I asked Uncle Vince why he didn't take his shot-gun and shoot it instead of taking the axe to it, he replied, "Shot-gun shells cost money."

After we settled in at Silver Lake in 1938, I took a bike ride south to the lake bed. It was dry except for puddles here and there. There was such a puddle just west of my vantage point which I spied down through some tree branches. Down to the lake bank I go to check things out. This puddle was full of carp fish two and one-half to three feet long, they were swimming around with about an inch of their back sticking out of the water. I picked up a nice swinging club, entered the water and mud and proceeded to whack hell out of carp. I had seven or eight of them lying out on the bank without the slightest idea of what I was going to do with them when I finally noticed a tall slender black kid approaching from the west along the water. It was the first black person I had ever met face to face, I was a bit uneasy, but he put me at ease by offering to help me do for the rest of the carp. We chased and whacked carp for thirty minutes or more until we had them all laying out on the bank. The black kid's name was Warner Jones, was a year older than I and would be a sophomore in high school this coming fall. I went home for dinner and didn't think anymore about the carp laying along the lake bed until after supper, I jumped on my bike and pedaled down for a look-see, thinking about the stink they would raise in two or three days. I eased over the bank, arrived at the puddle and not a damn carp was to be seen. I highly suspect that Warner loaded all those carp in a car or small truck, drove to the black part of east Topeka twelve miles east of Silver Lake and sold them for a nice profit. Warner was a good looking young man, well-mannered, and both an excellent student and athlete. He and I became and remained good friends throughout our high school days together.

My freshman year in high school was very difficult. A different room for every class with three minutes between classes was a rush I wasn't accustomed to. Almost all my class-mates were farm boys and girls, only two of the boys gave me any problems. One from south of the river tried to run a bluff on me, I called him, found out he was yellow. He out-weighed me by forty pounds, but after squaring off he backed down. Another from south of the river was quite different, his name was Kent Rhoades, well muscled and a ladies man. I hadn't entered the puberty stage as yet and when dressing into football togs or taking a shower, he would address me as the hairless babe in front of my school-mates. I finally took exception, Kent offered to take me outside and knock hell out of me. I took water, backed down and thought to myself, "it's not over yet, Kent, when I get some size, I'm going to clean your plow for you." Kent's Dad sold their farm south of the river and moved twenty miles north of Silver Lake to Oskalooska, but I didn't forget Kent Rhoades. When I was a senior, Silver Lake went up to Oskie for a football game, I could barely wait to meet ol' Kent on the grid-iron or after the game. We were in our dressing room getting into our football togs when in came Kent Rhoades, he looked neither right nor left, walked over to me, offered his hand and said, "George, I'm sorry the way I treated you at Silver Lake and I want to apologize." I readily accepted, shook his poffered hand whereas he left as he had entered the room. When I was a freshman I doubt if I weighed ninety pounds. The freshman lockers were located on the basement floor where we freshman boys usually stayed before classes began in the morning, at first we would stand in front of our lockers waiting for the bell to ring. About the third day of school, I noticed a large senior come down the stairs and proceed to introduce himself and shake hands with each freshman boy. He would say, "I'm Alonza B., shake," and proceed to crush one's hand. When he came to me, I kicked hell out of his shin as he grasped my hand, he didn't come downstairs after that.

    Across the alley east of our home lived Scotty and Orville Lister in a revamped barn which was still very drafty looking. They were motherless and their Dad worked on a Union Pacific extra gang as he was seldom home. Orville was my age and Scotty was a year older. These two brothers had quick tempers and would often engaged in fist-cuffs between themselves. One summer morning while in my back yard I heard a commotion and cursing, out into the alley came Orville in a controlled feinting run dodging a little left and then right with Scotty close behind almost an arms length. Orville led Scotty towards a natural gas meter which Scotty couldn't see being so close on Orville's heels, Orville dodged around the gas meter and Scotty hit it full tilt and immediately rolled in pain on the ground. Orville laughed to beat hell while standing over his brother, usually they got along well. I got along well with the Lister boys and could call them friends. I met Roland Whiteman in my class that year, he was interested in airplanes as I. His model airplane building was excellent and would fly as designed where mine were rough looking and barely air worthy. In late summer we had some steady rains and the lake was three or four feet deep. Roland decided to build a boat out of a sheet of corrugated tin eight feet long and three feet wide. First he built a rectangular frame of two inches wide boards three-quarters inches thick. The long lengths of the tin were folded up to meet the wooden frame and nailed in place, then the ends were crimped up and forced together to form the front and rear of the boat. The nail holes in the old piece of tin were soldered up, a paddle of half a broomstick with a paddle size piece of flat wood nailed at one end served as the paddle. As Roland was completing the construction his Dad, and next door neighbors, the Mowers were interested spectators. They readily followed Roland and I to the lake a short distance away to observe the fun, after we placed the little canoe boat in the water Roland eased in and cautiously paddled out a ways into the lake, the little canoe boat was very sensitive as Roland's paddling was slow with no sudden movements, he made it back to shore with no problem of a wet ass. I thought I could do the same as I settled my butt into the little vessel. I gingerly paddled out about twenty feet with a feeling of trying to walk on a bed of steel ball bearings, when I attempted to turn around and head back to shore the fun for the observers began, first I would correct my weight balance one way, over correct, ship water, then repeated the same mistake until finally I was swamped and ended up carrying the little vessel and paddle back to shore in water ass deep. My three observers were over come with mirth, but later on I mastered that little canoe boat though, in and around the small willow trees around the lake doing some fishing and just exploring.

 I thought I was finished with the study of the violin, but Silver Lake had hired a new music teacher by the name of Lloyd Mordy, he was well versed in all phases of music, band, orchestra, voice, choral groups, brass, wood-winds, and his specialty was violin. Mordy was eager and a promoter with plenty of drive. The first thing he did after getting acquainted with my parents was to convince them of my need for a better violin which they readily agreed to. They paid Mordy seventy-five dollars for his old violin he had played in college. When Mordy was studying at Kansas State college to attain his degree in music, an old aunt of his promised him an old violin that she kept in the attic of her home if he received his degree in music. True to her word she presented the violin to him upon graduation. Inside the violin was the signature in Italian, "made by Nicolas Amati." Mordy took the violin to Kansas City, Missouri for appraisal where it was declared authentic and valued at thirty-five thousand dollars. It was refurbished and was a thing of beauty. I played upon it many times but it was a violin for a master. Mordy soon had me taking a lesson a week, practicing at least an hour a day with a lot of public appearances. Every spring I went to the Kansas University Spring Festival to perform for K.U. music professors, in four years I never advanced beyond the rating of good. My senior year Mordy had me enter the bass voice competition at K.U. even though I had no formal voice training, I came up with a rating of good again. Music was a big part of my highschool life and taught me to appreciate the old masters.

My freshman year saw my first time at organized football, the equipment was old and too large for me, I looked like a pile of moving football equipment with an old dented helmet sitting on the shoulder pads when entering the practice field. On completing my first tackle on the tackle-dummy, I ended up looking out of an ear hole of the helmet. None of us freshmen saw game action that year as we were very small, but we scrimmaged among ourselves with ferocity. My sophomore year saw me with a weight of one hundred pounds, by then I had picked up the basic of blocking, tackling, and the single wing formation. Coach let me run back a few punts in games when Silver Lake had a large lead. One such game was with the Boys Industrial School in Topeka. Most of the B.I.S. team was composed of black kids, big and fast with no coaching. I received the punt, headed up the field, advanced from twenty to thirty yards, angling for the side-lines when four or five of the big black kids were going to smear this little white boy. I wasn't scared of contact and enjoyed carrying the football.

The potato farming industry around Silver Lake abounded, the Hook brothers being the largest producers. I spent two summers picking those spuds and became very adept at it, we were paid four and one half to five cents for every bushel picked, when the spuds were good I could pick over one hundred bushels a day. The men who came by with the truck to pick up the bushel sacks of potatoes were drawing two dollars and fifty cents a day as were the men working on the sorting dock and loading the one hundred pound sacks of potatoes into box cars. If we pickers could draw more money than the salaried day workers we had had a good day. All these years I had worked in the fields for the farmers was towards clothes and books for school, what little left over was my spending money, my red-haired Mom was a task-master. After my junior year of high school, my potato field job was that of hefting the sixty pound sack of potatoes up to the flat truck bed, I had grown considerably by then, about five feet six inches tall, carrying a weight of one hundred fifty pounds. I also loaded the one-hundred pound sacks into the box-cars, it took good strength to hoist-kick the top layer of sacked potatoes up to the near roof height, after a day of this one knew one had finished a good day's work with good clean honest soil all over you. The potatoe farmers barely broke even in those days as the market seldom went about one dollar a hundred pounds of top-graded Kaw Valley Cobbler potatoes, but I enjoyed standing in the door of a box car and viewing our work for the day, only a farm oriented boy could enjoy the neat stack of potatoes in their new gunny sacks going off to market. After a day in the potato fields about six or seven of us boys would head up to Dolphie's pond one-half mile north of Silver

Lake, a pond of at least eight acres. We would ease through the barbed wire fence, run forty yards hell bent for lection down the hill, jump in tennis shoes, clothes, straw hat, and all. Upon coming to the surface one would sail his straw hat on the bank then proceed to thrash around and swim for five minutes or so, by then the clothes were much cleaner. We would emerge from the water, shuck out of our clothes and shoes, lay them on the bushes for drying, when dry the swim was completed. After leaving the pond one could see we were five shades lighter in complexion with cleaner overalls and shirts although the tennis shoes were squishy as yet. No one wore shorts or T-shirts in those days except to school so drying under-clothes was no problem. There was an incident at Dolphie's pond which shocked me a bit. Duane "Droopy Drawers" Maupin, Droopy for short and I were swimming one late spring day, a little chilly but not bad if we stayed in the water. We planned to swim only for ten or fifteen minutes and were thinking about getting out when down the hill from the road came two women with their two boy friends. Droopy and I ignored them for about thirty minutes, freezing our asses off in the process, we finally decided to get out before we died of exposure. As we were struggling to pull wet pants over wet legs quickly, one remarked to me that I didn't have much of a dick. The cold water and air had put me in the category of drip dry peter, too short to shake. Droopy was well endowed and the elements hadn't affected his manhood too much, but he damned near fell off a large rock back into the water as he struggled to pull his pants up. The woman remarked to Droopy that he wasn't too bad. When we had our clothes on and were lacing our shoes, the two women and men left without saying a word. On a Sunday summer morning, Dad got word a man had been hit by a train one mile west of Silver Lake, he told me to accompany him to the accident scene which I did with some reluctance as I had seen a shooting victim when we lived at Linwood, Kansas. I was expecting a pile of human body parts lying along the railroad tracks, but on alighting from the car, following Dad and peering around him, I saw a man's body lying close to the railroad crossing along the tracks. When we arrived close to the scene I could see his head was cleaved in a V down to his ears, minus his brains which were lying in pieces down the tracks a ways. The ambulance arrived, the crew proceeded to remove the body, picked up the man's brain parts in a towel then left the scene. The deceased man was a young farmer from north of Silver Lake who walked into town for a few drinks Saturday night, apparently had a few too many and while going home had apparently passed out on the railroad crossing. Mom had prepared dinner while we were gone, my appetite wasn't worth a damn but Dad's wasn't phased, he had learned to live with such scenes during World War I.

During my freshman year I took a class in general science, we had a good instructor, Mr. Wyman, but I was having difficulties understanding the subject matter as were most of my class-mates. The end of class year was nearing, seeing most of us flunking the course. Mr. Wyman knew some of us were interested in airplanes and announced if each of us could build a model that would fly, he would give us a passing grade. I selected a balsa wood kit titled Monocoupe for twenty-five cents. I built the little airplane for six weeks before completion. It was a little wing low while at rest, but wasn't too bad for my first effort, I wouldn't fly it for fear of it crashing before Mr. Wyman could see it fly. We class students took our kit airplanes to the gym with Mr. Wyman as the official observer, we individually wound up the propellers and launched our airplanes. Mine climbed nicely, turned left when the rubber band unwound, continued turning left in a descending turn completing three hundred and sixty degrees and straightened out while doing a nice landing. Roland Whiteman was also in this knuckle-head class. His airplane was much more exotic than most and flew the length of the gymnasium. All of us passed the general science course, I retained more of the subject matter than I realized as I found out a few years later. I took a physics class during my junior year, managed to pass it without too much difficulty. I enjoyed mathematics, in fact I took the three classes that Silver Lake offered. At that time, the instructor, Skinner Boise knew math, but getting it over to me was another matter. I remember one late autumn day, the windows were open and Skinner was part way through explaining a theorem to the class when a flock of ducks flew over the school house on their way to the lake quacking as they went. Skinner ceased the explanation, ran to the window looking out to check the direction of the ducks to the lake, that was another theorem I didn't understand. Late summer before my junior year in high school, I was down at the lake where a rope was tied to a tree limb so that one could swing out over the dry lake bed and small willow trees. Lola Horner, the oldest of the Horner girls was there also swinging away. I swung a few times with Lola on the rope, holding onto the rope and Lola also, enjoying the hell out of it. We were doing this for thirty minutes or so when Scotty Lister and Homer "Hoge" Mongold appeared on the scene, they elected to take a swing, we willingly obliged them. Scotty tried first swinging far out over the lake bed, as he was swinging out over the bank for the third time, Hoge timed the swing, took a running leap at the rope, grasping it just above Scotty's grasp, out over the lake bed they swung with Hoge hollering his patented "KUH-H-H-H HUH-H-H-H." On the farthest extent of the rope over the lake bed, the damn rope broke with Hoge's HUH-H-H-H disappearing over the bank. When Scotty and Hoge came up the bank, Hoge was holding his left wrist, with the look of distressed pain on his face I knew he had broken it. They had fallen on an upright fence post at the bottom of the bank. My junior year of football was supposed to be one of the best football teams Silver Lake had ever fielded, and Hoge was to be our starting fullback. He came back to play in our third game of the season out of shape but ever charging as usual with a cast on his wrist wrapped in cotton padding. After a game the cast was literally shattered. In my estimation, Hoge was the best all around athlete to ever graduate from Silver Lake High School. We had a big team that year, averaging one hundred sixty five pounds in the line. We were undefeated and un-scored on. We employed the single-wing formation which featured various ways of offensive attack. I played the quarter-back, called the plays, threw my blocks as assigned and ran back punts. This team could make any play I called work.

The summer before my senior year two of my boy cousins, Norman and Robert Boyd from St. Louis, Missouri came to visit us for two weeks. Those kids thought potatoes grew on trees and one picked them as picking apples. I proceeded to show them the lake with it's snakes and other wild life, while at the southern end of the lake where the flood-gates to the river were located they wanted to go swimming. The lake water was too dirty for swimming, the creek five miles north of us, Dolphie's too deep, so that left the river close by, with the little farts word that they would keep their mouths shut we proceeded to the river. I selected a back water stretch of water with little or no current, sandy bottom, water six inches to a foot deep, marked a forty foot square of water out from shore with sticks, waded it out faithfully, then stood guard while they shucked their clothes and got their asses wet having a ball for thirty minutes. I was sitting on the lounger on our closed-in front porch reading the paper when I heard little Robert say to Mom, "Aunt Agnes, we went swimming in the river." Mom immediately confronted me the river was forbidden for swimming. I told Mom I would swim in the river if I wanted, Mom walked back to the kitchen saying, "Wait till your Dad gets home." I was still sitting on the lounger when he got home, while he washed up, I heard Mom tell him, "That big kid says he can go swimming in the river whenever he wants to." I then heard those work shoes clomping through the house in my direction, with soap all over his face and hands, he snatched me from the lounger by the front of my shirt and proceeded to shake and man-handle the livin' hell out of me. As I sat in a disarrayed disheveled heap on the living room floor, Dad said, "So you think you're your own boss?" I meekly replied "No." Those little cousins got no more entertainment tours or play from me, as far as I was concerned, they could play with my little brothers and sisters.

My senior year was enjoyable as I was one of the big boys now, I found that girls were approachable and somewhat different from my sisters. I was the only one returning from our excellent football team the previous season, our current club was very small. Line and backfield averaged about one hundred fifty pounds, but most of the time we executed well, although losing a couple of games due to injuries. I finally made the first team in basketball due more to tenure than ability, but I could play good defense and make good feeds to shooters. I always loved baseball, but Mom stuck a pin in that balloon, she was afraid I'd break my violin playing fingers. Coach wanted to make me his catcher as I was of solid build and had a good strong accurate throwing arm.

Uncle Joseph Spacek, our beloved little Uncle. North of Emmett, Kansas where Grandma Spacek and Uncle Joe lived was the small town of St. Claire, Kansas where world heavy-weight champion, Jess Willard stayed often between bouts. Uncle Joe often visited there also, probably to see Jess Willard. As related to me, Jess upon spying Uncle Joe would grasp Uncle Joe under the arms with his hands and lift my Uncle from the ground swinging and tossing him around as if he were a child. I can hear Uncle Joe saying, "Jesus Christ, Jess put me down."

Uncle Joe with my youngest brother, Larry, then Sammy, and youngest sister, Marcia. Photo taken at Emmett, Kansas.

An abandoned farm home, photo taken during 1935. The fence line shows box-car grain doors used to cause blowing dust to drift before doing same on the tracks of Dad's section. The Dust Bowl photos taken near Natoma, Kansas out in western Kansas.

Mom took this photo of drifted dust and an abandoned farm house. Photo taken a few yards from the right-of-way of the U.P. railroad of Dad's section.

Chapter Three

Cadet Days

Classification and Pre-Flight

December 7, 1941. As I'd often suspected, we were in a war again.

We senior boys speculated as to what branch of the service we should join. At that time, it took two years of college to enter the Army Air Corp Cadet program. Knowing it would be financially impossible for me to attend the required two years of college right then, I thought of what other branch of the service I could join. After considering the various possibilities, I spoke with Mom and Dad.

"As soon as I graduate from high school, I'm going to join the Army Infantry like you did, Dad," I proudly announced.

"Like hell you will," was his immediate reply.

"How about the Marines then?" I wondered aloud.

"That's just as bad."

"George, join the Navy," my mother suggested suddenly. "You'll always have a nice clean bed and good food."

I told Mom that I didn't like to swim that much.

Since I wasn't scheduled to graduate from high school until May, I still had some time to make a decision. I had a hunch that the Army Air Corp Cadets would soon be opening up to high school graduates, and I was right. In March of 1942, it finally happened. My lifelong dream of learning to fly was about to come true. The only hitch was the need to pass the entrance exams. Upon graduation I secured the initial application form, filled it out, and sent it off to Fort Riley, Kansas.

A June morning of 1942 saw me on th local train to Fort Riley, using Dad's railroad pass as train fare.

I was told it would take two days to complete the written and physical exams.

As I descended the train car steps, I became aware of the military atmosphere, so different from the civilian environment I had left an hour or so ago. I proceeded along a military street, checking the building numbers as I looked for the correct building where I had been told to report. I finally found it, reported in, and was told to return at thirteen hundred hours for the written exam. That left me about an hour of free time to explore a bit of the post.

Passing a large circular building, I could hear a loud voice reciting the pedigree of someone. I peered curiously through a large doorway and observed a sergeant in the center of a large ring, with a man on a horse circling the outer perimeter. It was my first and last observance of the old cavalry.

Thirteen hundred hours saw me in the written examination room, answering 150 questions on the subjects of current events, mathematics, physics, and English authors and characters. The test was closely monitored and the applicants were spaced quite a distance apart in order to keep everyone honest. While seventy-five points was the lowest possible passing grade, I only scored seventy-three. Damn! Two lousy points had proven my undoing. After being told that I could retake the test in three months, I boarded a train back to Silver Lake. When I arrived home, Mom asked if I had passed.

"No," I told her disconsolately.

"I prayed that you wouldn't," she said.

I spent the summer months of 1942 in the potato sorting shed, butt-kicking one hundred pound sack of spuds to the ceiling of box-cars.

On September 15, I again took the written exam at Fort Riley, this time with a bit more confidence, since I'd had a period of three months in which to study. Although it was a totally new and different exam, I managed to pass with a score of seventy-eight.

The following morning was spent taking a thorough physical examination, tough even by today's standards. I passed with no problems and was sworn in during the late afternoon. We were told to expect call-up in six months, a rather depressing announcement to one who was eager to go at once!

I arrived home feeling three feet taller, which made it easy for anyone to see that I had passed, even before I told them.

During the long six month wait, I worked part-time at Fred Ward's I.G.A. Grocery Store. One night I was helping Fred check customers through the checkout counter when some of my farmer friends came in. They asked me what I was going to do in the war. I told them I had been accepted into the Army Air Corp and that I was going to be a fighter pilot.

A man standing behind my friends suddenly said, "It takes a *man* to be a fighter pilot."

The remark, with its unmistakable connotation was enough to put me in a fighting mood, but Fred was quick to restrain me, and later I was told that the joker was a known "wise-ass". What surprised me was that this man was a veteran of World War I, and had seen a lot of infantry combat in France.

The job at the grocery store ended for me in late autumn. Dad came home from work one evening and announced he had a job for me on a railroad signal gang. Since the gang's bunk cars and equipment were in Silver Lake at the time, I reported for work the next morning. The work was both menial and difficult. After eight hours of it, I was ready for bed and a good rest. Since the other men were all older than I, I was frequently the butt of their good-natured kidding, on the order of no shave, no drink, no women. I did have a steady girl by the name of Donna Frey, whom I dated whenever I had the chance. Since the meals in the gang meal car were excellent and well-rounded, I could never understand why some of the men complained.

When March 1, 1943 rolled around—time for my call-up to the Cadets, I bid the railroad gang farewell, went home, and sure enough, the letter arrived the next day.

March 13, 1943. Here was the day I had looked forward to with mounting anticipation. After bidding my little brothers and sisters good-bye, my parents and I walked down to the bus stop where, with tear-filled eyes, my Mom gave me a hug and kiss, and told me to write often. As for Dad, he told me to look out for the clappy-assed whores, and then shook my hand as the bus pulled up before us.

I boarded with my small pasteboard suitcase, and started off to Kansas City, Missouri on what I perceived would be one hell of an adventure.

I know Dad had wanted to impart a bit more information on what I might expect in Army and combat life, if only to help me survive, but it would have been pointless, since I had never experienced such a life.

When the bus arrived in Kansas City, I checked into a decent hotel near the Union railroad station, and spent a night in fitful sleep. Not knowing that the hotel desk would gladly have given me a wake-up call, I feared I might miss my first contact with the army at 8:00 a.m. the next morning. Even so, I was at the train station at 7:00 a.m., and went to the train gate specified on my orders, where many other young men in civilian clothes were waiting. During those days, the large railroad stations were literally over-run with men in military uniforms, and the station master was constantly calling out arrival and departure times. I witnessed a number of joyous reunions and sad partings as I waited for my eight o'clock call out.

A sergeant, after attaining an elevated position at my gate, proceeded to call out our names in alphabetical order, whereupon we stepped forward and walked through the gate.

A modern pullman train waited us as we moved down the cement platform, and were assigned to our compartments, where we introduced ourselves and settled in.

It took two days and one night to reach San Antonio, Texas, and during the ride, I was introduced to the card game of Hearts, which cost me a total of six bits.

In this modern pullman train, meals were taken in the dining car, and there was a porter to pull down and make up your berth. It was a luxurious form of travel that I would soon be leaving behind.

Late at night we arrived in San Antonio at the cadet

classification center where we would spend about six weeks and later be segregated as: pilot, navigator, and bombardier trainees.

The first thing we were required to do was to go through the short-arm line at the dispensary, where one could hear the words: "Skin it back milk it down, next." One aspiring cadet trainee with positive symptoms was washed out before he had a chance to get started.

We drew our clothing, and while everything was a size too large for me, the sergeant assured me that in a few months, I would fill it out.

We were given basic instructions on the wearing of the uniform, on military courtesy, and close order drill. Then the testing and physicals began.

While I thought I'd had a good, thorough physical at Fort Riley, the one at San Antonio was a grueling experience.

Part of the exam included an interview with a psychologist. At the start of my interview with him, I was asked to hold out my hands, palms down. I later learned that biting one's fingernails was enough to invite immediate rejection. He then proceeded to ask a series of probing questions, and everything was going along fine until the subject of masturbation came up.

"When did you start?" he wanted to know.

"Start what?"

"Masturbating."

"I don't know. What does it mean?"

"Jacking off."

"Oh. Well—as soon as I could."

The next question the psychologist asked me was if I had experienced sexual intercourse. When I told him no, he looked at me in a way that caused me to blurt out, "Well, I haven't!"

"All right," he said. "I believe you." At that point, I think he did.

The next question I was asked concerned my reason for wanting to become a fighter pilot. I said it was something I had always wanted to do—ever since I was a kid. Apparently this reason wasn't good enough for I was sent to another room to think over my real reason for wanting to fly. Fifteen minutes later, I was called back in and once again I was asked why I wanted to become a fighter pilot.

"Because I like competition," I said, which was good enough for the psychologist, and he immediately passed me.

After that, I participated in a series of psycho-motor tests which were very tedious. One involved holding an ice-pick device into a hole in a vertical metal plate. When the pick touched the sides of the hole, a noise like a shorted electric wire was emitted and recorded. The problem was that the hole was a shade larger than the pick and one was required to hold the pick at arm's length.

Another test involved a turntable device that had a small metal disc in it, a little larger than a dime. As the turntable rotated, the disc was to be touched by a hand-held device a foot long, with a short arm, like a detachment hanging down. I soon discovered that the turntable sometimes rotated on-center, and sometimes off-center. There was no way of predicting its behavior. The short arm hanging down from the hand-held device was almost a full swivel, and the time off the disc was also recorded. During the time these tests were being given, an enlisted man walked among us, shouting in a harassing tone.

For our eye examination, we were taken into a dark room where an optician looked into our eyes. Any fault here was also good for an early wash-out.

I had my teeth checked before I left for the cadets, and while my dental check was good, I later experienced an intense toothache while undergoing one of the many psychological, mechanical and mathematical aptitude tests. Upon seeing the dentist, I knew some drilling and filling was in order. After drilling out two molars to such a degree that I could actually insert the tip of my tongue into them, the dentist said the teeth were impossible to save, and promptly extracted them. Since this was done without the benefit of novacaine, it was a truly agonizing experience. Next came a thorough physical exam, which included checking for hernias. I heard on doctor ask a cadet, "Son, haven't you been doing anything to develop this pecker?" even as another rectal specialist remarked, "I wish some of these kids would learn to use toilet paper." While in classification, most cadets were to experience the inevitable kitchen police duty. When my turn for K.P. came, I was asked if I wanted to work or go on the China Clipper, which I recognized as the elite form of inter-continental flight travel at that time. Going on the China Clipper sounded intriguing, and the Gulf of Mexico wasn't too far from San Antonio, but it didn't seem plausible that a flunkie like me could hope to do such a thing, so I politely declined. As it turned out, the china clipper they were referring to was the dishwashing machine, and so I ended up with pots and pans and garbage pails for twenty-four hours—which turned out to be my one and only experience with K.P.

After six weeks of instruction and testing in classification, we were called to Squadron Headquarters to learn of our training assignments. Most of us wanted to train as pilots. I was elated when my name was called for pilot training, while others, much to their chagrin, were selected for bombardier or navigator training.

A few days later, we pilot trainees were formed up by squadrons and marched west across the road to pre-flight, while our two packed barracks bags were taken over by truck. As a whole, we didn't look too bad on our way over. Before we went across the road to pre-flight, we were taken on a ten mile march carrying our gas masks. We were gassed by a BT-13 airplane halfway through the march. When some of the cadets jerked their masks out of their containers, apples, oranges, cookies and cake went flying. This march turned out to be a good way to break in a new pair of G.I. shoes. While some of the cadets couldn't complete the march, I had grown up walking, running and riding a bicycle, and so, I rather enjoyed it.

May 1, 1943. As we marched through the gates of pilot pre-flight, and entered the barracks area, upper-classmen were standing along the roads, making threatening and demeaning remarks. It was the last time I would avert my eyes during my entire military life, for my peripheral vision became acute. We filed into our assigned barracks where one of the upper-classmen waited to lecture us. As he explained what we might expect, he looked in my direction, and I grinned. I promptly received an ass-chewing since pre-flight was no laughing matter.

We learned that all under-classmen had to double-time when not in formation, square corners when necessary. When we later picked up our two barracks bags a block away, double-time and square corners were necessary. Some of the under-classmen couldn't handle the bags and double-time too. They paid for it later.

Our first night in pre-flight was the last peaceful night we enjoyed for a month. Upon our arrival, the upper-classmen were required to stand our guard mount, which made them irate. Our upper-classmen, who were the same as commissioned officers to us, lived on the second floor of the barracks. The next morning they returned from our guard mount but weren't able to get at us as we marched off to classes and lectures. But after the day's routine had been completed, they had ready access to us, and I thought I had descended into Hell. I had been assigned to "B Flight 2nd"squadron-Group 12, one of the roughest, toughest groups on the hill. During the ensuing month, they made a believer out of me. At times, under-classmen from other groups were sent to Group 12, for testing of their mental endurance, I assumed. I witnessed many a grown man leave my barracks sobbing after Group 12 upper-classmen were finished with them.

Each upper-classman was assigned an under-classman, and mine sought me out the second day. He told me what to expect, gave me two pages of typewritten material to commit to memory, then left me alone for the entire month. But six or seven of the other upper-classmen made life miserable for all of us. In my own case, the first thing they took exception to was that my belt buckle still had black paint on it. Over a week's time, I finally managed to rub it off with the help of a blitz cloth. Meanwhile, I was subjected to a week's worth of push-ups, duck waddles, and braces. The whole damn lower floor was a madhouse for a month.

One upper-classman went above and beyond the call of duty in the course of his instructions. His name was Schmidt and he would put you in a brace, then get an inch from your face and berate the hell out of you in a high, screaming voice. All the while, you were expected to remain expressionless, with your eyes staring straight ahead. Schmidt thought he had the right stuff to be a pilot—and so did I, but he was washed out in primary flight. When I was an upper-classman, I remember that he came back to our barracks, complaining about how hard it was to fly the airplane, watch your instruments and keep a general eye on things while the "goddamned instructor kept chewing out your ass." I'm sure that Schmidt went on to become one hell of a navigator or bombardier.

For purposes of clarification, the brace is a rugged position of attention—back straight, shoulders back, gut sucked in, chin pulled well in toward the throat, and reaching for Texas with very stiff arms. Some upper-classmen demonstrated a good brace one night near my bunk. A fellow upper-classman put this cadet into the brace, which he performed so vigorously that he was starting to turn a light shade of blue, and would undoubtedly have passed out if not told, "At ease."

In order to assure that an under-classman kept a military posture at all times, a piece of your belt was required. The procedure involved putting you into a brace, and as an upper-classman to your right held onto your belt still threaded through the buckle, a command of left-face was issued. What the upper-classman had in his hands was the portion you cut off and presented to him. This little exercise taught you to keep your gut sucked in, and your shoulders back. Unfortunately, the belt-tightening process sometimes got out of hand, and ended with grave results. One under-classman's kidney was damaged, and a few days later, he died.

Another upper-classman named Schroeder gave me a pretty bad time, which resulted in many push-ups, duck waddles and braces. Schroeder was the southwest conference wrestling champ at 175 lbs., and then there was Rice, our squadron Cadet commander. His hazing was accomplished on the sly, by observing someone averting their eyes while in formation, or not carrying their hands as if holding a teacup while on the march. Once, while sitting in the barber's chair, getting my close burr haircut updated, Schmidt came in and approached me in a menacing manner, with the thought of putting me in a sitting brace. The barber was trimming around my right ear and asked Schmidt, "Do you want me to cut this kid's ear off?" Somewhat dismayed, Schmidt walked to the other end of the shop and sat down.

Even our meals were consumed "at attention". We sat with our butts perched or hooked on the first two inches of the chair's seat. The meals were eaten in a square manner, and eating utensils were moved vertically from the plate. When opposite to one's mouth, the utensil was moved horizontally into same, and then the maneuver was reversed as the utensil was returned to the plate to pick up more food. During this entire eating procedure, the eyes stared straight ahead, another exercise in developing peripheral vision.

All my favorite foods were served: American fried potatoes, beans, corn, peas, pork chops, beef, home-baked bread and butter. I was still growing and had a healthy appetite, but I damned near starved to death until I finally mastered the square meal procedure.

Making one's bunk bed properly required much effort, since forty-five degree angles on the sides and at the foot of the bed were required, together with folding back the sheet and blanket to exact specifications. Then one had to dress up the blanket folded under between the mattress and lattice support. If it was pulled up tightly and evenly, it was possible to bounce a quarter off the blanket. The pillow was an art in itself, tight and uniform by a fold and with a lengthwise crease in the pillowcase to ensure tightness. When taps sounded at night, one gently placed the pillow on the foot locker and slept on top of the blanket. On the boom of the reveille cannon, one needed only to tighten the blanket between the lattice work and mattress, replace the pillow and proceed to the latrine. When flushing the commode in the latrine, it was common for one to yell "Bombs away!" which warned anyone taking a shower that they were about to receive an extra influx of hot water.

Some of my fellow classmates were older, married men of twenty-three or twenty-four years. They dearly felt the loss of a comfortable married life, and a steady job. One such man was Brotherson, a master mechanic, who I felt would surely crack at the hands of the upper-classmen, but he managed to hang tough. Another was Ed Carpowich of Kansas City, who became the barracks weatherman since his bunk was closest to the back-side door. When the reveille cannon boomed, Ed would rush out to the back porch landing and check the weather. Then he would come back in and give his forecast, which often included the need for raincoats or other appropriate garb. One morning, Ed miscalculated his forecast and we all got soaked in a downpour. I thought the damned upper-classmen would kill him from so much hazing.

The only words an under-classman was allowed to say to an upper-classman were: "No sir. Yes sir. No excuse, sir." An inquiry had to be made in the following manner: "Sir, aviation cadet George J. Brooks 17099958 requests permission to ask a question."

While an under-classman in Group 12-Squadron 2-Flight B, you popped to when an upper-classman from Squadron 2-Flight B entered the barracks calling, "Attention!" One would also wrack the shoulders back a little extra upon hearing "2-B". One afternoon, after noon mess, I was spending a minute of leisure time writing letters back home to my folks and my girl Donna; an upper-classman who happened to be an English major walked into the barracks. I called attention as I popped to. As he walked by me, he said, "To be or not to be." I recognized the phrase as one of Shakespeare's and thought nothing of it as he often quoted the classic poets. He had actually said 2-B or not 2-B, and I had not wracked my shoulders back. Luckily, this particular upper-classman wasn't much of a hazer, just mischievous. He returned to my position, faced me with a grin on his face and said, "Gotcha, didn't I?" I replied, "YES SIR!"

Another classmate in our barracks received a lot of attention from the upper-classmen. Red Carlson was a small man but well-muscled. Because he couldn't carry a tune in a bucket, he was instructed to just move his lips when we were singing on the march. The upper-classmen delighted in standing Red and I face-to-face, after which we were told to sing the Army Air Corp song to one another. While I managed to do a decent job of this, Red's version was truly appalling. To laugh or even smile meant an evening of constant calisthenics, so to Red and I, the singing of the Army Air Corp song was a damned serious business.

Bill Carter, another classmate from Arkansas City, Kansas also received a lot of attention from our upper-classmen. He got so many gigs that he was continually walking them off while the rest of us were on open-post. Bill had a good-looking wife, a college degree, and a private pilot's license. I figured he was a sure bet to get his silver wings.

The first two weeks of pre-flight were truly nerve-shattering. Going to church provided the one sanctuary where the upper-classmen couldn't get to you. In years past, I had attended both church and Sunday school amid groups of pleasant, relaxed people, but in pre-flight church, all one could see was a congregation of strained and harassed young men. Even so, the atmosphere inside the church was a welcome relief and I attended every Sunday.

There were classes all morning, drill and physical training all afternoon, with endless films on military courtesy and venereal disease, to fill out one's day. The class of aircraft identification saw me with an almost perfect score, but naval identification was more difficult. In the course of taking the tests, I sank several of our own battleships. There was a two-month course in the receiving of the Morse Code. Twelve words per minute were required. I hit a hot streak and passed it in five weeks.

I thought I had the mathematics course well in hand but flunked it as the high percentage question concerned itself with a navigational problem. I somehow got the deviation and variation turned around, plus the cross wind. The recheck test was tougher, but I passed with a good score.

After two weeks as an under-classman, we were granted an open-post since we were all pretty well on the way to being on the ball. But before going on open-post, we had to submit to a personal inspection by our upper-classmen, in formation, on the streets by the barracks. We stood at attention, with the bill of our caps two fingers above the nose, shirt on sides pleated and folded back to insure a smooth front appearance, with the shirt buttons lined up with the fly of the pants, G.I. shoes gleaming an hose supporters in evidence. Upper-classmen requested permission to touch in order to confirm the presence of supporters; they could not touch an under-classman without first asking permission. They were very strict about this.

San Antonio was an old city with a Spanish flavor. A good party was in evidence every open-post, and the Gunter Hotel was the place of action. I looked in the party room and it really scared the hell out of me. All that booze, cigarette smoke and women was more than I could handle at the tender age of nineteen. The VD films we'd seen didn't help matters much; any woman you didn't know was a potential time bomb. During one open-post I went to see the movie "Cabin In the Sky". I'd never before seen a film with an entirely black cast. Rochester, who had made his mark on the Jack Benny show, came across altogether differently as a movie actor. Lena Horne was as talented as she is today. Visiting the Alamo was a must. That old fort told me a lot about history and the strength and preserverance of the human spirit.

Because the weather in Texas during May could get quite warm, we were issued shorts to sometimes wear instead of our regular khaki pants. Even so, we were required to wear our hose supporters, which was something of a comical sight. It made one want to burst out laughing to see a formation of cadets marching down the street, singing 'Alouette', with all hose supporters in perfect cadence.

Every Saturday there was stand-by inspection in Class-A uniform, then a line abreast by the flight pass in review. I found that standing at attention in the hot Texas sun wasn't all that difficult if one relaxed the knees a bit. Once you passed out and hit the ground, your career as a flying cadet was ended. Our tenure as under-classmen came to an end on the last day of May, 1943, and the battle of B-Flight was to be fought the evening before the upper-classmen left for their primary flight schools. We were to storm the stairs leading up to the upper-classmen's quarters. No G.I. shoes were to be worn. Under drawers were the attire of the day, with no fisticuffs allowed. As the time came to advance up the stairs, we shouted, "Are you ready?"

"Come and get us, you bastards," was the immediate answer.

The idea was to man-handle and subdue them down the stairs and into the showers. I said "Dibs on Schmidt," but one of my fellow classmates said, "Like hell. That son of a bitch almost killed me spiritually and physically. He's mine."

"Fine," I said. "I'll take Schroeder."

We advanced up the stairs and were met with soppy wet paper balls of baseball size which stung like hell. We knocked over the foot lockers they were using as a barricade and charged into their quarters, throwing wet paper balls back at them. Soon the floor was as slick as ice. I had broken the rules of the battle and had my G.I. shoes on. I was glad I did as they gave me excellent footing during this slam-bang affair. One of my classmates took a running flying tackle at an upper-classman, but missed him and knocked over three double bunk beds in the process. Meanwhile, I singled out Schroeder, advancing on him with a wide grin on my face. Being a college wrestler, he knew his weight and balance, but I was determined, and managed to pin him. Then I hoisted him from the floor to my shoulder, walked the length of the barracks, down the stairs, and dumped him in the shower.

The battle was over in ten minutes. Schmidt took his lumps but he was game. Rice was locked in his private room at the front of the barracks, denying us access to him. A couple of us stood outside his door and loudly discussed his pedigree, then departed. Some time later, Schroeder sought me out and shook my hand. "I didn't think you were that strong," he said, with a note of surprise in his voice. The labor in the fields and on the railroad had finally paid off.

As upper-classmen we could participate in sports, touch football, track, basketball and pick-up games of volleyball between the barracks. I played on the squadron touch football team with mediocre success. Our basketball team was undefeated. My good defense and ability to feed the best shooters enabled me to play a lot. While I was a good dash man in track, I never could beat a guy by the name of Bates from St. Louis, Missouri. His success was due to getting out of the chocks. I remember that Bates beat everyone on the hill, and that he was also an avid Duke Ellington fan.

I had always considered volleyball a girl's game, but at the urging of my classmates, I agreed to play. They had all played in college and were well-oriented, certainly better than I. I was positioned in the back court, away from the net. To my surprise, I found the game to be a great deal of fun. Keeping the ball in play required quick reflexes from off-balanced positions. Eventually, I was rotated to the net, and the first time I went to block a shot, the ball bounced off my forehead. After that, I crossed my arms in front of my face when blocking a spike.

Calisthenics thirty minutes a day had become a fact of life since they were so important for one's muscle tone and coordination. Cross-country runs of three to five miles were run at least twice a week, and were occasionally timed. While running, I could see many short-cut paths, well-worn with use, but I ran the full course in order to build up my endurance.

During my tenure as an upper-classman, we were taught the manual of arms with the old Enfield rifle—first at attention, then while on the march with fixed bayonets unscabbared. We looked pretty good after only an hour of instruction, but the "to the rear, march," made one want to flinch a bit.

When pre-flight for my class 44A came to an end, our under-classmen wanted a turnabout day, but were denied since they served as under-classmen in name only. The class system had been abolished just before my classmates and I became upper-classmen. No hazing of under-classmen was allowed; a quiet lecture of instruction sufficed. I thought they were a bunch of raunches, for we didn't get to instruct or haze them.

June, 1943. My classmates and I had survived pre-flight and were now being assigned to various primary flight schools. We were on the ball, had a military bearing, and were thinking the military way. We were in excellent physical condition with self-confidence, and looking forward to finally getting our butts into the cockpit of an airplane.

The last of June, class 44A left for various primary flight schools, my flight traveled to Mustang Field, El Reno, Oklahoma, twenty to thirty miles west of Oklahoma City, Oklahoma. The over night train ride was uneventful except the farther we went north the drier the land looked, Oklahoma was in a period of drought with the inevitable hot temperatures to go with it. Buses transported us from the railroad station to Mustang Field, on the Field complex there was dry grass, no trees, recreation hall, mess hall, and finally the flight line with PT-19 trainers. Class-rooms were in evidence also, half of our days would be spent there in this hot weather, rotating every week from morning to afternoons and back. A cool day was below one-hundred degrees Fahrenheit, I didn't mind it though, I had spent many a day in the fields back home under such conditions.

The primary flight school was a civilian run operation with a staff of fourteen military officers to keep us on the ball. I thought perhaps military discipline would relax a bit, but commandant of cadets, Lt. E. Hughes Scott saw to it otherwise. He was a tough disciplinarian and more formidable than any upperclassmen I had previously run up against. When our study periods during the evenings was in effect one had best be studying as he might be outside the open window observing and

Author as an upper classman in pre-flight June, 1943, on open post hanging-out around the Alamo.

listening. One morning my flight had fallen out in front of our barracks preparing to go to classes, we were called to attention by our cadet flight leader with Lt. Scott standing by observing. There were PT-19 airplanes taking off over our heads which was very distracting, the basic rule of not averting the eyes was in effect whether under observation or not. A classmate of mine, Marvin Alford averted his eyes a split second to the PT-19's which Lt. Scott detected, Alford was called out in front of the formation where his infraction was stated to him and ordered to do fifty push-ups, the rest of the formation remained at rigid attention. Lt. Scott was a military figure to be sure, sharp as a tack in dress, carriage, and bearing, he damn well kept us on the ball.

    I took my first flight in the PT-19 June 29, 1943 with my civilian instructor, Mr. Willet. The PT-19 was a low wing aircraft of wood construction and ply-wood skin with a 175 H.P. engine, a good trainer for aspiring pilots, but quite formidable to me as this flight was my first ever. Mr. Willet entered the front cockpit and I the back, he after showing me how to buckle the shoulder and lap safety harness. Another cadet inserted the crank on the left side of the engine aft of the propeller, Mr. Willet soon had the engine running smoothly. We taxied out to take-off position doing S-turns all the way, after the engine run-up I got a thrill as Mr. Willet applied full throttle but upon leaving the ground I felt a big let-down as my stomach wasn't adjusting. This being an orientation flight Mr. Willet did most of the flying showing me the area, after twenty minutes or so he instructed me on gentle turns which were very sloppy as I was very timid about moving the controls. Upon landing after thirty-five minutes I noticed my stomach still hadn't adjusted, I wasn't actually throwing up air sick just very nauseas. I attributed this feeling to my first flight in an airplane. Mr. Willet and I flew again June 30, 1943 for forty minutes, communication between instructor and student while in the aircraft was by a rubber tube system, a funnel like gosport device hanging around the instructor's neck with a hose leading back to the student's flying helmet.

    The first six hours of my flying career saw my pedigree degraded to no end. My former upper classman Schmidt's rendition of primary flight training was absolutely correct, learning to fly the aircraft, looking around, checking the instruments all at the same time with an instructor chewing on your ass was very difficult indeed. I got to take off our second flight after performing the engine run-up and magneto check. Upon applying full throttle I immediately started slewing left, over correct with right rudder then slew right, as more speed was attained the aircraft straightened out somewhat and became airborne. Mr. Willet took over and did the climbing turns out of the traffic pattern to altitude where he taught me turns and stalls. My turns were sloppy and skidding, keeping the same altitude for me was impossible. I spun out of most of my stalls, after twenty minutes nausea took over, total concentration was impossible for me. We came in and landed after forty minutes for which I was grateful.

Mr. Willet flew with me three or four more times, my progress was below average, turns and stalls somewhat better, most of by landings were too hot and of the kangaroo variety. Between Mr. Willet's aggravation and air-sickness. I became concerned about my ability of learning to fly. During my last flight with Mr. Willet while attempting to park the aircraft he took it away from me and parked it himself, after he switched the engine off he turned to me and said, "Mister, you would forget your ass if it wasn't hooked on to you." This was the last time Mr. Willet flew with me.

Mr. T.V. Blake few with me my next flight, the turns and stalls, were fair, towards the end of our flight period Mr. Blake took the aircraft from me and dove to a speed over two hundred miles an hour then gave it to me and immediately pulled the throttle back then said loud and clear, "forced landing." I slowed the aircraft down to about one hundred fifty miles an hour as the wind was fairly rushing by my open cockpit, picked out an emergency field, set up a pattern and approached same still at one hundred fifty miles and hour, way too fast as the speed approach of the PT-19 is about eighty miles an hour. As the field disappeared beneath us he turned around and glared at me shaking his head in disgust. Mr. Blake looked like a fierce eyed eagle ready to devour me, his disgust was fully warranted. He took the airplane over, flew back to the field and landed. His very brief critique was a statement as follows, "Mister, why in the hell didn't you pick up altitude with all that excessive airspeed you had then look for an emergency landing field?" My reply, "No excuse, sir." He walked away still shaking his head, he never flew with me again.

My air-sickness problem didn't improve at all, I finally discussed it with a class-mate who had soloed a day or two before, he strongly suggested that it was psychologically induced and to forget about it and concentrate on my flying. My next instructor was Mr. H.K. McClune, he reminded me more of a big brother than an ass-chewin' instructor, from our first flight he displayed confidence in me and let me do all the take-offs and landings, talked me into doing well coordinated turns of all varieties by using the correct application of stick, rudder and ailerons. He straightened out my landings by having me slow down my approach speed so that I wouldn't balloon when I broke my glide for a landing. I progressed well under Mr. McClune to a point when shooting landings at an auxiliary field he stepped out of the front cockpit, re-buckled up the safety harness and said, "George, take her around, shoot me one landing and taxi back to here." Up to this time I had been dependent on my instructors to keep me out of trouble, now I was on my own. I taxied to a point short of the run-way, turned forty-five degrees to the run-way making sure Mr. McClune wouldn't get dusted off when I run my mag.-check. I checked the sky for any approaching aircraft, pulled out to the center of the run-way and applied full throttle. Just after leaving the ground I realized Mr. McClune wasn't up front but forgot about him as I made the first climbing turn to set up a rectangular pattern for a landing. I did everything as we had practiced, correct altitude and airspeed on down wind leg, turning to base leg at proper time to insure a safe glide to point of landing and coming back on the throttle forty-five degrees to point of landing. I accomplished all these prerequisites, set up the correct landing approach speed, broke my glide as I came over the end of the run-way, held her off five feet above the run-way and dropped in to a three-point landing. I slowed down, did a one hundred eighty degree turn and taxied back for Mr. McClune, he got back in the front seat, buckled up and allowed the landing was pretty good then said, "Take us home." Now I could pin the Army Air Corp small insignia wings and propeller on the left front of my cap designating me as having soloed after ten hectic hours of intense instruction. I was one of the very last to solo from my class.

The chow at Mustang Field was excellent, prepared by civilians, varied and balanced. My air-sickness had sub-sided to where I was eager to get into the sky, having finally soloed changed things around completely. Mr. McClune flew with me two more times, an hour of dual instruction then a few solo landings on an auxiliary landing field. During our next to last flight together Mr. McClune let me shoot the landing at the home field, we were one of the last aircraft to land, the flight line in front of the dispatcher's building was crowded with cadets and instructors watching the late arriving aircraft land.

I entered the traffic pattern at the correct altitude, maintained the correct airspeed, set up a good approach with no cross-wind whatsoever, broke the glide over the approach end of the field, came back on the throttle, held her off a few feet above the ground, brought the stick back gently as she settled in to a nice three point landing. As I worked the rudders to maintain a straight roll out the aircraft veered left sharply which I attempted to correct with full right rudder and brake which only seemed to hasten the three hundred and sixty degree ground loop to the left. The RANGER engine quit as we sat there contemplating what I had done wrong. Mr. McClune turned around and said, "George, I trusted you." I unbuckled, secured the hand crank from its storage compartment in the aircraft, the engine was reluctant to start and took a lot of cranking. At least half the flying personnel on the field had a grand stand seat to my mis-adventure from which I received a lot of kidding. Mr. McClune flew with me once more, I did well for him shooting many landings. He must have been a trouble-shooter instructing cadets with border-line flying problems.

My new instructor was Mr. A.B. Connell who chewed on my ass for twenty minutes during the early part our first flight together. When I learned to do things his way, he let up and used a normal voice to instruct.

At this time I was having a problem with spin recovery, I wasn't vigorous enough with the controls while executing the procedure. After a Friday afternoon flight Mr. Connell informed me the following Monday I take an elimination ride, if I passed it would-be considered my twenty hour check-ride. That left me a weekend to sweat it out on an over-night pass to El Reno a couple miles from Mustang field. A classmate, Milton Anderson, and I hitched a ride to El Reno after Saturday morning inspection to view the local girls. As we were walking down the short main street two P-51 Mustangs commenced buzzing the town, there were no high buildings in the town so the Mustangs came in close to the roof-tops. They beat the town up for a good five minutes. On their last pass, they each did a quick roll off the deck. I'll bet that Mustang field had been their primary flight school six or seven months previously. This flying exhibition reminded me again what my ambition was, my determination to beat the elimination ride was much strengthened.

Monday morning after falling out at the flight line everyone immediately files into the dispatchers office to check the daily status board, S for solo, D for dual. After my name was D for dual with Warrant officer Wollem, he was already in the PT-19 as I reported and saluted before cranking us to a start. After I buckled in he told me to taxi and do the take-off which I did a good job of then continued on doing climbing turns to five or six thousand feet of altitude, then leveled out for further instructions. About then another PT-19 made a pass at us, W/O Wollem took the controls from me, a dog-fight lasting at least twenty minutes unfolded, tight turns, vertical reverses, climbing turns, diving turns, everything a PT-19 was capable of doing was exhibited for me. Neither of the PT-19 aircraft could gain an advantage as each of us went our separate ways. W/O Wollem looked over his left shoulder as the other aircraft departed, getting an identification number I'm sure. We had lost a thousand feet of altitude during the friendly dog-fight, W/O Wollem instructed me to climb back up, while doing so I realized I was completely relaxed and enjoying the hell out of this aviation. After regaining altitude he instructed me to do a three turn spin to the left for him. I cleared the area by doing a couple of steep turns then lined up on a road as I throttled back and stalled the aircraft, stick in my gut I eased in left rudder, dropped off in the spin holding left rudder in, stick back in my gut, when two and one-half turns were completed I shoved in right rudder then shoved the stick to neutral. I went a half turn beyond three turns before recovery which wasn't too bad but it wasn't good enough for the Army Air Corp. I climbed back up to altitude where W/O Wollem demonstrated a spin for me, he narrated to me all through the maneuver, as he was making the spin recovery he told me to be more vigorous applying opposite rudder away from the spin and to say son-of-a-bitch when I popped the stick forward to the neutral position and little bit forward of neutral so that one could feel a little bump as the aircraft came out of the spin. W/O Wollem had me do two spins for him to the right then left of four turns each and that he wanted to hear me yell son-of-a-bitch. I cleared the area as I was climbing to altitude then demonstrated the spins for him yelling son-of-a-bitch as I popped the stick forward, my spins came out on the nose.

During the entire flight I kept my head on a swivel, I had started to master the art of searching the sky, scan the instrument panel on the sweep and fly the airplane also. W/O Wollem shot the landing, after taxiing to the ramp and parking he told me there was nothing wrong with my spins which gave me renewed confidence plus I had passed my twenty hour check-ride. After my flight arrived back at our barracks I asked some of my classmates why W/O Wollem was a warrant officer instead of a lieutenant. Heresay says he did a roll on approach to landing once thus rank demotion. I hope he ended up in a fighter plane overseas, to my estimation he was one damn fine pilot.

The routine at Mustang was demanding, classes and physical training in the morning, the afternoon was spent on the flight line, as aforementioned procedure was reversed every week. To me physical training was a relaxation period, exercise, games of basketball, volley ball, soccer ball, then a two mile run to top it off. The two classes I remember was navigation using the E6B computer for dead reckoning, we soon dubbed it the E6B confuser. I managed to pass all my classes except engine mechanics even though I had a master mechanic sitting next me in class. Cheating on tests never entered my mind, Dad always told me to do my own work. I attended study hall every evening during my stay at Mustang field, with tutoring from my classmate A/C Brotherson, the master mechanic, I passed my re-test on engine mechanics.

While I was an underclassman at Mustang field, we were required to wear a red name tag above our left shirt or flying coveralls pocket. On the flight line an upperclassman could select you to crank his PT-19 for him, some of these upperclassmen used the wobble-pump too much during these hot summer days thus a flooded engine. I wore blisters on my hands while cranking one such flooded engine, A/C Brotherson gave me a procedure to clear the engine which saved me many a blister. Everyday when we arrived at the flight line a small cross breed dog greeted us, while sitting on the benches in front of the dispatcher's office waiting on our appointed time to fly, this little dog would come down the benches greeting us individually, he consoled us while we were sweating out our check rides. His name was wobble-pump, he reminded me of my dog Tony back home.

My special buddy in Primary flight school was Milton Anderson, a six foot tall Swede from Minnesota and a ladies man. A couple of young men from Texas whom I played with and against during physical training sports was Teddy Kerr and Otto Develvus Jenkins. I asked Jenkins if he wanted to be called Otto, he replied, "Everyone calls me Ditty Wah." Teddy and Ditty Wah were buddies, inseparable. Another tandem, Russel Campbell and Rex Cox from Des Moines, Iowa were buddies.

El Reno, Oklahoma was a small town of perhaps two thousand people, they accepted us into their homes, churches, and businesses. The largest building in town was made into a Cadet club for us, soft drinks and snacks were readily available to us.

Saturday morning inspections were hectic for us, every bit as rough as pre-flight days, a stand-by white glove inspection of our four man bay area in the barracks, and in rank personal appearance inspection in front of our barracks, then a pass in review on the athletic field. White gloves was a regulation at the Primary flight school, and the TAC officers meant white gloves. Most of us soaped and rinsed our white gloves then dried them on our bunk steads but one cadet by the name of Burton lavishly put talcum powder on his then clapped his hands together to knock out the excess and spread it around the gloves a bit. Before we were called to attention for the personal inspection one cadet would say to another, "Ol' Burton has washed his gloves this week." The whole damn flight smelled as though we were all freshly talcummed.

My first pay day at Mustang field was made in cash, seventy-five dollars all in one stack, I had never seen that much money before and it was all mine. I immediately arranged for a bond and savings allotment, I couldn't possibly spend that much money all in one month.

Mr. Connell was still my flight instructor. He taught me chandelles, lazy lights, then acrobatics. Loops, cuban eights, slow rolls, snap rolls, and immelmans. Immelmans were difficult to do in a PT-19 as the 175 horse power engine wasn't quite enough to insure a good roll-out on top of the maneuver. I was also instructed on the pylon eight coordination exercise. I faithfully practiced all these maneuvers plus the stalls and spins every time

I went up solo.

One evening after our study period the inevitable bull session about flying took place, one of my class-mates told us his instructor demonstrated an inverted spin to him. By now all of us still in primary flight training were well versed in the conventional spin maneuver but not the inverted spin. With his hand in the air depicting an airplane upside down he related his experience, the airplane was stalled out upside down then the rudder shoved in, stick held forward, as they spun earthward upside down my classmate said he thought his eye-balls were going to pop out. The recovery was made by shoving in opposite rudder, popping the stick back into the gut thus going into a conventional spin, then the normal spin recovery was made. I could tell by my class-mate's face that this had been a very sobering experience for him.

We lost one cadet with his instructor during our stay at primary flight. The student and instructor flew into the side of a hill. I thought nothing of the accident, we were too damn busy with classes, P.T., and learning to fly.

I passed my forty hour check with no problems, the PT-19 and I were on better terms by now. During one of our nightly flying bull-sessions someone told me of the thrill of buzzing, up to now I had refrained from such antics, it was a sure way to wash out if caught. The next day I was scheduled for solo, after I took off, the urge hit me when I was well away from the field. I selected an old house out in the hills of Oklahoma, after clearing the area for other aircraft, I redlined the air-speed and swept over the house, as I pulled up and away I looked over my shoulder and saw a young teen-age girl bolt from the house, during my second buzz and pull-up a second girl appeared waving wildly, on my third pass their mother joined them, all waving. I gave them one final buzz job, pulled up and away then departed the area hoping they didn't get my aircraft number, I'm sure they enjoyed the buzzing as much as I did.

We were permitted to solo from the front seat at about fifty hours of flying time, it seemed strange flying from that cockpit, the line of sight for shooting landings was much different, I bounced most of them.

Towards the end of my time at Mustang field I got the urge to visit my home at Silver Lake, Kansas, the limits for a week-end pass was one hundred miles radius from El Reno, Oklahoma. Silver Lake was much farther but on checking on the fast train schedules I was confident I could do it. After Saturday morning inspection and the week-end pass in my shirt pocket I signed out an proceeded on my daring do journey home. I had previously confided in a lady at the field's post exchange of my plans, she agreed to give me a ride into El Reno, leaving before the official time of departure. I was at the rear door of my barracks waiting as she came driving past slowly, I made a dash for the car, the door was opened by another cadet on the floor of her car, I piled in, staying on the floor with the other cadet until we were away from the field, then we sat on the seat. I boarded the Sante Fe railroad stream-liner and was home by two o'clock Saturday afternoon. Mom and Dad were very surprised when I came walking in, Mom noticed that I wasn't smoking cigarettes as yet. Dad thought I had filled out. To arrive home I had taken a cab from the Sante Fe train station to the city limits of Silver Lake, while driving west through Topeka I shared the cab with two enlisted men recently arriving from North Africa and the war in that theater. They had been infantry men at the battle of Kasserine Pass. Being very curious about actual combat I asked them how it was, they replied that it had been like a football game, the Germans had pushed us back to our goal line where we held then got the ball and pushed them back and scored. My fellow cab riders got out in west Topeka, they had a bottle and were out for a good time.

    A friend of mine from high school days and his girl friend dropped by the house so that Donna and I could attend a movie with them. The next morning was spent around the dining room table talking about military life and flying. I told my folks I was almost through primary flight school with only my sixty-hour check-ride to pass. I felt very confident and related my thoughts to them. The folks drove me back to the Sante Fe station to catch the stream-liner back to El Reno, Oklahoma. After I boarded and the train was pulling out I was walking down the aisle looking for a seat, a nice looking little WAC had a vacant aisle seat beside her, sitting down after asking permission we struck up a conversation. We had been talking for thirty minutes or so when I saw a military policeman approaching from down the aisle, he stopped at our seats asking for travel orders. The WAC handed him her official travel orders, as for me I felt as though I had been caught stealing watermelons again, a one hundred mile radius week-end pass wasn't much for travel orders but I produced it anyhow. The M.P. studied it, thought a moment then asked me if I was headed back for my base, to which I replied, "Yes, Sir." He handed the week-end pass back to me then proceeded on down the aisle, I thought he gave me a break.

    Monday morning I went up with a first Lieutenant flying officer for my sixty hour check-ride, I was doing a decent job with my airwork until asked to perform some pylon eights for him. I selected two telephone poles a mile apart, then attempted to keep the wing-tip on each of them as I circled one at forty-five degrees to the left then proceeded diagonally to the other telephone pole circling to the right thus completing a pylon eight. I had no sooner completed the attempted maneuver when the Lt. took over and demonstrated one for me, he kept the wing-tip on the pole by using the rudders. I had attempted the maneuver by coordinating the stick and rudder which made my forty-five degree bank vary plus the altitude.

The Lt. didn't flunk me on my sixty hour check-ride but put me up for a re-check as soon as I learned to do a good pylon eight. I talked to Mr. Connell about the situation, we immediately took to the air to iron out my pylon eights plus other required maneuvers. I flew another five hours solo practicing everything I had been taught so far before the sixty-hour re-check. The Lt. and I were in the air for about twenty minutes where I demonstrated a couple of good pylon eights for him which graduates me from primary to basic flight school.

Primary flight school had been very eventful for me, it took me almost ten and one-half hours to solo under three different instructors, I learned how to pick a good field for a forced landing, setting up a good pattern to enter the selected field. I could now let the ass chewing slide off my shoulders, when to raise my knees when the instructor tried to whack them with the stick. When I was flying with Mr. Willet he related some wisdom of flying to me, I quote as I remember it, "When you can put an airplane where you want it, how you want it, when you want it, then you can fly, mister." The flying time at primary flight school was almost equally divided, thirty-two hours dual instruction, thirty-three hours solo. The wash-out rate at primary flight was around forty-eight percent, as a survivor I thought I had the potential to be a good fighter pilot.

Basic Flight

After nine weeks at Mustang Field we rode by bus north to Strother Field, between Winfield and Arkansas City, Kansas; only one hundred sixty miles from home as a crow flies.

We piled off the buses, fell in, come to called attention, then marched off to our assigned barracks to settle in. The barracks were of wood construction covered with tar paper, a pot-bellied stove in each end for heat, the floor were so uneven one would trip if you didn't pick up your feet while walking. G.I. soap was used every week, applied with a scrub brush, then rinsed clean with water. A stand-by inspection again was required every Saturday. The latrine and showers were centralized outside the barracks complex, no cement walks, just coarse gravel to walk upon.

After making up our bunk beds we were called out of the barracks, marched to an open area where the bird colonel commanding the cadets addressed us. We were told training would be no easier for us, stay on the ball or suffer the consequences. The TAC officers were in evidence watching us like hawks as usual. The chow at Strother field wasn't too good, I don't even remember the mess-hall.

Upon reporting to the flight line I got my first look at a BT-13 trainer, a low-winger, fixed landing gear, four hundred and fifty horse-power radial engine which was started by a toggle-switch from the cock-pit. Tandem cockpits were enclosed with a glass canopy, radio communication for inter-communications and air to ground communications. The throttle quadrant was different from the PT-19, the BT-13 had a variable pitch propeller control and mixture control. There were more instruments to watch and the needle-ball coordination instrument wasn't tapped over as in primary flight.

I was assigned to an instructor whose name was Lt. Marconi, a school teacher from Massachusetts with the New England speech accents. Lt. Marconi was a man of small stature, the minimum of five feet, five inches tall, an excellent pilot and an even better instructor. On our first flight together I was buckled in and waiting for Lt. Marconi to give me the let's go phrase, I turned around to see how he was progressing and was surprised to see him framed in bright yellow pillows. The pillows were constructed of a canvas type material, two and one-half feet long, eighteen inches wide, and about five inches thick. They were very comfortable and excellent for the purpose of situating one properly in the cock-pit. Lt. Marconi became situated and said, "Let's go," I started up, left parking ramp area to the taxi way, doing abbreviated S turns to clear the path while taxiing to active runway. Mustang field was all dirt and dust, here everything was cement except angled areas between the run-ways which were over grown with wild Kansas sunflowers. After engine run-up at the active run-way, Lt. Marconi told me to call the control tower for take-off permission, I took the mike off the hook, depressed the transmission button as I held it to my mouth to do so but I couldn't utter anything but buh, buh, buh. When the tower called us, "Aircraft in number one take-off position, say again." I knew I had mike fright which I overcame immediately and stated my request. After take-off I knew I had an excellent instructor, no ass-chewing, every flight maneuver demonstrated with a running commentary all the way through it. Lt. Marconi was very low-key, after five and one-half hours he soloed me in the BT-13 on September 14, 1943, somewhat better than the ten and one-half hours to solo in primary.

The nickname of the BT-13 was the Vultee vibrator, this became evident when it was pulled up into a complete stall, it would literally shake if held in the stall. But like the PT-19 a good airplane for novice pilots learning to fly.

After soloing and ten hours dual with Lt. Marconi I was making an approach to landing after a rigorous acrobatic dual flight. We were landing to the north with a forty-five degree fifteen mile an hour cross-wind from the right, my approach was good and I maintained a good crab into the wind to stay lined up with the run-way, when I broke my glide and pushed left rudder to land, the left wing stalled with the wing-tip striking the runway which bent it up almost to the aileron. I applied full throttle, became airborne immediately, and was prepared to go around and try again when Lt. Marconi told me he was taking over. He immediately came back on the throttle, veered left of the runway, as he was landing the sunflowers came up to the leading edge of the wings then immersed the BT-13 and us completely as we settled in for a landing. As I was unbuckling to leave the aircraft, I took a look for the control tower. I could barely see it through the Kansas sunflowers. The sunflowers surrounding the airplane and those knocked down by our landing approach were all mine. It was embarrassing walking back to our ready room, no one said a damn word to me, I expected an elimination ride the next day, I was sweating it out when a classmate told me of a conversation he overheard between Lt. Marconi and the squadron commander. The squadron commander asked Lt. Marconi if he wanted to put me up for an elimination ride. Lt. Marconi said the cross-wind was strong enough and the angle of such degree that the runway for landings should have been changed, also that he was in the back seat, and finished his statement by saying the kid can fly. This was good news for me but I continued to sweat it out for a week.

    The regimen away from the flight line didn't let up from pre-flight and primary. Standby inspections were required every Saturday morning, up to now I had not acquired enough demerits or gigs to walk a one hour tour, five gigs meant an hour walking back and forth between the rows of barracks in the coarse gravel, a halt and an about face required at the end of the prescribed line of march, military posture carried at all times. This tour walking was accomplished in class A uniforms, and on week-ends when everyone else was on weekend passes. The TAC officer inspected my bunk, foot-locker and clothes closet one Saturday morning, as he walking away he turned and said, "Mr. Brooks, I'm going to get you." I made every effort to see that I didn't get a tour in the gravel and damned if I didn't succeed while in basic flight training. There was many a six inch deep path made by cadets walking off tours in the gravel. We had a one hour drill period every week day, the eight piece field band supplied the march music. Their favorite march was the Colonel Boogey which I still enjoy hearing today. The physical training was as intense as ever, still relaxing to me.

    The link instrument flight trainer was put on our schedule, the first time I pulled the hood over me and attempted a climbing turn I spun out. It didn't have the feel of an airplane but taught us the rudiments of instrument flight, in all we accrued fifteen hours of link trainer time under excellent sergeant instructors. To coincide with our link training an instrument flight instructor was instructing us in the BT-13. I forget my instrument instructor's name but he was young and enjoyed instructing, always had a grin or a smile on his face. He always gave us a good workout while under the hood in the back seat. He delighted in putting the BT-13 into unusual positions then say, "You got it," being upside down, approaching a stall in a steep climbing, or diving in a steep spiral were not uncommon. He also stressed needle-ball, airspeed, and compass in case one tumbled the gyro artificial horizon and gyro compass. After one such flight while turning on an approach to a landing which I thought was too high in altitude to my judgment, he told me to crank my canopy open as he was going to demonstrate a side-slip to me. He did a side-slip to the left by holding full right rudder, stick to the left and a bit forward. He glanced over his shoulder at me, he had a gleeful smile on his face as I held my cap and head-phones on with my left hand as the wind rushing through the canopy opening almost tore them from my head. He kicked the BT-13 strait a few feet above the run-way and settled in for a perfect three-point landing. When entering the traffic pattern one had to first get in the entry leg, to do so, one had to wait one's turn so as to not cut another aircraft out of the entry leg. My instrument instructor would lurk along the entry leg about two hundred feet higher than the traffic pattern, if there was the slightest gap between aircraft he would dive into the gap cranking like hell to get the flaps down so as not to over-run the aircraft in front of us, then crank like hell to get the flaps up when he had the correct distance established. He enjoyed doing this maneuver and so did I but he warned me not to do it while flying solo. We got ten hours of backseat instruments, a good foundation for further instrument instruction in advanced flight training. Ditty-Wah Jenkins and Teddy Kerr were in my training squadron while in basic flight training. Ditty-Wah told me how his instructor pulled the throttle back during one flight and declared a forced landing. Dirty Wah selected a good field, set up a good pattern and turned on his approach to land, broke his glide as if to land when the instructor will push power to maintain flight. Ditty-Wah said he kept waiting for the instructor to push the throttle but he never did so he landed the BT-13 in the field. I asked Ditty Wah what they did then, he related they did a one hundred eighty degree turn after completing the landing roll, taxied back to the approach end of the field, shut off the engine, unbuckled, climbed out, lit up their cigarettes, set under the wing and did a little hangar flying. Later on I heard Ditty-Wah's instructor and another talking about their students, Ditty-Wah's instructor related as to how Ditty-Wah never made a movement with the stick ever so minute that he also made a coordinate movement with the rudders. He said Ditty-Wah was going to make one helluva fine pilot.

We had been practicing dual formation flying for two one hour periods with our own instructors in the rear seat, gentle turns of no more than forty-five degrees bank. It required intense concentration with very small manipulations of the controls and throttle. I thought I was catching on well to formation flying until I was scheduled to go solo with a strange instructor in the lead BT-13. He set us up in a "V" formation, a cadet flying on each of his wings. At first he did gentle turns of about forty-five degrees bank then proceeded to do ninety degree turns of bank where he lost me as I was every place but in the correct position on his wing. He deemed me as dangerous and sent me back to the home field. My instrument instructor somehow heart of this incident as he was waiting for me after I landed. We immediately went up in two BT-13s where he gave me a workout in formation flying, steep turns, diving and climbing turns, I felt much more competent after this one hour workout.

The rudders exercise stall was a flight maneuver we were required to master while in basic flight. The ordinary stall procedure was easy to recover from by pushing the stick forward when the stall is detected. When performing the rudder exercise stall one had to hold the stick back in the gut and walk the wings level down through the horizon. My instrument instructor was teaching me this type of stall, my first two attempts ended by falling off on one wing or the other and damn near spinning out. After those two bad attempts we proceeded on to other maneuvers but after landing during the flight critique he explained how to master the rudder exercise stall. When you have the aircraft in a complete stall with the stick back in your gut and a wing starts to fall imagine that by kicking the opposite rudder you are kicking the ass-end of the airplane over under the falling wing. The next time I went up solo I practiced this type of stall for an hour, I demonstrated some good ones for Lt. Marconi later on.

There was an instructor on Strother field who graduated with class 42X, an odd designation for a flying class. I was told that they took their primary flight in BT-13s. This instructor would make a normal approach to a landing and would do a rudder exercise stall from ten feet above the run-way to a three-point landing. I got pretty good at this type of stall but nothing to approach his expertise.

To practice our instruments flying we cadets were assigned to buddy rides, one cadet in the rear seat, the other in the front seat doing the take-off and landing and observing for other aircraft. After landing after one such flight and walking the ramp back to the ready room I over heard Russell Campbell chastising Rex Cox. Rex was flying the front seat with Russell in the back seat under the hood. Rex asked Russ if he was all set and Russ allowed he was, Rex then did a full circle of the cockpit with the stick, scared the hell out of Russ. If they hadn't been such good buddies, I'm sure Russ would have given Rex a whipping on the spot after landing.

After accruing thirty-five hours of flight time in the BT-13, dual and solo combined, we were checked out in night flying. An instructor I hadn't met before checked me out, I took off, made one circuit of the landing pattern, shot a landing for him that consisted of a couple of small bounces then the main gear alternately touching and bouncing as we lost flying speed. I endeavored to do better the next landing, but while taxiing by the control tower he told me to stop. He immediately unbuckled, standing on the wing he rebuckled the safety harness and stepped up to the front cockpit where he deemed I had shot a good landing for him. He turned me loose for solo at night, I soon realized I had extraordinarily good night vision. My first day solo had been a high point thrill, my first night solo exceeded this by far. I always kept my cockpit instruments lights turned way down, this technique insured good night vision while keeping the head on a swivel, turning the head from left to right sweeping the instruments on the way and visa versa. Our squadron commander, a captain from the south often called us raunchy, no one can say raunchy like a Southerner. He stated that some of you misters look like a library when you come flying over.

While shooting a landing stage at an auxiliary field and after the critique I was designated to take an instrument flight check with a Gulf Coast Command instrument flight instructor. I buckled in as he taxied to take-off position, after doing this he instructed me to pull the hood forward over the cockpit. I knew immediately what he had in mind and I had never practiced an instrument take-off. He took the run-way, lined us up in the middle of same, gave me the correct compass heading of the run-way to which I set the gyro-compass. I applied throttle as if doing a visual take-off, managed to get air-borne but the gyro-compass kept indicating a swing to the left, I was not correcting for the torque of the engine. I did manage to set up a decent climb rate eventually as we left the area of the field. My air-work on instruments was passable though not good, the instructor's ass-chewing was as good or better than my primary flight days. He habitually chewed a half-smoked cigar constantly, even during the process of speech, I swear bits of chewed cigar came from my head phones into my ears as he chewed on my ass. The instructor finally told me to fold the hood back over my cockpit after thirty minutes or so then proceeded back to the auxiliary field doing level coordinating turns of forty-five degrees banks and direction, first left and then right. He managed to get me air sick, but I held on, I didn't want to let this instructor whip me. Upon landing I felt as well as ever. The check-rider taxied over near a small one room ready shack, shut the engine off, motioned me forward to his cockpit and proceeded to tell me how bad I had performed on the check-ride. He had my complete concentrated attention when a BT-13 taxiing along between our right wing and large wooden landing T taxied into the landing T. The check-rider turned his head to look at the accident but I kept my attention focused on him and his critique. He immediately snapped his head in my direction to get my reaction of the accident, he got nothing of emotions from me, just my undivided attention. He then said, "I feel mercenary today, I'm going to pass you on the check-ride."

The pilot who taxied into the landing T was the commanding officer of Strother field. I stepped from the wing root of the instrument check-rider's BT-13, came to attention, gave him a salute, did an about face and walked into the little one-room ready shack, there I observed four of our astute instructors literally rolling on the floor or bent over in mirth. I didn't join them, perhaps a grin, I left to join my fellow cadets standing off a ways showing somber expressions. We flew our BT-13s back to the home field during late afternoon, while relaxing a bit in our Sqd. ready-room in came the instrument check-rider, he spied cadet Alford sitting in a chair with his chin on his chest catching a short snooze. He walked over to Alford, popped him to attention, put him into a brace, then chewed his ass out for sleeping on the flight-line. True to character the check-rider never took the half smoked cigar out of his mouth.

Dad, Mom, my oldest sister, Dorothy, and my girl, Donna, drove down from Silver Lake to visit me. We were scheduled to fly Saturday night so an afternoon pass was all I could secure that week-end. My buddy, Milton Anderson, accompanied me to the motor court for this reunion. We had a nice visit of three or four hours then returned to the field to get ready for night flying.

Our night flying that night consisted of landings at the home field. I never closed the canopy while shooting landings as per orders. We had been issued our winter flying togs, sheep skin pants and jackets, sheep-skin boots and a billed sheep-skin cap. As I was doing my second circuit of the landing pattern to shoot a landing I stuck my head a little too far out of the cockpit into the slip-stream while looking around, off went the cap plus my ear-phones. I thought about landing and securing a replacement but continued on with the landings calling in on base leg as usual. When the night flying session was over I told the instructor I had lost the items while shooting the last landing, he merely told me to see the supply sergeant to secure replacement items.

There was another session of night flying at an auxiliary field, all the cadets were decked out in the sheep-skin flying togs, it was a bit chilly out but not that cold. The run-way was black top but where the airplanes were parked was dry grass and dust, after ten minutes there was a ten foot high layer of dust over the entire field. Some of the cadets were landing on that layer of dusty haze, it's a helluva feeling expecting to touch the run-way then fall another fen feet before doing so. I was scheduled to fly later that night and was aware of the situation. Our Sqd. commander was the run-way controller, communicating through a two-way radio mounted in the back of a jeep, advising caution about the dust haze layer. There was a loud speaker attached to the radio where all communications between air and ground could be heard. I found it interesting and exciting hearing my flying buddies calling in. Two BT-13s came over the field above traffic altitude flying close formation, the Sqd. commander merely told them to knock it off.

Cadet Green from New England called in advising the commander that his windscreen was covered with oil and had difficulty seeing to land. The Sqd. commander ordered all aircraft to stay up in the traffic pattern, clearing Green to land, he felt his way down through the haze and executed a decent landing. Later on that night I did my landings, I never did like using the landing light as one had a tendency to fly down the beam into the ground, but the first landing I flipped on the light switch and sure enough that haze layer looked like the actual run-way. There on out I finished my landings without use of the landing lights.

Towards the end of my tenure at Strother field they turned us loose on an evening and night cross-country flight to FT. Riley, Kansas. There wasn't much for land marks on the way up but we all checked in at the FT. Riley field on schedule. On the way back we were required to shoot another strange field landing; it was a grass strip in the middle of no where, the strip was dimly lit with a flood light shining across the run-way at the point we were to touch down on landing. I called in to get clearance to land which was granted, entered the pattern, called in on the base leg, set up a good approach and did a three-point landing in the glare of the flood light. The instructor sitting in a BT-13, acting as run-way control officer said as I touched down, "That's the way to land that airplane." Everyone made it back to Strother field, although a couple of cadets had difficulty finding the grass strip.

While shooting night landings at the home field one night one of my class-mates pulled back the mixture control by mistake while on a landing approach. He realized his mistake as the engine quit, put the mixture control back to right, but was in the tops of trees before the engine caught again. There was leaves and small tree limbs in the engine cowl, dents along the leading edge of the wings and one shook-up cadet. I didn't get to talk to him until the next day, he was still concerned about his off-the-ball mistake. This incident was the only near-miss fatality while my class was at Strother field.

One of our school classes was weather, the study of the phenomenon of weather was in its infancy in 1943, but isotopes, cyclones, anti-cyclones, weather fronts, and different cloud formations was taught to us. I found this class very interesting, studied and concentrated much, and completed it with a good score. The instructor emphasized ground fog, what causes it, and when to expect it. How to identify a cold front was also emphasized and never, never attempt to penetrate one.

The wash-out rate for my class at Strother field was around thirty-five percent. My buddy, Milton Anderson washed back a class because of a physical disability which required a little time to heal away from flying. My small pre-flight buddy, Carlson, was to meet an evaluation board when we left for advanced flight training. At Strother field we received thirty hours of dual instruction, forty-two hours of solo, gradually we were permitted to fly solo more as we progressed. My instructors in basic flight were damn good, taught me well and I learned much.

Advanced Flight School

First part of November, 1943 we departed for single-engine advanced flight school, some of my class-mates went on to twin-engine advanced flight. The change of stations was made by pullman train, pretty plush for novice pilots. The train stopped for a while in Houston, Texas, on departure the word quickly spread that Ditty-Wah Jenkins had left the train, seems as though he had an estranged wife or girl friend.

The next morning we arrived at Victoria, Texas, near-by was Foster Field known as "University of the Clouds." We filed off the train, fell-in, called to attention by our Cadet officer as the TAC officer approaches. He welcomed us to Foster Field, first TAC officer I had seen smile as he addressed us, told us that we had worked hard to progress to advanced flight, to wash-out we would have to screw-up royally, then he told us to stand at ease, smoke if you wish. The barracks were partitioned off into two-man rooms, linoleum floors, curtains, painted walls and ceilings, central heating and latrine plus showers were down the hall at the end of the barracks. The regimen was still with us, classes, physical training, from one point to another in formation, and a TAC officer to observe us. Saturday morning stand-by inspections were still in effect, I still enjoyed the drill-field one hour a day. We were allowed a day to settle in then reported to our training squadron on the flight line. We assembled in the pilots ready room to be addressed by our Sqd. commanding officer, a captain about my height. In civilian life he was a minister, a collegiate boxer, his eyes were dark and piercing. He had my complete respect immediately. He expected discipline and to carry ourselves as the young men we were. He also stated that if anyone didn't like what he was saying or how he run the training squadron to speak up, he would go outside with them and settle it by fisticuffs behind the ready room. He then remained silent, observed us all, complete silence prevailed.

My assigned instructor was Lt. Roland C. Dart, a man of my height. He assembled five of we cadets around him to acquaint himself with us. He stated to us that it was rumored the cadet pilots entering advanced flight training now were not as good as our predecessor, he finished the statement by saying, "Don't you believe it, you re just as good." We then went to an AT-6 airplane for a familiarization lecture, the AT-6 was a low-wing, tandem canopied seating, 650 horse-power Pratt Whitney engine, variable speed propeller, and retractable landing gear, to my estimation, more like a fighter-plane than our previous trainers.

Ditty-Wah Jenkins arrived on a later train the same day the main contingent arrived, reported to the field commanding officer, stated his reason for leaving the train, and continued his life as an aviation cadet. Affairs of the heart can be compelling at times.

I took my first dual flight in the AT-6 with Lt. Dart November 9, 1943. He showed me the local area, I performed some stalls and other air exercises for him, then entered the traffic pattern to shoot a few landings. I felt confident about flying the AT-6 as it was similar to the BT-13 only faster and more responsive to the controls. I set up a good base leg, came back on the throttle forty-five degrees to spot of landing, turned on the final approach, dropped fifteen degrees of flaps, set up my final approach speed, as I neared the run-way I broke the glide and commenced to hold the AT-6 off for a landing, Lt. Dart pushed the throttle forward and said over the intercommunications circuit, "Mr. Brooks, this airplane lands better with the wheels down, that will be five stars." We climbed up to pattern altitude where I did lower the landing gear then proceeded to shoot a normal landing. There is a loud warning buzzer just aft of the front cockpit but I didn't hear it as my concentration on the landing was intense. I didn't worry too much about the stars, five dollars was cheap for the boner I pulled.

The mess hall at Foster Field was excellent, they usually had four or five choices of salads for the supper meal.

After three and one-half hours of dual Lt. Dart soloed me in the AT-6, lowering the landing gear was standard operational procedure to me by now. Up to now we had been taught three-point landings, at Foster Field we shot wheel-landings, upon making contact with the run-way a little throttle was applied, stick slightly forward to keep the tail in the air and the main landing gear on the ground, then a fast taxi to the first turn-off taxi-way. Upon approaching the taxi-way one had to use extreme caution while lowering the tail surfaces by retarding the throttle a bit, coming back gently with the stick, braking to slow down for the turn-off still keeping a little throttle on to keep the tail surfaces on the run-way. As one turned off on the taxi way one could look back up the run-way and see three AT-6s directly behind. This type of landings and clearing the run-way at Foster Field facilitated the heavy flight schedule employed during advanced flight training.

We had no sooner soloed than our instrument flight training continued, both link trainer and flight training. The art of flying the beam was introduced to us plus the let down procedure for a landing.

A beam radio station emitted low frequency signals, located in close proximity to the flying field it is serving. An inverted cone of silence extended vertically up from the station to alert the pilot he was close to the field. Projecting out from the cone of silence were the actual radio beams, usually in directions, north, east, south, and west or close to those vectors. Between these beams were the quadrants identified by the Morse code dah dit for A and dit dah for N. The actual beam was identified by a steady hum which increased in volume as did the quadrants as one flew towards the radio station.

Towards the end of November, 1943, Lt. Dart checked me out for night flying in the AT-6 after about forty minutes, he gave me a good work out before turning me loose on my own. Shooting night landings at Foster Field started with complete runway lighting, as we progressed through training the runway lights were hooded, they could be seen only as one was breaking his glide for a night landing. This was invaluable experience, quite to my liking as I enjoyed night flying. One cadet in my class at advanced flight was extremely afraid of night flying, he told me once in strict confidence how he flew an hour of night landings. When he was scheduled he merely went out on the flight line, climbed in an AT-6, turned on the radio, called the tower when on the supposed base leg and repeated the hoax for an hour. He succeeded on this hoax as the landings were touch and goes. He must have been miserable flying his night cross-country flights.

Formation flying in advanced flight progressed well for me, going from an echelon right to an echelon left presented no problem except one day Lt. Dart had all his cadets up for formation flying. Lt. Dart was in the lead plane in the back seat, a cadet doing the flying in the front seat, I was flying the lead airplane's wing in an echelon to the right, my intense concentration undivided on them when Lt. Dart pointed a finger down the echelon, for an instant I looked at my instrument panel then back to his airplane thinking he had pointed at me wanting to bring something to my attention. My instant of inattention caused a little adjustment on down the echelon right, one should never take one's eyes off the aircraft whose wing you are flying formation on. Lt. Dart led the echelon over the run-way of an auxiliary field where we peeled off for landings using the three hundred sixty degree overhead traffic pattern. Everyone parked their aircraft, walked to Lt. Dart's airplane for the critique. I received mine first from Lt. Dart as follows, "Mr. Brooks, for almost killing the man flying your wing, you are fined five stars." Then he continued on with the critique for the group as a whole.

A fellow cadet asked me to accompany him into Victoria one Saturday to see a girl friend of his, we proceeded to the out skirts of town to an old bar. We crossed a dusty dirt road to the establishment, an unpainted board building with a lean-to-type porch extending over the board-walk in front of it. I felt as if a gun-fight could take place at any time as the entire scene could have been Texas back in the eighteen hundreds. We entered the bar, my friend inquired of the girl and received a negative answer as to her where abouts, then asked me if I would care for a drink of tequila. I could handle a bottle of beer stretched out over an hour's drinking time, hard liquor I knew nothing about, but I had to start sometime. My friend ordered two short glasses of tequila with the salt shaker and lemon wedges. He demonstrated for me the way to drink tequila by pouring a small portion of salt on the back of his hand, licking off the salt, drank the shot glass of tequila then sucked on the wedge of lemon. I waited about five minutes before I tried it, only I sucked the lemon wedge first then followed the tequila shot with salt from the back of my hand. It took my breath away, that was the first and last drink of tequila for me. It reminded me of kerosene.

An integral part of our pre-gunnery training was shooting at clay pigeons on the skeet range. An old sergeant in charge of the skeet range versed us on the Browning semi-automatic twelve gauge shotgun with a modified choke then proceeded to demonstrate each station on the range to us. Each station required a different lead on the clay pigeon from the high or low house. I broke sixteen out of a possible twenty-five clay pigeons my first round of shooting. The old Sarg. asked where I had learned to shoot, I allowed I had been raised shooting at quail with Dad's old Model 97 full choke 12 gauge Winchester shot-run, he nodded at me approvingly with a wistful look of remembrance on his craggy face. During our skeet training I averaged twenty-two or twenty-three clay pigeons out of the possible twenty-five, one day towards the end of this training I had a perfect score until I arrived at the station between the two houses, I missed the target coming from the house on my left, I ended up with a score of twenty-four. There was a very short placard type listing of perfect twenty-five shooters hanging on the range house wall, Cadet Alan Blest of our group made the listing.

During one of our night cross-country solo flights two cadets of my squadron used abusive language while on this flight. As we took off at staggered intervals, I was far enough ahead and out of radio range I didn't hear these two cadets talking back and forth over the radio. Our Sqd. C.O. had a radio in his home as did some of the instructors, their wives could listen to all the conversations which took place. The very next morning our Captain was waiting for us when we arrived at the flight line, he addressed us all in the ready room wanting to know who used the abusive language on the radio. No one spoke up. He promised to knock the livin' hell out of the raunches if he ever found out. He was one very irate man with good reason.

Towards the end of my advanced flight training as I was just leaving the ground on take-off I lost all power, immediately realized the throttle quadrant was loose. The throttle was full forward in my left hand but the propeller control and mixture control had vibrated to the rear, having long fingers I managed to get the two retarded controls in the forward position regaining full take-off power. A quick glance at the quadrant told me the wing-nut was loose on the quadrant, I held the stick in the crook of my right elbow while reaching across with my right hand to tighten the wing nut. This could have resulted in a serious crash but fortunately I correctly diagnosed the problem then proceeded with my climb out to practice acrobatics. I leveled off at abut ten thousand feet with the canopy still rolled back. I was doing fairly steep turns one way then the other to clear the area prior to acrobatics when I noticed my safety belt wasn't buckled, one slow-role and I would have made my first parachute jump.

The middle of December saw some of Lt. Dart's cadets going to Matagorda Island, fifty or sixty miles southeast of Foster Field to shoot aerial and ground gunnery in the AT-6. As he read off the names of cadets going I must have had an expectant look on my face, he called every name of our group but mine, he finished up his statement by saying, "Mr. Brooks, you will stay at Foster and fly night and day cross-countrys." I replied, "Yes, Sir," thinking to myself perhaps this was a good omen, they might check me out in P-40s a week or so from now. The AT-6 aircraft they flew at Matagorda had a single thirty caliber machine gun in one of the wing's leading edge. It seemed the field was almost deserted the week they were gone. I flew cross-countrys to Houston, Waco, San Marcus, and Columbus, following the flashing beacon light lines at night, dead reckoning during the day. On local flights I sharpened up my acrobatics, coordination exercises, and wheel landings. When the gunnery group returned from Matagorda everyone was talking of Henry Bates, he shot expert, achieving high scores consistently. After a dual flight with Lt. Dart, he told me of a sea turtle he had machine-gunned while at Matagorda Island, after landing his AT-6 he walked the gulf coast until he found the turtle to observe his hits. While he was doing this observation an old gentleman approached, stopped and asked Lt. Dart if he had machine-gunned the sea turtle. Without looking up from the turtle Lt. Dart allowed that he had, when he did look at the older man in the wrinkled khakis he recognized him as the commanding officer of Foster Field. The Lt. stood for a good ass-chewing.

Some cadets were chosen to check out in the P-40, I wasn't among them, if and when I achieved my wings I could already see myself flying gunners around in the AT-6, shooting the hell out of a towed sleeve target while standing up in the back seat. The cadet who was afraid of night flying was chosen to fly the P-40, he did a good take-off, did some required air work then came in for his first P-40 landing. Most of we cadets who weren't going to be checked out in the P-40 had completed our scheduled flying for the day were intently observing the action. This cadet touched the P-40 down and immediately started to kangaroo down the entire length of the run-way before advancing the throttle for a go-around, he did the same thing three or four times, as a matter of fact he even scared the hell out of me. A flight instructor standing near our group was heard to say, "I guess we will have to roll out the flak guns to get him down. The control tower talked the cadet down to a decent landing eventually. Rex Cox from Des Moines, Iowa was also selected to check out in the P-40, Rex had trouble with his landings also, but knowing Cox I felt he was quite capable of doing a good landing. While having difficulties with one of his first landings a WAC in the control tower was telling him how to land the P-40, Coxy told her to shut up as he was flying this god-damned airplane. Rex did a go-around, set up a good approach and stuck the P-40 on the run-way doing a perfect three-point landing. After watching these antics I was glad I didn't check-out in the P-40 at this time, if I was lucky, perhaps later I could talk someone into checking me out.

Lt. Dart gave me my final instrument check ride, it lasted two hours. Immediately after take-off he told me to pull the hood forward over the canopy and proceeded to have me do all the required air-work on instruments. The unusual position he put the aircraft in was a barrel-roll, while we were up-side-down he said, "You got it." I felt the maneuver all the way and completed the barrel-roll to straight and level, re-set my gyros, getting ready to continue the check-ride. Next he tuned in the radio beam and said, "Take us home." The first thing to do is definitely identify the correct beam station then set the volume control moderately to definitely ascertain a fade or build-up of the beam signals. The signal I was receiving was a dit-dah or an N, I knew I was in the northeast or southwest quadrants of the beam station, I took up a northeasterly heading and soon detected a fade in the volume which definitely put me in the northeastern quadrant, I also knew the beam was to my left and field one hundred eighty degrees to my rear. I took up a heading of two hundred forty degrees to intercept the beam closer to the field, getting a definite build-up of volume all the way, turning down same so as not to hurt the instructor's ears. I intercepted the beam, verified by the steady hum, turned to a heading of one hundred eighty degrees, volume building up again, turned it down again, then entered the cone of silence directly over the station, entered outgoing beam leg, by timing and pre-determined compass headings and rate of descent. I knew I was over the run-way. I wiggled the stick to signal Lt. Dart I thought I was over the run-way, the Lt. pulled the hood release in the front cockpit, as the instrument hood folded back over my head I looked out and down, I was over the run-way. The forty-five hours I had spent in the link-trainer and in the back-seat in the air tutored by excellent instructors had paid dividends, I had passed my final instrument check with confidence.

December 31, 1943 I flew two hours solo during the morning, came back to the barracks in the usual formation, fell out for dinner chow then we had the afternoon off to prepare for the graduation and New Year party combined. It was a good time to catch up on some letter writing, I was engrossed in this small chore when my room-mate, Wheels Beals, left our room, I paid no attention, went on with my letter writing. After a minute or so I looked out the window for inspiration to continue a letter and observed all the cadets falling in in front of the headquarters building, I had heard no announcement over the cadet public address system. I grabbed my shirt, tucking it in on the way to the formation double timing all the way, everyone was already at attention when I arrived. First formation I had ever been late for, the TAC officer announced loud and clear this lateness would cost me fifteen demerits, three hours on the ramp, commencing immediately after dismissal of formation. I reported to the TAC officer immediately after falling out, I was issued a shot-gun then proceeded back and forth between headquarters and supply walking off my three hours, hoping I wouldn't miss supper chow, my main meal. After doing an about face at the supply building, marching back to headquarters I saw the TAC officer approaching, I came to a stop and executed the manual of arms salute. He stopped and told me to report to the gymnasium to complete the two hours of tours remaining, I executed another salute, continued on to headquarters, checked in the damn shotgun, then proceeded to the gym where they were decorating for the dance and party. I hung up a little crepe-paper, a few lights, then retired to the barracks across the road. Back in basic flight a TAC officer stated he would get me and get me they did.

Around eight o'clock on New Year's eve a fellow cadet and I attended the dance when we heard the band start playing, my buddy asked me if I would join him drinking a bottle of beer, I allowed I would. I was standing against the wall of the gym watching some of the cadets dancing with their dates looking like the wall sunflower that I was, taking my time with the beer. After an hour's time my buddy returned with a glass from the punch bowl, going on about how good it tasted. I finished the bottle of beer, proceeded around the dance floor to the punch bowl table where a tall glass of the mixture awaited me. I returned to my place along the wall sipping the punch drink, damn but it was smooth, I could barely taste the liquor. After thirty minutes I had consumed half the glass, nothing to this drinking I thought. Slowly but surely the lights began to dim which was good, the couples dancing could dance closer together. I sensed all was not well with me when the gym floor began to tilt one way then the other, so much that I thought the dancing couples would slide from one end to the other. The feeling of airsickness took over my stomach, I needed to get to my sack in the barracks as fatigue overwhelmed me. I went through the door of the gym closest to my barracks, down the three or four steps holding on to the railing, I made it across the road to the barracks, three steps forward, two backwards, negotiated the three or four steps to the barracks. On through the latrine then bounced off the hall way walls getting to my room and that good ol' sack, I managed to undress except my shorts, slid between the sheets thinking I would sleep forever. During my young flying career I had accomplished many a spin but the ol' sack just wouldn't make a recovery whether my eyes were open or closed. My stomach dictated that throwing-up would be in order to rid myself of the beer and punch, down the hall I go hand over hand on one wall this time to the latrine. I couldn't throw-up so I sat on the adjoining stool leaning over the neighboring stool waiting for the inevitable relief. I was there for thirty minutes or so when one of my buddies came through and suggested I drop my drawers before I sit on the stool, I told him I was waiting to throw up. He wanted to be helpful so he raised a couple of windows to help me sober up. Texas is damn chilly in December and there I sat until after mid-night literally freezing my ass off. A couple more buddies came through inquiring if I would be alright, to which I replied, "Aw Roger." The cold air did help my spinning condition. I walked slowly down the hall to my room desperately fatigued, the ol' sack never felt so good. New

Year's Day was a much needed day off for us, no flying or classes, upon arising with my very first hang-over I asked my room-mate, Wheels Beal, what was in the punch. He related that the TAC officers had mixed the concoction and managed to get drunk while doing so. They had used all types of fruit juices plus bourbon, gin, rum, and tequila. I'll bet that one could fire up the Pratt-Whitney engine on an AT-6 with it.

The WACs held an open house New Year's Day, Wheels and I sauntered over to see the gals at close range, their area was strictly forbidden to any male personnel all other times. A little WAC met us at the door and took us to their egg-nog bowl for a drink, the bourbon smell nauseated me, I declined respectfully. A good supper New Year's Day left me in good shape for tomorrow's flying schedule.

I took my final check-ride with Lt. Dart January 2, 1944, it lasted one hour and twenty-five minutes. I did everything he had been teaching me the last two months, from straight ahead stall to an immelman turn. As I touched down to a decent wheel landing into my ear phones came the statement, "Mr. Brooks, that was a good ride." The first time any instructor had issued such a statement on my behalf. I didn't consider it as a compliment, merely progress.

January 3, 1944, our Captain, the squadron commanding officer rode with every cadet in his squadron as was his tradition. We were scheduled in alphabetical order, when one cadet had finished his ride, the next one immediately followed after observing the military courtesies. My turn came, as the preceding cadet departed the front cock-pit, stood back a ways, saluted, did an about face, I took his spot on the ramp, came to attention, saluted, received same, hurriedly took the three or four steps to the wing-root, buckled my parachute leg straps, eased into the front cock-pit. While buckling the safety harness the Captain was taxiing to take-off position. I received tower clearance for take-off, effected the take-off, making sure we were airborne before pulling up the wheels. I didn't want to give the impression I was a hot-rock. I climbed to three thousand feet where he instructed me to do a couple of stalls and a few steep turns, we then descended to one thousand feet for a return to the field.

The captain asked me if I had ever seen an AT-6 loop from a cruising speed of one hundred fifty miles an hour, I shook my head no as I looked back at him. We were still a couple of miles from the field heading in a northerly direction when the captain said I got it, he did two clearing turns, then adjusted the throttle and prop pitch to cruise at exactly one hundred fifty miles per hour airspeed. He pulled back smoothly on the stick, adding full throttle and propeller pitch almost at the same time, up and over we went with the captain coming back on the throttle and propeller pitch on the way down, we leveled out at one thousand feet altitude at cruise speed of one hundred fifty miles an hour. My butt barely left the seat as we were upside down in the loop, I looked around at him and grinned, I appreciated the expertise of a master pilot. I shot him a good landing, taxied in where the next cadet was waiting, I did the military courtesies then departed to the ready room. Not every cadet who rode with the captain experienced the loop from cruise speed.

    The evening before while in the barracks I heard a commotion in the hall out side our room, Cadet Nixon was loudly voicing an opinion of sheer wrath, it seems his instructor had made the statement to someone that Nixon was afraid of the AT-6 airplane. After cadet Nixon rode with the captain the captain was heard to say, "That was the damndest ride I ever had while still in the traffic pattern." Nixon demonstrated to the C.O. that he sure as hell wasn't scared of the AT-6 aircraft. After the short ride with the C.O. I flew a day cross-country to Austwell, Texas and back requiring four and one-half hours of flying time then finished up the day with three hours of night flying, the sack again felt good after eight hours in the air. Another cross-country of three hours and thirty minutes plus two hours of local solo flying saw my flying career as an aviation cadet come to a conclusion. In advanced flight the instructor was in the back seat only fourteen hours plus ten hours of instrument instruction. The remainder totaling eighty hours was solo.

    The middle of December 1943 we were given two hundred fifty dollars uniform allowance, the tailor in Victoria did an excellent job on my officer's uniform of greens and pinks, he even asked me how I wore my trousers, up high or let them hang on my hips.

    January 7, 1944, we all donned these nice new uniforms with insignia to match, sauntered to a large hall where our wings were pinned on us. On the way back to the barracks the grouments came out of the visored caps, hell we were now Army Air Corp. pilots. One of my buddies tossed his cap in a small creek we were crossing, retrieved the cap, shook off the water and set it back on his head in a rakish manner.

    Now for the trip home to spend ten days before my next assignment. I was satisfied and happy when I received my orders to report to Marietta, Georgia for gunnery training, transition to fighters, and subsequent assignment to a fighter unit. Ten months earlier at Kansas City Union railroad station while waiting for the sergeant to call our names out I noticed a tall kid also waiting with his girl friend plus his parents. He received his wings as I did and being located seventy miles apart back home we decided to travel home together. A fellow cadet who graduated with us by the name of Roy Coats, West Plains, Mo. offered us a ride home or to the southwest extremity of Missouri where he turned east for West Plains. We gave Roy some money for gasoline after signing out to leave Foster Field, put our luggage in the trunk, got in the back seat. Roy's wife, Nita, occupied the passenger seat front. My traveling companion was Bill Florance of Kansas City, Missouri.

Roy's car was a 1939 or 1940 Ford V-8 in good shape, I noticed that flat-head V-8 purred when we started for points north. After two hours or so of travel it began to snow, in no time I realized we were in the middle of one of those cattle killin' blizzards that roared out of the pan-handle of Texas in a north easterly direction. It was getting damn cold in the back seat, I asked Roy to turn on the heater, it didn't work as he couldn't get a thermostat for the engine due to the war. Nita was setting close to Roy for being old married folks, they got some heat through the front floor boards.

I finally took off my shoes, crossed my legs and folded my legs thereby sitting on my feet, not much improvement so I put my shoes back on and did the same thing. I watched over Roy's shoulder as he negotiated those treacherous roads, down shifting, very light on the brakes, doing an excellent job of keeping the car moving through the drifts of snow. The circulation in my legs told me to straighten them out, but my feet were somewhat warmer. I noticed Bill Florance was sitting on his feet also. We finally arrived at the town where Roy and Nita turned east for West Plains, he bid Bill and I good-bye when they left us at the railroad station. I warmed up a bit in the station then took a stroll along the station platform where I run into second lieutenant Brotherson who had received his silver wings from a twin-engine advanced flight school, his wife was with him. We were standing there shootin' the breeze about this and that when a G.I. private walked by without saluting. Lt. Brotherson nailed the G.I., proceeded to chew his ass out about military courtesy. I was appalled by this spectacle, turned and walked away, I had received so much ass-chewing the past ten months I didn't feel like doing the same. I hope Brotherson didn't end up in a combat unit with that attitude.

The seating on the train north was negative, I found another use for the B-4 bag, not a bad seat if one had a back-rest. Upon arriving in Kansas City, Bill's folks and girl friend were awaiting him, this scene was different than ten months ago. I bid them good-bye, taxied to the bus depot and got on a bus for Silver Lake. It was good to see Dad, Mom, and the kids again, I had a lot to tell them. Dad asked me how an airplane actually took to the air and stayed up, I explained the Venturi theory to him, he understood it instantly as he had a mind like a steel trap belying his five years of formal education. I smoked a pack of cigarettes a week by now. It upset Mom when I shook one out and lit up. She also suggested I go to the ration board to secure ration coupons for my stay at home. The ration board was lenient and gave me ration coupons for ten extra gallons of gasoline. My little brother Larry was coming along real well with his swearing especially when provoked by his brother Sammy. Just for the heck of it I tried on my sports jacket I had graduated from high school in, I could barely button it, I had grown from a size thirty-eight to forty-two in less than a year. Mom and I agreed to give it to a cousin of mine who was in need.

    I spent a lot of time over at the high school where Donna was a sophomore. My under classmen friends who were now seniors seemed like juveniles to me, no purpose or direction, but their time was fast approaching. They all were to be in the marines, infantry, and navy, one was to enter army air corp pilot training. My old swimming buddy, Droopy Drawers Maupin, was destined to be the pilot.

    The leave at home went very fast, but I was eager to get on with my training, I became very restless before the ten days were up. I saw a lot of Donna those ten days, she was concerned by me flying airplanes and eventually going into combat. I thought about giving her an engagement ring or even getting married, but I was scared to approach her folks for her hand. Country girls only love once. Donna would have been a good wife to be associated with. Just before I left for Marietta, Georgia, Mom made the statement that I should have gotten married while at home, also that I should enjoy some married life before going overseas.

Chapter Four

Marietta, Georgia

Through the First Four Missions

Dad secured a tentative line-up of train schedules to Marietta, Georgia for me. There would be a short bus ride as Marietta didn't have railroad service at that time.

After changing trains at Kansas City, Missouri, I stowed my B-4 bag in the overhead luggage rack, and was in the process of getting acquainted with my fellow passengers when I noticed an M.P. coming toward me. I felt I looked damned sharp in my uniform, consisting of pink pants, green shirt, and a tan tie tucked between the second and third buttons of my shirt. In addition, the brass was shining and my shoes were gleaming. After looking at my orders, the M.P. informed me that I was out of uniform. I was supposed to be wearing my dress blouse when traveling. After fetching my B-4 bag from the luggage rack, I proceeded to the men's smoking room to make the change. The M.P. followed me the entire length of the car and stood in the doorway of the men's smoker watching while I changed into a tan shirt, retied the tie and then put on my green blouse. The smoker was filled with men at the time, which didn't help my feelings much.

Once the change had been made to the M.P.'s satisfaction, he ambled on down the aisle, as happy as a dog that had just pissed on a tree stump. Had this only happened a year later, the outcome would have been extremely interesting.

Upon arriving in Marietta, Georgia, I found myself at a single-engine advanced flying school. Since I hadn't flown for almost three weeks, the itch was strong to get back into a cockpit. I talked to operations, requesting to be scheduled as soon as possible.

The next morning, I was up in the air over Georgia, climbing away from the busy field to do a few coordination exercises, stalls, and even a few acrobatics. My altitude was about 8,000 feet. As I executed my clearing turns, I looked up and down for other aircraft and noticed another AT-6 about 2,000 feet overhead. Slackening my turn, I kept my eyes on the AT-6 as he started a spin to the left. He spun down about 200 hundred yards in front of me and was still spinning when I lost sight of him below.

After completing my scheduled hour, I landed, parked and then proceeded to check in my parachute. I asked about the pilot who had been doing the spins and was told he was a little Jewish kid who had to wait another two months to receive his pilot wings. Although he had completed the required training and was a really hot pilot, he wasn't yet eighteen years of age.

After a week of virtual inactivity, our group was bussed east to a small auxiliary field for fixed gunnery in the AT-6. Up to this time I hadn't met any of my old cadet flying buddies. The field was near the Atlantic coast in the middle of nowhere, with a concrete north-south runway and parking ramp. The barracks were almost as bad as those of my basic flying days back in Kansas. The field commander, a captain, addressed our group in a no-nonsense tone, stressing that raunchiness would not be tolerated on the ground, in class, or in the air. Just like cadet days, I thought. But I had no problem conforming, whether there was a gold bar on my shoulder or not. Silver pilot wings were of the utmost importance to me.

My gunnery instructor was a low-key and all business sort of guy. After I'd attended a few hours of classes, he took me up for actual dry run gunnery passes. He gave me a good demonstration which I observed from the front seat.

A training gunnery pass at a towed aerial target was typically executed as follows: Parallel the tow aircraft at approximately 1,000 feet higher and ahead of same about four or five aircraft lengths. The distance from the tow plane was about one mile. If a pass was made on the towed target from the right, the gun sight and one .30 caliber machine gun switches were switched on. Then a descending turn was made to the left, picking up speed, then a good reefin' turn to the right, approaching the towed target ideally at a 45 degree angle and at the same altitude. Hold three-fourths of a radii lead ahead of the target and fire away, needle and ball centered being of the utmost importance. When the angle of attack decreased to ten or fifteen degrees, cease firing, break down and left to safely clear target, climb to the left side of the tow aircraft and position for a gunnery pass from the left side. The .30 caliber machine gun was mounted in the top of the engine cowling, firing through the propeller. Since the firing mechanism sometimes malfunctioned, holes in the propeller were not uncommon.

Two of the instructors were really hot pilots. It was possible to feel the torque just by listening to them talk. I often played basketball against them on a dirt court during our physical training period. Since they knew every trick in the book, I spent a lot of time in the dirt looking up at the goal.

One morning as I left my aircraft after returning from a gunnery mission, I noticed a first lieutenant, nicknamed Buck. He was walking up the ramp with his seat pack parachute hitting the back of his legs. This was his punishment for a minor infraction he committed while flying a gunnery mission. I talked to him later and learned that a second lieutenant instructor had put him on the ramp for a period of four hours. The next morning Buck had charley horses on the backs of his legs. Buck went through flight training as a first lieutenant, and so, did not experience cadet life. But he was an amiable man and a darn good pilot.

We progressed through aerial gunnery on to ground gunnery, which was much easier. In the latter case, one approached the target at a 45 degree angle, firing when the light pip in the middle of the gunsight reticule was on the bullseye in the middle of your numbered target. At times there were a few pilots who shot at the wrong target, and the hits counted. Good coordination was essential and the smooth air of the morning was extremely beneficial for good scores.

After returning from a ground gunnery mission, I left the cockpit and noticed that damned near the whole field had congregated around an AT-6 airplane. I questioned a ground crew man about the crowd and was told that it was the reception for a woman pilot of the WASP organization. Walking up that way I was soon able to confirm that this was indeed a woman, and a damned good-looking one as well. But she was way out of my league for I was still a teen-ager.

I was scheduled again that afternoon for ground gunnery and the lady pilot was going to shoot with us. The air in the afternoon was rough and bouncy so keeping the piper on the bullseye was difficult if not impossible to do. After we'd all expended our ammunition, we returned to the field and landed. The general consensus among the male pilots was that none of them had hit the target, and when the scores came in, it was quickly confirmed that no one had. But the woman pilot, having scored one hit, could honestly say that she had out-shot all the men.

After two weeks, my group left the auxiliary field. I didn't get an ass-chewing for flying up the tow plane pilot's tail, firing away.

In aerial gunnery, I shot well. Hunting quail with a full choke twelve gauge shotgun when I was in high school, and the skeet range in advanced flight school definitely improved my proficiency in aerial gunnery.

A few days after arriving back in Marietta, the word came through that the two hot pilot instructors had allowed their egos to exceed their ability and judgment, and both had hit the ground attempting a slow roll off the deck.

The schedule saw my group being bussed out to another auxiliary field to fly the P-40 type aircraft, a definite transition from trainers to fighters. This field was also out in the wilds of Georgia, and upon alighting from the bus, I noticed a black-top landing strip running south to north with a taxi strip alongside as wide as the landing strip. Scrub brush was all around, and it gave me the feeling of being at a combat strip. The P-40's were somewhat dispersed here and there, still in their camouflage olive drab paint. The strip commander addressed us in the small weathered board pilot shack. I felt as though I was still a cadet, still learning everyday as one should.

Our assigned instructor took his fledgling pilots out to a P-40, explaining the aircraft and cockpit to us. He was a very friendly and helpful man who had our best interests at heart. Learning the cockpit was the first task we encountered in the course of acquainting ourselves with the P-40. Before we were allowed to fly this aircraft, we would need to pass a blindfold cockpit test. After one hour of sitting in the cockpit, I had it down pat. The actual test was given to us while we sat with taped goggles over our eyes.

The first day was taken up with orientation and chalk talks on the P-40. The next day, as we got off the bus, we knew that we would be flying a true fighter plane. I wasn't one of the first to check out but I did fly in the morning.

I buckled up my seat pack parachute, entered the cockpit, buckled up the shoulder straps and lap strap with our instructor hovering close by. I started up, and once the 1,125 horsepower Allison engine had settled down, I throttled back to idle and that little ol' engine just chuckled like my Uncle Vince's farmall tractor engine. After my instructor had clasped my shoulder, he left the wing of the aircraft and suddenly I was on my own.

A requirement of our first P-40 flight was to stop at the runway control tower. It was constructed of weathered boards atop four four-by-four posts about 30 feet in the air. There was room for one man with his radio equipment. The tower's roof was like something I had once built over my treehouses when I was a kid. We parked where the tower officer could peer down into the cockpit as we went through the cockpit check, then would rev up the engine for the magneto check. It took much more brake pressure to hold the P-40 than it had to hold an AT-6, and the engine roar was much greater, which required turning up the radio volume. I received permission to taxi to the south end of the runway for take-off, S-ing more than usual to see along the long nose of the P-40. Before take-off I checked the rudder trim tab for the correct right trim to offset the torque, checked for P-40's on the approach, called the tower, stating that I was clear and number one. When permission for take-off was granted, I took the runway, lined up in the middle, applied the throttle steadily; at full throttle the acceleration was something to experience. The P-40 flew itself off the runway. With just a little back pressure on the stick, we were soon boring a hole in the sky.

Our first flight aerial maneuvers consisted of the various stalls, power off-power on, wheels and flaps down, and a split-S maneuver. Accomplishing the split-S entailed cruising along at

220 miles per hour, rolling the aircraft over and pulling back on the stick to pull out of the ensuing dive, thus ending up in direction 180 degrees from the original course. I finished the first hour doing turns, trying to get better acquainted with the P-40 fighter aircraft. Toward the end of my first hour, it was time to return to the strip for my first landing in the P-40. When I put the nose down in a gentle altitude-losing dive 325 miles per hour appeared on the airspeed quickly, but on approaching the landing strip, a bit of retardation on the throttle on leveling out at traffic altitude cruise speed was attained. The entry leg to the traffic pattern required more loss of air speed to approximately 150 miles per hour to lower the landing gear. I gradually slowed to 110 miles per hour on the base leg, the turn on approach to landing lowering required flaps maintaining about 95 miles per hour on the final approach to landing. Nearing the runway, I caught a slight crosswind from the right which blew me over the taxi-way. Since there were no other aircraft on the taxi strip, I proceeded to three-point the P-40 in a cloud of dust, completed my roll-out, did a 180 degree turn and taxiied back to the parking area. I had no sooner shut the engine off and opened the canopy than the tower officer jumped onto the left wing. He was as irate as any human being could possibly be.

"Why in the hell did you land on the taxi-way, and neglect to open the coolant shutters for ground operations?" he wanted to know. He finished up by stating that a transfer to bombers was in the offing for me. I could already picture myself sitting in the co-pilot's seat of a bomber cruising straight and level through the flak and enemy fighters. Damn!

The old "Yes sir, No sir, and No excuse, sir" served me well during this ass-chewing. As I trudged to the pilot's shack, I was very pissed off at myself for pulling such a head up and locked stunt.

Upon approaching the pilot's shack, my instructor met me, hustled me out to another P-40 and into the air. I went shooting good landings on the landing strip. We accrued ten hours in the P-40, a good taste for fighters, but still a long ways to go to be considered accomplished in one of these planes.

The wheels and flaps controls on the P-40 were located on the left side of the cockpit on a ledge about lap high. They were toggle switches about one and a half inches long and were plainly marked and easily accessible to the left hand. Nonetheless, it was easy to inadvertently make the wrong selection when one was concentrating on the traffic pattern and the turn on an approach to a landing. The hydraulic actuating mechanism was merely a ring of one inch radius attached on the forward part of the control stick just below the hand grip. Attached to the ring was a strip of metal about 3/16's of an inch wide, 1/4 inch thick that ran down the control stick to the hydraulic actuating mechanism.

Halfway down the control stick a pivot stood the lever mechanism out forward of the control stick. When the toggle switches' position were set to the desired selections, it was necessary to put the small finger in the ring and press to acquire the toggle switches' selection. A couple in our group had the wheels retracting and the flaps coming down on an approach to a landing. It looked funny as hell but an on-the-ball tower officer averted any serious mishaps.

The coolant shutters were operated by a lever not unlike what I used to see on my Uncle Vince's corn cultivator. It was located close to the cockpit floor, right of the pilot's seat. One had to reach a bit to grasp the handle, squeeze it, and move it up or down to open or close the coolant shutters.

The P-40 had an excellent combat record and prepared us well for our first flights in the P-51 Mustang.

When we left Marietta, Georgia for Tallahassee, Florida Air Base, I was still sweating the tower officer's remark about being transferred to bombers. At Tallahassee, we were marched around in formation to various lectures, personnel appointments and other functions. I had an itch to get on with the flying of the Mustang and found all of these other activities extremely boring.

The college at Tallahassee was an all girl's college. Some of us went to the campus one evening and were immediately invited to the Spring Prom.

My buddies paired me off with a young lady named Ann. On the way from downtown Tallahassee, someone secured a couple pints of bourbon from a porter at a hotel. I had a shot during our walk up to the campus, which left me with a nice glow. While we waited for the girls to make an appearance, one of the guys came up with some bottles of Coca-Cola. After my first coke high, I found that I felt even better. The gals were a damned good-looking bunch of Southern belles, although Ann looked a trifle apprehensive as we sauntered into the ballroom. Although I had never been on a formal dance floor before, I felt that Fred Astaire had nothing on me. After taking four or five labored steps, I managed to step on the hem of Ann's gown, and heard a loud rip. This abruptly brought a halt to our dancing and I watched as Ann fled from my side. As I stood around with a country boy's grin on my face, I began to feel the bourbon. The effects were similar to air sickness, and I quickly found an easy chair in a secluded sitting room where I stayed until I'd begun to sober up. After that, I proceeded back to the barracks along with the other guys. Some of the pilots had apparently really lucked out at the college for they came back with grass stains on the knees of their trousers.

After gunnery and fighter transition, we arrived at Bartow Army Air Field in Bartow, Florida where the famed P-51 Mustang was the standard training aircraft. Bartow is situated in the center of the Florida peninsula, and upon alighting from the bus at the main gate, I could see the palm tree lined road leading into the base proper beyond a small sentry house. After walking up this blacktopped road and arriving at the headquarters building, we sensed that we had entered a very relaxed atmosphere. It turned out to be true enough. There was no reveille, no evening lowering of the colors, or taps. Two training squadrons comprised the entire function of the field, and there was a turnover of approximately 75 trained fighter pilots every month.

I proceeded to the low-roofed barracks assigned to me. My roommate in this 15 x 20 ft. room was a fellow by the name of Elmer William Fogelquist. He originated from the state of Washington, and as soon as I'd shaken hands with him, I knew we would become good friends. I asked how he would like me to address him and he said, "Just call me Fogie." Fogie was about an inch shorter than I was, and had the muscular build of a diver, having competed in this sport in the Junior Olympics. He was liked by everyone as he was very amiable, with an infectious smile and the face of a cherub. There were times when he would talk with a thick Swedish accent, and he also had a habit of standing toe-to-toe with people while engaged in conversation. Fogie could get by with asking a lot of penetrating questions for that grin of his was so totally disarming.

Another close friendship I developed while at Bartow was with Norman Ott, a pilot from Massachusetts. Ott was from a staunch old New England family, and while he sometimes appeared a little brusque, he was actually quite sensitive and deep.

On the morning after our arrival, my training squadron sauntered down to the flight line where we each received some flying coveralls, a throat mike, a cloth helmet and some goggles. Only one instructor was placed in charge to see us through a specific phase of our training. Then our transition instructor took us out and introduced us to the P-51 Mustang. Damn, what a sleek aircraft it was, sitting on the flight line in its olive drab war paint. The razor-back and square wing tips, plus the squared tail surfaces suggested great speed even while it sat perfectly still. The coolant and oil cooler air scoop underneath gave it a highly distinct appearance. It was, in all respects, a most unusual plane.

We were told as we began our cockpit familiarization study that the P-51's controls had been laid out according to the advice and suggestions of veteran fighter pilots, and this was altogether believable for everything came easily to hand.

The next morning we went through our cockpit checks by simply placing our left hand over our eyes, and then touching the various instruments or controls as the instructor called them out.

My turn to check out finally came about, and after the instructor had observed me buckling in and starting the engine, he quickly touched my left shoulder as I closed the canopy and then left the wing.

The date was April 14, 1944. Thirteen months earlier I had started cadet training. Nine months earlier I had soloed back in primary flight. I hadn't realized that we would be given only this short time span in which to accomplish an initial flight in the P-51 Mustang.

While S-taxiing on the taxi strip to the active runway, I was aware of the smoothness of the 1,125 horsepower Allison V-12 engine. Receiving permission from the tower, I took the active runway and smoothly applied full throttle. The immediate acceleration was astonishing, for it was much quicker than the P-40. The Mustang effortlessly broke ground with very little back pressure on the stick. After setting throttle and propeller pitch for climb out of the traffic pattern, I realized that this airplane was capable of climbing like a homesick angel. It seemed able to anticipate my moves, and as I did my transition airwork, the roll rate of the ailerons was much quicker than anything previously experienced. The first hour went by in a rush, and for my first landing, I lowered the nose and eased back the throttle from cruise in order to maintain a constant descent. Damn, it still gained speed quickly. Its given name had been well-earned. I did a couple of 360 degree turns to kill off the diving speed and looked around for other aircraft. Then I entered the traffic pattern, peeling off after flying over the end of the active runway, executing a 360 degree overhead approach, flying at 1,000 feet. After peeling off, it was necessary to immediately retard the throttle to reduce the speed to 150 miles per hour to lower the landing gear, all the while continuing to turn to the left, and further reducing the airspeed to 110 miles per hour for the final turn to approach for a landing. My first landing in the Mustang was too damned slow as I used a little throttle on the approach until I touched down. My second landing was much better for by then, I had a better idea of the Mustang's rate of descent on the approach. The aircraft came down like an elevator with closed throttle, wheels and flaps down.

Eight hours were allotted for transitional training and by then, I felt reasonably comfortable in the Mustang. After the first four hours of transition, a bi-place check with an instructor was required in the BT-13. By then, I had come to hate the idea of flying an aircraft with an instructor behind me. The Pratt-Whitney engine provided one continuous roar, and cruising below 250 miles per hour wasn't particularly exciting. When we checked out in the Mustang there weren't any technical manuals to read, just a few do's and don'ts compiled on some tattered sheets of paper that had been glued to a strip of cardboard.

A black man kept our rooms neat and tidy. He made our beds and saw to our laundry and dry cleaning, and even shined our shoes. When Fogie and I decided to go into Bartow one evening and asked this man for a ride, he was glad to oblige. Fogie entered the back seat rather hurriedly as I slid in the front seat, coming eye-to-eye with a pigeon who was perched atop the seat back between the driver and passenger side of the car. There were quite a few streaks of white where the pigeon sat, but none where the driver or front seat passenger sat.

When I gave the driver a questioning look, he said, "It's all right. He sits there all day until I get off work."

The chow at this air field was excellent. And the weather was getting very warm, which made the Mustang's cockpit insufferably hot—well over 100 degrees. While I didn't have much of an appetite, a bottle of cold beer certainly hit the spot after a couple hours in that cockpit.

Sunday was a day of rest, and often Fogie, Ott and I would hitch a ride into Bartow to attend church. After the services were over, many local families would approach us on the front steps of the church and invite us to their homes for dinner. A family by the name of Jordan sort of adopted me for a while. Margie, the youngest of their two daughters, made a point of taking me under her wing for the next two months.

On weekends, the gals in Bartow frequently held dances in a public park. Although the dance floor was protected with a roof, it was still very much an open-air structure. Even so, a lot of attractive lighting managed to set the proper mood. There was even a swimming pool close-by where Fogie, Ott and I took a quick dip before going on to the dance. Fogie showed me a few dives off the low board which I attempted, but they were poorly executed and I remember stinging the hell out of my back and chest.

"God, this is painful!", I said. "How in the world did you stand it when you were first learning these dives?"

He admitted to me then that he had worn long underwear until the dives had been perfected.

At the dance I was content to stand around and watch until Fogie finally began to shove me from behind into a waiting Margie's arms. After that, Margie managed to teach me a few basic steps, and while my sense of rhythm was pretty bad, I nonetheless enjoyed having a lovely young girl in my arms.

A mile or so out of Bartow was a swimming hole called Kissengen Springs. After the dance, Margie and some of the other girls invited us out there. I envisioned something comparable to Dolphie's Pond north of Silver Lake, but upon arriving there, I was amazed to see a crystal clear pool of water approximately 60 feet across. There was a sandy strip of beach around the entire pool and there was hardly any movement on the surface of the water. On one side of the pool was a low solid wooden fence 5 feet long by 1 yard high that allowed the water to escape at a constant rate over the top. The water's high sulfur content created a smell of rotten eggs in the air, although it did not cling to a swimmer's skin. Margie said she often shampooed her hair where the water flowed over the gate and that the sulfur had proven extremely beneficial to her hair and skin.

After swimming at Kissengen Springs several times, I concluded that I should be able to touch bottom in the middle of the pool where the water came up from the earth's depths. I went straight down, as far as my lungs would permit me to go, able to see clearly all the way. But then common sense told me to turn around and so I did. I doubt if anyone has ever touched bottom in the middle of that pool.

Margie wore a bathing suit that was quite daring for its day. It had a halter bra, and bottom that laced up the sides. I threatened to buy a pair of shears and cut through the lacings, and while she was not inclined to believe that I would, she would nonetheless run for the bath house whenever my fingers made the slightest little clipping motion.

I took many a relaxing swim at Kissengen Springs, enjoying the company of the gals from Bartow. It was one of the nicest associations I ever experienced with the civilian population while in the military service stateside.

Another place of interest was Cypress Gardens, a very large lake surrounded by cypress trees close to the water's edge. The proprietor's name was Dick Pope, and I was told that he had started the enterprise on a shoestring. The lake had a beauty all its own, and water skiing was the dominant sport. The gals who did the water skiing were good athletes an damned good-looking as well. They worked as a team behind speedboats, and were pulled individually with tow ropes. One afternoon five other pilots and I managed to talk these lovely gals into teaching us to water ski. As service-men, we were allowed to enter Cypress Gardens free-of-charge. We donned our swimming trunks and then listened carefully to our instructors. After a few tries, most of the guys managed to get up on their skis and even made a circuit behind the speedboat. My instructor was a little sixteen-year-old named Nancy Stilley who, unfortunately, was never able to teach me much of anything. After nearly drowning myself a couple of times, I finally gave up. I had no one to blame but myself for Nancy was an excellent instructor, and also the Women's National Water Skiing Champion in the late 1940's. Her picture had even appeared on the cover of Life magazine.

Another pilot and I went to Cypress Gardens one Saturday afternoon to watch the gals practice for a show. Afterwards, we stood along a road that was bordered with orange groves, hoping to hitch a ride back into Bartow. In Kansas I had often helped myself to some fruit off the apple trees, and decided to sample an orange. I had been told to select one with a slight amount of mold on it, and after I'd done this, I walked back to the road and tasted my stolen wares. It was without a doubt the sweetest orange I had ever eaten. Afterwards, my hands were a bit sticky but my handerkerchief and a bit of spit soon took care of that.

After our transition in the P-51A Mustang elementary formation flying was started, I finally developed a knack for getting in tight formation and staying there without too much difficulty. I had never experienced this while flying formation in the AT-6. As the air flowed over the Mustang's leading surfaces, a vacuum was created behind these surfaces, such as the wing one was flying formation on. Once I'd tucked my aircraft in there tight, a little pressure on the controls was required to keep the aircraft from flying into the lead plane. In the race car world it is called drafting.

The instructors gave us a good workout flying formation. The finger four was the dominant formation and also the basic one used in combat. The two aircraft element should always be maintained in aerial combat as it is very flexible if flown properly.

The P-51A Mustang was a quick aircraft. With just a little urging, it would change positions in a hurry, and I soon became acclimated to its responses.

We started our aerial gunnery with camera gunnery at about 10,000 feet, using the standard training command gunnery pass. The initial gunnery training was flown in the P-51A, and while the engine power would fall off dramatically at 10,000 feet, from there on down to the deck that plane had no equal in the world.

Lt. Dow was our gunnery instructor, and he was all business. His talents were known far and wide for he was a crack shot.

Once they were satisfied with our camera gunnery and technique, they allowed us to have a loaded .50-caliber machine gun in each wing. Lt. Dow cautioned us about flying up the tow plane's ass before we took off with live ammo for the very first time. I felt pretty good about my passes, correct lead and good coordination.

After landing, we gathered in the ready room and listened to Lt. Dow's critique as the scores came in. Lt. Dow's colored bullet holes in the towed sleeve were the only hits recorded and he had many. There hadn't been one damned hit by my colored bullets, and the other two pilots on this training mission did no better. Lt. Dow again stressed technique, the correct lead and coordination. "Work on these fundamentals and you'll qualify," he said.

Our instrument flight time was kept current with flights in the BT-13's back seat under the hood, and in the Mustang, head in the cockpit flying fighter instruments while another Mustang flew alongside, keeping an eye out for other aircraft. Short round-robin navigational flights were flown also. The check points came up much faster than my AT-6 cross-country days.

On May 11, 1944, I was checked out in the P-51B Mustang with the Rolls-Royce Melin V-12 engine, rated at 1,390 horsepower. This engine had a turbo super-charger that cut in at about 13,000 feet of altitude. Upon starting up, I noticed a more deep-throated engine sound from the exhausts. While S-taxiing out for take-off, I thought the engine cowling was a bit wider than that of the P-51A. The cockpit layout was the same as the A model, except that the coolant and oil shutters could be set at automatic after being airborne. During take-off, I noticed the P-51B was a bit heavier, but after attaining altitude and setting the throttle and prop pitch to cruise, the performance was about the same. Climbing on up to where the super-charger cut in was a revelation for suddenly a real surge of power was felt. It was sort of comical to be in a flight of four climbing up to high altitude to see P-51's surging ahead—first one, then another. At this point, it was always wise to loosen the formation until all of the super-chargers had cut in.

Altogether we spent twenty hours firing aerial gunnery plus eight hours camera gunnery before firing live ammo. It was necessary to hit the target on three consecutive gunnery flights in order to qualify. It was frustrating to hit the towed target on a couple of flights and then to come up with a zero. But with concentration and practice, I managed to score well on my last three gunnery flights and so I was able to qualify. Some of the pilots were required to shoot extra in order to qualify. On one gunnery flight I was assigned a P-51A. Our flight of four flew out to the tow aircraft which was flying at about 15,000 feet. I managed to get the P-51A up to 16,000 feet and in position for a firing pass from the right. The initial turn into the tow plane and target gave me some needed airspeed but when I reversed the turn to approach the towed target, my gun sight slid to the rear of the target sleeve. I compensated by gently pulling the stick back. Although I had the throttle and prop pitch full forward, there wasn't enough power at 15,000 feet to pull the Mustang through the 90 degree steep turn. Just as I was pulling the gun sight reticule past the target sleeve, the aircraft did a quick flip to the right into a spin. Kicking the left rudder and popping the stick forward enabled me to recover after making one turn. I climbed back up to make a pass from the left side of the tow plane, this time from a higher altitude to gain more airspeed for the final turn onto the towed target. The oxygen masks we used at Bartow for high altitude flying were the old type. They would slide down onto the chin during violent maneuvers, especially if a person had sweat on his face. The Florida sun shone hot and steamy through the canopy, and over a period of two months, I managed to lose fifteen pounds of puberty fat.

One mid-afternoon, after we'd returned from a gunnery flight, we were hanging around the flight line watching the rest of our squadron peel off and land. As the second Mustang of a flight started to peel off, there was a rapid Pow! Pow! Pow! sound. The pilot flying wing on this Mustang told the other pilot to go to the control tower and count his hits. It might have been a serious situation but it brought a chuckle as the voice came out over the loudspeaker on the flight line. The fact was, the hot weather sometimes cooked off a few rounds unexpectedly.

Toward the end of our aerial gunnery training we also shot ground gunnery. I shot well but damn near flew into the banked up ground at the rear of the target. While making a pass at the target, I thought I would hold my dive a little longer so the convergence of the guns would hit the target dead center. I knew I had good hits as the dust came up from the banked earth behind the target, but as I made my recovery from the dive, I got a ground effect sound in the cockpit, all engine noise. I knew I had come close to hitting the earth, and the range officer later verified this by giving me an ass-chewing call on the radio.

We also had quite a bit of strafing gunnery. Our instructor warned us before we took off not to get too low as we flew around the gunnery patterns since a tree could reach up, grab a wing and send us cartwheeling into the ground.

After arriving at the range, the instructor made the first strafing pass. Pulling up to the left of the target, he proceeded to set the rectangular pattern we were to follow, making his turns at 100 to 150 feet of altitude. We student fighter pilots had our wing-tips on the tree tops in our turns. It was our first chance to legally buzz since coming to Bartow.

On our last strafing training mission, our instructor told us: "You kids can make those turns with your wing-tips in the trees if you want. As for me, I'm going to stay up where it's safe." This particular instructor was a veteran of many combat missions, and I'll bet he had his wing-tips below the trees on many an occasion.

While at Bartow our link trainer instrument training was continued. There were fourteen hours of it, and we also studied Morse Code, which I had almost forgotten since my preflight days.

One afternoon as I left the link trainer building, I heard a commotion coming from the flight line. I didn't think much of it at the time, but later I learned that a pilot from Texas had attempted a landing in a Mustang and hit a slight crosswind. He had a bad bounce and applied full throttle and prop pitch. The torque was too much to hold with the right rudder as his left wing caught the ground. After cartwheeling he ended up on his back. By the time others had reached the crash-site, there was a strong odor of high octane gas, and a hot engine ticking with heat. A faint voice was heard from underneath the Mustang, someone yelling, "Get me out of this sonofabitch!"

The crash crew immediately went to work and soon had extracted the pilot. I came away thinking that it would undoubtedly be impossible for anyone to handle a Mustang after a bad landing bounce in a crosswind with full flaps down and full power applied.

That evening, I approached the Texas pilot in the bar of the club. He seemed a bit more subdued than usual as he sat sipping his beer. I noticed that there were a few scratches on his forehead. I asked him how he was feeling and he said he was feeling fine. After that, he brought me a beer and there was no further discussion. While many people didn't like to approach a pilot who had experienced a mishap, I was more inclined to make myself available in case they cared to talk.

On the field was a model P-51 period, unpainted and looking sleek in its aluminum skin. The flight line personnel had apparently been keeping it in a hangar, preserving it with the care one would normally give to a collector's item. Occasionally it was flown by certain selected instructors, but never by a fighter pilot trainee. Of course I was eager to fly it, as were many of the other men.

I was in a flight of four with this particular Mustang in the lead. The instructor had to throttle back so that the three of us could keep up at cruising speed.

Most of our instructors were combat veterans from the Mediterranean theatre of operations. They had flown the original P-51, designated then as the A-36 used as a dive bomber, the P-40, and the British Spitfire. The A-36 instructor was a former school teacher who had a lot of combat wisdom to impart. He had been shot down by flak and had used his parachute to survive. After a training mission he had led us on, we all gathered around for our usual critique. He mentioned that we should always be sure that our parachutes were properly fitted and then pointed to his front four upper teeth, which were false. He explained that the chest strap on his chute had once slipped up and knocked his teeth out when the parachute opened. The chute itself had been the seat type, the only type we had flown with during our training. I immediately tightened the straps on the parachutes I wore after that.

This instructor also told us how to make sure the bird cage type canopy of the Mustang would jettison if the need arose. It was simply a matter of sliding the air vent open that was located forward on the side of the canopy which created a draft-like action, ensuring the canopy's departure. This little piece of advice would prove invaluable to me later on in Europe.

Another instructor of ours was a southerner who had flown the Spitfire in the Mediterranean theatre. He was a lot of fun to fly training missions with. During our critiques, he would literally have us rolling on the floor once the serious talk was over with. He told us abut the flak in that theatre, about seeing too much of it too often. Finally, a flight surgeon sent him to the flak camp for a rest. He spent a few days there getting his nerves calmed down, then he returned to operations. On his first mission after returning, a flak burst turned his Spitfire upside down, so back he went to the flak camp.

After returning from one of our training missions, we three pilots filed into the briefing room, checked our parachutes in and then joined our instructor for the usual critique.

With a perfectly straight face he said, "I just shot a landing out there that was so smooth that I had to call the tower to see if I was really on the ground." The three of us damn near spun in right then and there, laughing with uncontrollable mirth.

After a good rat race he would call us into formation for the flight back to the field. We had to be on our toes for he would sometimes come back on his throttle while we were catching up to him with our throttles advanced. One could anticipate when joining formation, usually sliding into an assigned position with clockwork precision when the lead aircraft was at cruise throttle. When the instructor would pull this tactic on us, he would watch us slide just below him with a look of comical disbelief on his face. Other times he would gently move his control stick backward and forward to give us the bumps, but he taught us how to safely join up in formation, and always join a formation from below and from the side so that he could watch us. It was important to never blank out the aircraft whose wing you were flying by turning away from him. If you overshot him, the correct and safest method was to slide on by underneath.

While flying his tour in the Mediterranean theatre, our instructor spoke of hearing a radio transmission while on a mission. It seemed the pilot was going to abort the mission because of a rough engine but then an authoritative voice instructed him to get his black ass back in formation. This small episode came out of the 99th Fighter Squadron, an all-Negro fighter outfit. I'd heard of them while flying in Europe and knew they were damned good.

Toward the end of our training, our squadron commanding officer led a flight of us on a combat exercise. I was flying number four position, usually called tail-end Charlie. We were flying at about 13,000 feet when our C.O. told us to loosen up the formation. As he nosed over into a 45 degree dive, and we began to hurtle down, I glanced at the airspeed which read 500 miles per hour. As our C.O. leveled out, he looked around and saw that we were all with him. These Mustangs we were flying were war-weary with a maximum speed below five hundred miles an hour as indicated by the red line on the airspeed instrument. I thoroughly enjoyed it for this was the fastest I had ever flown. The C.O. put us into echelon right for the peel off for landing. Prior to take-off he had briefed us to land close behind one another. As I was breaking my glide for a landing, I could see the other three aircraft ahead of me on the runway, and they were properly staggered, with the C.O. on the left side of the runway, his wing man on the right, and my element leader on the left. I, of course, was to land on the right. As I was settling in for a nice three-point landing, the gremlins took a hold of the Mustang. Suddenly I had the stick back in my gut with full left aileron, at the same time applying full left rudder and brake for an instant to straighten out my landing roll. A runway landing light flew out from under the right wing. I wasn't concerned as I had shot a good landing and thought no more about it. The gentle wind had been straight down the runway and had blown all the turbulence and prop-wash back for me to contend with, another small problem for a tail-end Charlie. I told the crew chief about it after shutting the engine off.

Gathered around our C.O., we discussed the landing light I had hit and I was simply told to "watch it". Then he talked some of gunnery, and his closing statement was, quote: "Deflection shooting is fine but it is a known fact that if you stick the barrel of a gun up a jaybird's ass and pull the trigger, you are going to blow him him to hell," unquote.

A married fighter pilot from the other training squadron approached me one evening in the club, asking if I wanted a blind date. He vowed that the girl was extremely good-looking. We left the club and drove into Lakeland, Florida to pick our girls up. Sure enough, my date was a knockout. She was almost as tall as I and very slim. The four of us spent the evening at an out-of-the-way lover's lane. Since I didn't even know the girl I was with, all we did was talk.

The next morning, which happened to be a Sunday, I crawled out of my sack, inhaling the faint aroma of orange blossoms that drifted in through the window. After showering and dressing, I proceeded to the club for a light breakfast. Afterwards, I sat down in the lounge and was reading the paper when suddenly an M.P. began paging me. It made me wonder what I could possibly have done, or if there might be a problem at home. After standing up and identifying myself, I was told that there was a damned good-looking woman at the main gate waiting to see me. We walked to the main guard gate where I found my date of the previous night sitting in a convertible, dressed in a halter and tight brief pants. Another date was promptly arranged, which once more included the married pilot and his girlfriend.

That evening, as our car stopped briefly at a stoplight in uptown Lakeland, my date suddenly slid down in the back seat that she and I were occupying.

"What is it?" I asked. "What's the matter?"

"There goes my husband in the white shirt and dark slacks," she said.

Looking ahead, I noticed a man crossing the street. He was well-groomed, with an athletic build and at least an axe handle's width across the shoulders.

We promptly took the girls home for I had been taught to respect the institution of marriage, and as it turned out, my partner's date was also married. After that, I went back to the Bartow girls, for the ground was a little firmer there.

The club at Bartow Army Air Field held some really fine Saturday night dances. At one such dance I was sitting at a table with my date, Margie Jordon, and several others when I noticed a really handsome couple who appeared to be looking for a table. The pilot's name was Beder, but the girl was unknown to me. I asked some of the guys at our table if we couldn't make room for them. I was told no, that they were Jewish. We had flown several training missions together and I knew him to be an excellent pilot, and very friendly. Rising from our table, I presented myself to them and got an introduction to Beder's pretty wife. Finally, a pilot at another table invited the couple to join him, which made me feel a great deal better about things.

Gradually, I was becoming a little less naive and a bit more worldly-wise. In the space of a very brief time, I had nearly gotten myself involved with a married woman, and also, been exposed to Anti-Semitism.

Fogie fell for a Bartow girl by the name of Dorothy Butts. After confiding his feelings, he asked if I thought he should present her with some sort of ring. He wasn't sure she would accept an engagement ring so he decided on a ring with a ruby setting, a token of their "being engaged to be engaged at some later time." Fogie had been dating this gal for quite some time. The manner in which she repeatedly rebuffed his advances made him all the more determined. One night he was invited to her home for supper. Needing all the moral support he could get, he wangled an invitation for me as well. I was only too happy to fly his wing on this particular mission and looked forward to sharing in a pleasant evening.

As we approached the front door of Dorothy's house, I noticed that the house itself was quite old but also extremely well-maintained. The same was true of the inside. Dorothy was a tall, attractive girl who strongly resembled her parents. We enjoyed a good home-cooked meal—meat, potatoes, gravy, vegetables and pie, which left me in excellent spirits. At this juncture, I felt fairly certain that Fogie and this girl might have a future together, so I was quite surprised when she refused his ring, refusing to consider any sort of an arrangement. By then, Fogie had become a close buddy of mine and I didn't like to see him hurt. Dorothy certainly missed the boat when she turned Fogie down for he was a damned fine young man.

In one of my letters home, I mentioned to Donna that I was seeing some of the local girls, that she was too young to be waiting around for me, and that it wasn't fair or logical to expect her to wait.

When we first arrived at Bartow Army Air Field, the Commanding Officer had instructed us to let our hair grow out for we weren't cadets anymore. Had we been wise enough to read between the lines, we might have been able to figure out that our final destination would be Europe, for the people on that continent all wore their hair long. I remember that I had to purchase a comb at the post exchange for this was the first time I had combed my hair since classification days thirteen months earlier.

One of my training missions was a two aircraft formation flight. Lieutenant Scipioni was my instructor. On take-off I tucked in tight and remained so up to altitude where he informed me to stay in tight formation through various combat maneuvers. For the next thirty minutes, the lieutenant did all he could to shake me up. As he was rolling out of a G-pulling steep turn, he told me to get my prop out of his ass, and upon rolling out to straight level cruise, still in tight formation, he got a "Roger" and a big grin from me. They don't send one back to the field for flying good tight formation.

Another phase of our training was synthetic gunnery, an excellent procedure consisting of a cockpit, stick and rudders, gun sight and throttle with engine noise varying when diving or climbing. An enemy aircraft was projected on a screen in front of the device, always in motion, and with varying types of background terrain, or sky and clouds. The problem was to place the lighted reticle of the gun sight at the correct amount of lead on the projected enemy aircraft, then to press the gun button on the forward part of the control stick. There was a staccato noise when the gun button was pressed. If you weren't hitting the aircraft, the instructor would project a lighted dot ahead of the aircraft where you should have been sighting your guns. A good rule of thumb was to lead an enemy aircraft four radii at 90 degrees deflection; he would probably be going as fast as he could.

Our squadron C.O. taught us the theory of one radii lead for every 100 miles an hour the enemy aircraft was traveling, plus the jaybird theory.

One evening while I was sitting at the bar enjoying my usual beer after supper, a pilot from the other training squadron sat down beside me. He told me about a gal he had met the night before. I found this rather strange for I didn't know this pilot at all. After a while, he took a closer look at me and promptly excused himself, hailing another pilot who had just walked in the bar, a pilot I suppose I vaguely resembled. As it turned out, there was quite a story behind my look-alike. His mother had been captured or interned by the Japanese at the start of the war. Later, he would be assigned to the Pacific theatre of operations.

Another topic of subdued conversation in the club that night concerned itself with the friendly dog-fight our instructors had engaged in with the fighter pilots from a naval base not too far from Bartow. Our instructors got their butts waxed, and while I don't know what the navy pilots were flying, it was probably the F4F, F6F, or the F4U, all damned good fighter aircraft.

Since my last name was Brooks, it always appeared high on the alphabetical list for details. When it was my turn to be Officer of the Day, I reported to the military police headquarters for instructions and probable duties about 0800 hours. There wasn't much to do during the day, and at night, there were a couple of tours of the guard posts with the Sergeant of the Guard. After our first tour, I asked the Sergeant if I could possibly attend the dance at the club, for Margie was waiting for me. I didn't much care to go there with the O.D. brassard on my arm and the hog-leg .44 pistol hanging almost to my right knee. The Sergeant suggested that I put the brassard and pistol in my bed, hiding it well. After that, he said, I could attend the dance and he would call me if my presence was needed at the guardhouse. I spent a nice evening, then later retrieved the brassard and hog-leg, before returning to the guardhouse from where the Sergeant and I began our guard post inspection. During our tour I asked the Sergeant where whiskey could be purchased.

"How much do you need?" he asked.

"Oh, about a case of bourbon," I told him.

I gave him the money required for a case of fifths as we continued our guard post inspection. Afterwards, he asked what barracks and room I was billeted in and said an automobile would deliver the booze in the darkness just before sunrise while everyone else was asleep. He was as good as his word and I quickly shoved the case of bourbon under my bed. That Sunday morning, Fogie sold all but three fifths. We could have sold four or five cases, if we had only had them. The pilots who knew their bourbon said it was pretty decent stuff.

During our two months of training at Bartow, we were issued one 24-box case of .12 gauge shotgun shells to shoot skeet. I went to the skeet range one morning when I wasn't scheduled to fly and asked the Sergeant if I could somehow get out of shooting the case of shotgun shells as I was getting all the shooting I wanted while flying. He went to the ammunitions storage, returned with the case of shotgun shells he had stored for me and suggested I send them home to my Dad. After crating the case, I supplied the Sergeant with my Dad's name and address and left the skeet range with a real good feeling, knowing that Dad and some of my uncles could shoot quail this coming winter.

One of the pilots occupying the room next to Fogie's and mine was a very small man from St. Louis, Missouri. His name was Kenneth Graeff. His height wasn't much above minimum pilot standards, and his build was almost frail. His forehead was wide, angling down to a pointed chin, and he wore his hair parted in the middle, and sported a small mustache. He could quite accurately be described as a ladies' man for that is what he was. He frequently came in late at night, and on weekends, sometimes not at all. Kenny had spent a year or two in the enlisted ranks before learning to fly. He knew his way around, particularly in the military structure. I had often seen him with different gals, some much taller than he. The gals were all damned good-looking and were always hanging onto Kenny as if they were afraid he might get away. Kenny was a great kidder which invited a certain amount of retaliatory remarks. Still, he never quite managed to get my goat and so we became pretty good friends.

After flying all afternoon in the hot Mustang cockpits, Kenny and I hit the showers at the same time. I noticed that he was rather modestly endowed and couldn't help asking how he managed to satisfy so many sexy little gals.

"Brooksie," he said, "I go around the edges so fast they think the middle is all filled up."

Of all the men I was to meet while in the Army Air Corps, Kenny was the most unusual and truly an unforgettable character.

May 31, 1944 was the first time I consulted the flight surgeon. Another pilot by the name of Slovak from Nebraska had teamed up with me for an instrument flight of two Mustangs to altitude. I had a slight head cold but thought nothing of it and flew all the same. We took off and climbed to 20,000 feet in our P-51B's. As each of us did a bit of flying, the other would watch for other aircraft. We ended up in a rate race to finish the flight of one hour. I gave Slovak a call on the radio, betting him a bottle of beer that I could beat him to the deck. After he'd accepted that bet, we nosed over and hurtled down, staying about even until we reached 10,000 feet where I came back on the throttle when my head suddenly felt as if it had been pumped up with air. A very uncomfortable feeling came over me. Slovak continued down to the deck, entered the traffic pattern, peeled off and landed. I eased on down to traffic altitude, entered the pattern, peeled off, coming around for an approach to landing.

At Bartow, a yellow line marked a third of the way down the runways, denoted a touchdown of your aircraft before reaching the yellow line. Overshooting the line would cost you five dollars. Since my approach was too high, it meant a go-around. I applied full throttle slowly, at about 100 feet. I could not hear that big engine at full throttle directly in front of me. I came around for another landing, this time touching down before the yellow line. After rolling out, I opened the coolant shutters, brought up the flaps, taxiied back to the ramp, parked where the crew chief indicated, filled out the aircraft form and then approached the crew chief. Although his lips were moving and I knew he was talking to me, I couldn't hear a word he said. After pointing to my ears, I walked directly to the flight surgeon's office. His message to me, which he wrote out on a notepad, was to lie out in the sun since that would probably clear up the congestion in my ears. I still owe Slovak that bottle of beer.

Being deaf for a while made me realize how my Grandmother Brooks felt, living in a world where communication was extremely difficult,

I flew with another pilot in the BT-13 for an hour, practicing instrument flight, going up to 6,000-7,000 feet slowly, then descending the same way. Of course this didn't help the congestion in my ears. By that time I was really falling behind in my training. My squadron flew three hours of night transition which I could only watch from the flight line with some of the gals from Bartow. As Fogie greased in two night landings, I found myself wishing that I might have been with him.

After four days of nursing along this condition with my ears, the operations officer suggested I wash back a training class. In order to leave for overseas with my group, I needed only another twenty hours of training. The next morning I went to the post exchange and purchased a Vicks nose inhaler. Returning to the barracks, I changed into my swimming trunks and lay in the Florida sun between the barracks where no breeze was blowing. I worked up a good sweat which was further enhanced by sipping some straight bourbon now and again. Three hours of this treatment was enough for one day. I finished things off with a real hot shower, then lay back on my sack until supper chow. After chow I noticed that my ears were crackling a bit, and that a little hearing had returned. The next morning I went to see the flight surgeon but he wouldn't clear me for flying. I kept seeing him in the mornings for another two days and finally he cleared me for flight duty.

On June 6th I went into Bartow to pick up a silver identification bracelet with my name and serial number engraved on it. As I was leaving the jewelers, the bells and whistles in

Bartow began ringing. When I asked a passersby what it was all about, he said that we had successfully invaded Europe. I had hoped to be in on the invasion, flying cover for the infantry as they hit the beaches.

On June 7th I talked to my squadron C.O. bright and early. I was determined to fly like hell to catch up with my group. He obliged me by scheduling me on five straight skip-bombing training missions that very day. Before taking off, I made sure that the Vicks nose inhaler was handy.

The Mustang's cockpit was well over 100 degrees and we didn't fly over 1,000 feet. I flew five hours on practice skip-bombing missions and by day's end, my ears and sinuses were well loosened up. The following day I flew another seven-and-one half hours. Three of those hours were spent skip-bombing and four-and-a-half were spent on a full military load up to Savannah, Georgia. Our flight of four landed at Tallahassee, Florida on the return flight to Bartow. It felt pretty good to be in a Mustang taxiing by the P-40's on the ramp.

On June 9th, I finished up my ground strafing requirements. The old car bodies in a field off in the wilds of Florida must have been well pulverized after so many classes of fighter pilots had strafed them.

I now had a weekend off before flying three hours of transitional night flying in the Mustang with the other training squadron.

The night of June 12th found me in the other squadron's operations building. My name was listed as to take-off time and assigned quadrant. I hadn't flown at night since January 3rd but that didn't bother me. I loved to fly at night, and being among strangers didn't concern me either.

During basic and advanced night flying we flew around the traffic pattern, shooting landings or participated in cross-country flights. The best way to describe quadrant night flying is in a visual way. It is necessary to imagine a multi-layered round cake, with the cake sliced once along the north-south active runway, and sliced again along the east-west runway. The pilots in the higher quadrants took off first. I took off climbing to my assigned northeastern quadrant at 4,000 feet. There were two pilots below me flying the same quadrant at 3,000 and 2,000 feet, respectively. There were one or two above me also. It was a beautiful cloudless night with thousands of twinkling stars. Temperature-wise, it was the first time I had ever felt comfortable in a Mustang.

Flying around my quadrant, I observed the bisecting runways, ever alert for other aircraft. It was possible to see the wing lights of other Mustangs as they flew in their assigned areas above and below me. The fire from the engine exhaust on the left and right in front of the cockpit was something to behold.

Occasionally, a small piece of burning carbon would streak by the cockpit. After almost an hour-and-a-half, the tower instructed me to come in and shoot my first of two landings. I came back with the throttle as I started a wide descending spiral left, watching like a hawk for other aircraft. I entered the field boundary, peeled off and commenced a 360 degree overhead landing pattern as I flew over the northern end of the runway. Next there was a quick check of all instruments: a full rich mixture, propeller pitch full forward, wheels down while circling to base leg, turn on approach, closing throttle to adjust approach speed, select the correct amount of flaps, then set the Mustang into a nice wheel landing. I held the tail surfaces up a bit with a little forward pressure on the stick to insure that I was going straight down the runway, gently lowering the tail-wheel to the runway. After a straight roll-out to the turnoff taxiway to the parking ramp, I parked, directed by the crew chief's flashlight.

I was in the pilots ready room lighting up one of my infrequent cigarettes when the squadron operations officer came storming in, every bit as irate as the P-40 training operations officer had been.

"Who in the hell told you to shoot a night wheel landing?" he bellowed.

"No excuse, sir," I said.

"In this squadron," he continued, "we shoot three-point landings at night and wheel landings during daylight hours. And another thing, roll those flying coverall sleeves down. Later on in your flying career you could have a cockpit fire."

After another of my quiet "Yes sirs," he finally left the room. This particular ass-chewing had been like water running off a duck's back after all of my pre-flight and cadet flying days.

In a short while I took off again, flew my quadrant for an hour-and-a-half, then came in and shot a decent three-point night landing.

During the daylight flying hours I had noticed the other squadron shooting wheel landings. It was nothing unusual. I had done the same landings while in advanced flight. The three-point landings at night didn't make much sense to me. My own squadron shot three-point landings during daylight hours, and wheel landings at night, which seemed like a much more logical system.

The three hours of night transition finished my training as a fighter pilot. All I needed now was some experience under combat conditions. I had just completed the most extensive competitive fighter pilot training my country could offer, and by any standards, the best. I felt confident, and ready and eager to take on the enemy.

Parting with the people of Bartow was a difficult thing to

do. I knew I would miss the meandering drives from the flying field to Bartow over the narrow blacktopped road with its Spanish moss draped oak trees.

When my group first arrived in Bartow, I had taken the bus into town to look things over. As I was walking down Main Street, a pretty little gal said, "Hey." In Kansas, "hey" was taken to mean that somebody wanted to talk to you. But here it simply meant "Hello." And that was how I happened to meet Margie Jordon.

My group journeyed up to Tallahassee by bus where we spent a week drawing brand-new equipment, plus a few lectures, going everywhere in formation again. The best and latest in flying equipment was issued to us. The leather flying helmet was of soft leather, with goggles, plus smoked lenses if desired. The oxygen mask covered the entire face except for the eyes. The microphone enclosed inside the mask was located in front of the mouth when the mask was hooked up to the helmet. A very fine leather flying jacket was also issued. The high altitude flying togs were olive drab in color, pile lined with a fur-like inside lining. Suspenders were also included to hold up the heavy trousers. Silk gloves plus fine leather outer gloves were issued, and sheepskin flying boots zippered up the front, with the fur to the inside. A Colt .45 pistol with two clips and shoulder holster was our issued sidearm. The .45 was swathed in protective cosmoline, wrapped tightly with thick waxed paper.

All of this equipment went into a new foot locker with two O.D. wool blankets, two sheets, two pillowcases and of course, a pillow. A new pair of overshoes were included with the issue plus a wristwatch.

After returning from a lecture, we were lined up in front of our headquarters, still in formation. The headquarters adjutant addressed us, and as he did so, he noticed when I shifted a wad of gum from one side of my mouth to the other. He told me to report to him, dismissed the formation and retreated to his office. I followed, and after waiting a minute, knocked once on the door. After entering, I came to attention, saluted, and remained at attention for the adjutant didn't give me an "at ease". He was a First Lieutenant, and rumor had it that he had crawfished out of flying combat overseas although assigned to a combat squadron. I riveted my eyes on the wall behind him as he verbally chastised me for chewing gum while in formation. When I finally looked at him directly, he apparently read my thoughts for suddenly he stopped his childish prattle and excused me. I left his office thinking that this joker would have made an excellent Cadet TAC officer.

During our short stay at Tallahassee, a three day pass was given to our group. I thought about going home to see Donna and my family but the distance was too great. And anyway, I didn't want to upset anyone with the news that I was going overseas.

Fogelquist, on the other hand, traveled all the way to Spokane, Washington, hitch-hiking across country and back on military aircraft. He was a real wheeler-dealer when it came to things like that and usually accomplished his objective. I was one of the few who didn't take advantage of the three-day pass. I took a stroll up to the college campus, but most of the gals had gone for the summer. I attended a movie on base one evening, after taking a leisurely shower. Although it was a good movie, it was uncomfortably hot and close in the barracks-like theatre. Afterwards, I enjoyed the fresh outside air for it came as a welcome relief. I thought that Kansas had an excessive amount of high temperatures and humidity but it was nothing compared to Florida.

My group of approximately 75 trained fighter pilots boarded a Pullman train in Tallahassee to head for a destination north. Troop movements were always kept secret, which invited a lot of speculation among the men. As usual, the Pullman train was first-class, meals were taken in the diner and there was a porter to make up the bunks.

This was my first trip to the East coast and it was at about midnight when the train stopped in a large city. There were those who suggested that we should take a look around for we were in New York City on famous Broadway. Though I was one of those who took a look around, I didn't think that Broadway was any more impressive than a lot of streets I'd seen in Topeka, Kansas.

Eventually, we arrived at Camp Miles Standish in Massachusetts. Norman Ott disappeared for a couple of days for his home was an easy traveling distance away.

I remember that the weather was beautiful with days in the mid-70's and nights that were cool enough for Class A winter uniforms. The chow was excellent and my appetite was suddenly greatly improved.

Every branch of the Army was represented at the camp as they awaited shipment overseas.

One evening a dance was given, organized and sponsored by a group of P-38 pilots. Some gals had bussed in from Boston, and a couple of my group and I sauntered in to sort of look things over. I remember that a brawl nearly broke out between us and the P-38 pilots when we tried to cut in on some couples who were dancing. Our egos were pretty pumped up at the time, which was altogether necessary in the view of what we would soon have to face.

At that particular time, I felt that I was in the best possible physical and mental condition and that I was ready for anything.

After a 24-hour pass was granted for a night in Boston,

Fogie and I walked around a bit before taking a hotel room downtown. Fogie called home to talk to his family, including a twin sister. As it happened, Fogie was the only son. After he'd finished his call, he handed the phone to me. I explained that my parents didn't have a phone, but of course we had neighbors who did. Still, I hadn't any idea how to place a long distance telephone call so finally, Fogie did it for me. I spoke to our neighbor, Mrs. Bridgeford, and asked if she would run across the street and fetch my Mom. Of course she was only too glad to comply.

I learned from my mother that Dad was working ten to twelve hour days, and that the kids were all fine and everyone was thinking of me.

"Take care of yourself," she said, and I promised that I would.

Although our conversation was relatively brief, my mother managed to find out where I was because the operator had said, "Boston calling."

We stayed at Camp Miles Standish for a week, awaiting shipment overseas. One of those days was spent at Boston's major league ballpark where we watched the Red Sox and Chicago White Sox play a game. Joe Cronin played first base for the Red Sox, and one of the Foxx brothers played as well. Although the players were a bit gray around the fringes, they could still play the game like it was meant to be played. There were eight or nine in our group and we all enjoyed baseball. Since this was my first opportunity to watch a major league game, I drank it all in like a kid. Joe Cronin came over to our seats behind the first base line with two autographed baseballs, and while I didn't get either one, I did get to shake the man's hand. He spent a few minutes shooting the bull with us, then wished us good luck and returned to the dug-out.

After Fogie and I had spent our 24-hour pass, we rode the train back to camp with five other fighter pilots from our group. It was very early in the morning but even so, we still had to stand in the aisle. The other guys had a gallon of whiskey—now half empty—from which they offered us a drink. As we politely declined, I watched one of the guys crook his finger through the jug handle, then hoist it to his mouth with the aid of his elbow. After taking a healthy swig, he said: "I'm a Rhode Island Red." We learned these fellows had visited the state of Rhode Island on their pass.

Once our shipping orders came through, B-4 bags were packed, shipping labels were affixed, all immunization shots were taken and finally, we were ready. Tom Heine, one of the pilots who couldn't tolerate shots, waited for me to clear the line, then forged the initial signatures from my shot record. He was taking a big gamble but shots put him in bed with the chills.

When I saw our ship in Boston harbour I told the guy behind me that it was the biggest boat I had ever seen.

"That's not a boat," he said. "That's a ship. Don't ever let a sailor hear you talking like that."

With our B-4 bags in tow, up the gang plank we went. The harbor smell was new to me and took a bit of getting used to. A salute was required when we came on deck, and then we were assigned to our cabins. I had been looking forward to these accommodations until I realized that six other men would be sharing them with me. All in all, our group consisted of three naval officers and four fighter pilots. One of the naval officers had been on a ship that was sunk in combat. His face was very red from burns he'd received while in the water, which was covered with a layer of burning oil. When he told us of his ordeal, I decided I was glad that I hadn't joined the Navy.

Eventually the ship was loaded, with a lot of planning and execution involved in the entire procedure. After leaving the harbor, we were informed over the public address system that nothing was to be thrown overboard—not even cigarette butts, since an enemy submarine could detect the course of a troop ship by following the trail of debris.

When the ship started across the open sea and began its constant roll, I remembered what my Dad had once said about getting so seasick that he wished he would die. Fogie and I asked a sailor how to avoid seasickness and he told us the best way was to never miss a meal and to spend as much time as we could topside amidship.

We soon found out that we were commanded by an English captain with an English crew, and that segregation between officers and enlisted men was strictly adhered to. There was a promenade deck for the officers, but for the enlisted men it was catch as catch can. Even on board ship they had duty rosters. I thought the lifeboat drill and life jacket usage would end our commitments, but they assigned me a duty for one meal, that of going to the enlisted men's mess to tell them to remove their caps before entering the mess. The way I accomplished this was to simply inform the first man and then I let him pass it on. I thought the whole thing was a chicken-shit kind of duty.

We were served two meals a day in the officer's mess. The British served a lot of fish, and the way it was prepared made it distinctly different from the fried catfish I was accustomed to.

One day as I looked out to sea, Anton Dvorak's New World Symphony came to mind. The excerpt from the Negro spiritual "Going Home" lingered for a while and I began to wonder if I would really be going home after the war. Then I decided to take a positive outlook on things. Hell, I was exactly where I belonged and right where I wanted to be.

On one of the days I spent topside I remember that I turned

from the rail when I saw a field grade officer come strolling along the deck. He had a very small terrier dog on a leash. Right in front of me, the dog began to gag and the officer hurriedly placed a newspaper on the ship's deck, and when the dog had finished vomiting, the officer rolled up the paper, put it under his arm, and he and the dog continued with their promenade. I figured the officer must have been closely acquainted with someone of high authority in order to be able to bring a dog aboard ship.

It took us a period of six days to cross the Atlantic Ocean and reach Liverpool, England and we zig-zagged all the way. It was very boring after the first three days and I decided that the sea was no life for me.

At Liverpool, the powerful tugs pushed our ship alongside the dock. It was late afternoon and we would not disembark until the following morning.

Early the next morning I was standing by the rail looking out over the Liverpool docks. The people here spoke a language that was new to me. With B-4 bags in tow, we disembarked and had a few minutes before our group was scheduled to leave by train for Hull, England.

Fogie approached a cockney dock worker for a bit of conversation. In no time at all, he and the worker were standing toe-to-toe as Fogie tried his best to interpret the funny-sounding words that were spoken in this unfamiliar accent.

Hull, England was located across the island and north on the English channel. Since we had a three or four hour layover in London, we decided that a little rubber-necking was in order. I very much enjoyed the old world architecture, the people who spoke the King's English, and the quaint little shops, although most were bare of merchandise. The air raid warning sirens sounded a few times and it made us a little jumpy, but when we saw that no civilians were running for bomb shelters, we began to take the sirens in stride.

The English train cars were segregated into compartments. Each compartment could be entered directly from the depot platform which made for an easy exit whenever the train stopped at stations along our way.

We arrived at Hull, England up in Lincolnshire late in the evening. Quonset huts were to be our barracks for a two week period as we finished our final outfitting and lectures before being assigned to various fighter groups.

The English weather this far north was extremely chilly, or so it seemed to me. Although it was the month of July, our trench coats felt good in the evenings and also looked extremely sharp. The first thing we did after settling into the huts was to walk to the surrounding villages where we viewed the English girls. Many were quite good-looking and in one of my letters home I asked Dad what he had thought about English women.

"Don't get involved," was his immediate reply. "They will marry you for the insurance. They know where you are going."

By now I had grown up a little and could see that Dad was a pretty sharp man.

I attended a few dances while at Hull. One dance was held on a pier that jutted out into the surf. The flooring was supported by large timber piles and was enclosed. The area was as large as a football field. It might have been a typical dance except for the fact that there were bomb shelters all along the seashore. During the blitz they were hit quite often, but some of our group used them for other purposes while at Hull.

While we were there, a brand-new back type parachute was issued and put into bags we had brought from state-side, to be fitted by the parachute rigger at our assigned squadrons. Escape and evasion photos were taken in civilian clothes to be enclosed in our kits of the same name. These kits were small plastic boxes about an inch thick and could fit in a hip pocket. They contained silk maps, concentrated food tablets, drugs to stay awake with, and a very, very small compass with a thin strong silk string attached for the purpose of secreting it in one's body. One of our E and E instructors told us of an airman shot down over Germany who was eventually captured. Part of the German interrogation included a physical examination. This airman was bent over with cheeks spread for the rectal exam and the German doctor was reluctant to pull on the black silk string attached to the very small compass secreted in the man's rectum. Another airman shot down deep in Germany rode a bicycle he had stolen all the way across Germany. While stopped at a stoplight, the bicycle's chain came off, and as he was putting the chain back on, two old German ladies engaged him in conversation. He answered some simple yes and no questions they asked as he placed the chain back on the sprockets, then rode away as the light turned green. Another airman was shot down over eastern France. His escape route was a string of French whorehouses and it was said that he literally screwed his way west across France.

Tom Heine, one of our group from Detroit, Michigan, visited a nearby P-38 Fighter Group and wangled a check-out flight in a P-38. He went to altitude for a good wring out, returned to the field, landed, and then parked the aircraft. The P-38 pilot asked Tom what he thought of the craft and Tom told him it would make a good cross-country plane. Rather obviously, Tom was proud to be a Mustang pilot. For that matter, so was I, but I don't think I would have made such a statement for the P-38 had an excellent combat record.

Another part of our training involved the correct use of the Mae West life preserver. We were required to jump feet first off a high diving board into the water, where we inflated the vest by pulling on a short cord which activated the small inflation bottle. The vest inflated outward from one's chest thus the name Mae West. When two of my friends confessed to me that they couldn't swim, I promised to come out and get them if their Mae Wests didn't open.

I had completely forgotten that our .45-caliber pistols were as yet in the cosmoline preservative. At Fogie's suggestion, we walked to the weapons building to clean them. In the cleaning room was a square metal tub about ten feet square, a foot deep and with an inch of cleaning fluid in it. It took a bit of soaking to loosen the cosmoline. Even after field stripping the weapons, the two extra magazine clips took additional cleaning also, but with a wire brush, a thorough cleaning was finally accomplished. Although I had almost forgotten how to field strip a weapon, the sergeant in charge soon put me back in the know.

During our two week stay in Hull, our foot lockers caught up with us. It seemed incredible to me that decent schedules could somehow be maintained on things of this kind.

Once our final processing was completed and our assignments were given, we became scattered all over England and the western part of France, which was now in Allied hands. There were about a dozen of us assigned to the 363rd Fighter Group. Ott, Fogie and I were assigned to the 382nd Fighter Squadron. Dressed in Class A green blouse, pink trousers, and shiney brown shoes, we departed Hull, England for France. The guys assigned to the 8th Air Force were calling us the Purple Heart boys as we bade them good-bye. Our Fighter Group was in the 9th Air Force on the continent of Europe. The 9th Air Force fighter strips weren't far from the invasion beaches. We boarded a C-47 transport aircraft after loading our foot lockers and B-4 bags. The flight across the English Channel took about forty-five minutes. The landing strip in France was in about a mile from Omaha Beach. We loaded our baggage onto a two-and-one-half ton truck, then proceeded on our way to report to our Fighter Group. As we were leaving the air strip area, the truck driver stopped the deuce-and-a-half, raised his head over the truck bed and informed us that there were snipers in the area. A second later, twelve fighter pilots in Class A uniforms were digging like hell into their baggage to find their .45-caliber pistols. Since Fogie and I were situated in the back of the truck bed, getting to our baggage was relatively easy. We put the shoulder holster strap over our heads, tucked the holstered .45 under our left armpit, withdrew the weapon, inserted the loaded clip, pulled back the ejector slide, released same, gently eased the hammer down and after that we were loaded and locked, and ready for the enemy. This procedure was accomplished by holding the muzzle of the weapon toward the sky and away from anyone near at hand. Half of the pilots had one helluva time arming themselves as some had no ammunition in the magazine clips, and others had not cleaned cosmoline from their weapons. When they released the ejector slide to load a round in the firing chamber, the ejector slide went forward as if in slow motion. All of this action was taking place as we cast wary glances toward the large trees that surrounded us.

After a short dusty ride, we found ourselves at our air strip, occupied by the 363rd Fighter Group and a squadron of P-61 Black Widow night fighters. We had a few minutes before reporting to the group colonel and used this time to put our weapons into our B-4 bags and dust each other off with our hands.

The Group headquarters building was an old two-story rock building with a corner of the second floor knocked off, plus a piece of the roof. It was more or less what I had expected to find in a combat zone.

We got word from the C.O.'s adjutant that the Colonel was ready to receive us. We filed in with our caps under our left arms, popped to, saluted, and were given "at ease". The Colonel came down the line shaking everyone's hand and told us a bit about our duties. We then trucked to our assigned squadrons to meet our squadron commander. Our 382nd Fighter Squadron C.O. was Major McWherter, a veteran fighter pilot who had flown a tour against the Japanese. We met some of our squadron mates who came from all over the United States. A veteran of the squadron, Don Frey, was from Kansas. I was assigned to C flight where our flight leader was James Brink, from Kansas City.

My sleeping area was in a German built wooden building consisting of four rooms. There was an embankment around the building approximately four feet high. The Germans who occupied this field north northeast of Cherbourg, France must have been raided often. The room I occupied with three other pilots had received a grenade blast from an American infantryman who helped liberate this field soon after D-Day. There were breastworks and trenches near all the buildings left standing after liberation.

After settling in, Fogie and I looked around our area. The runway was a heavy mesh wire laid from northwest to southeast. In places the wire mesh had rippled two feet up off the ground. There were no Mustangs in sight except for four parked along the runway, the pilots in the cockpit or close nearby, runway alert looked interesting to me. Then I realized how exposed they were. In case of a German aircraft attack on the field, they had to crank up those P-51's and take off to engage the enemy. I didn't think I would volunteer for such duty.

At the east end of the runway a dead tree trunk about fifteen feet in height stuck up into the sky with a wrecked

British mosquito bomber at its foot. I asked a ground crew member how the crew made out in the crash and was told "not very well".

The first order of getting ready for combat missions was the fitting of the back type parachute. A grizzled old sergeant was the parachute rigger. When fitting my new chute he told me to bend over, then he pulled the straps between my legs so damned tight that I could not even stand straight. I complained but the sergeant said it was a good fit and to be damned sure that the family jewels were between the leg straps when buckling up before entering the cockpit. A Mae West was put on before the parachute. A seat-pack dinghy was in all the Mustangs, one had to buckle it to each side of the parachute metal fittings after easing into the pilot's seat.

On July 29th we new replacement pilots were taken aloft by one of the old veteran fighter pilots. As he and I were walking to our Mustangs I asked him if it would be all right to shoot down German aircraft if they came our way while we were practicing formation flying. He said it would be all right, although I thought the old veteran pilots should have first crack at the enemy aircraft.

After two hours of practice flights around the local area, I flew my first combat mission—August 2, a patrol of the Cherbourg peninsula lasting two hours. I concentrated so much on my formation flying that I couldn't tell where we went or how we got back. During our practice formation flying before combat missions, a Capt. Buskey flew with us a bit. He had completed his tour flying the B-17 Flying Fortress. He bounced around a bit while flying formation; a B-17 took much more controls to keep in formation than a Mustang, plus four throttles to contend with. I flew my second mission on August 7th, a patrol over the Brest peninsula. Once again, I was tail-end Charlie. The new pilots often got the number four position in a flight of four, which was often called the coffin corner.

When the Germans fired the flak at the flight they usually didn't lead the first aircraft enough, thus the lead was about right for the number four aircraft. We were flying at about 500 feet, looking for a target of opportunity when the twenty millimeter flak came up. It was just off my right wing and I swear I could hear the white bursting balls. The flight leader called, "Flak! Hit the deck." I followed my element leader to just over the trees. He was flying between the trees whenever possible until we cleared the area. After strafing military vehicles, we climbed to 10,000 feet for the return flight to our landing strip. We had been briefed about the German submarine base along the Brittany coast. It was said that it was a hot spot that was well worth avoiding. I took a quick peek as we were opposite the base, then thought nothing more about it.

After landing, my element leader approached me for a bit of critique. He reminded me that when they said "hit the deck" they didn't mean on top of the trees; they meant below the tree tops whenever possible. Then he asked if I had seen the black flak burst off my tail as we passed the submarine base. Although I hadn't, I had experienced what I thought was some turbulence. I had been told that one could hear flak, the twenty millimeter flak sounded like a short string of firecrackers going off and the big black flak bursts were able to bounce an aircraft around.

Between my first and second missions, I was scheduled for a dawn patrol. After getting buckled in and waiting for press time or start-up time, the mission was scrubbed. This was a letdown for me as I had prepared myself for a mission. After my second mission I walked around the aircraft looking for flak holes. The crew chief had already found them. They were small holes on the right side in the tail section.

There were certain missions that the intelligence officers told us to wear our .45-caliber pistols on. I never did fathom their reasoning in this, for while I had qualified with the weapon I would probably have gotten into more difficulties than out of them.

Being off the mission schedule the same day saw Fogie, Ott and I east of our fighter strip looking at the battle remains of the ground action. There was a large German tank sitting in a small creek at a tilting 45 degree angle. I wanted to crawl up on it and have a look inside but there was always the possibility of booby-traps so I finally decided against it. It was a massive machine, much larger than our Sherman tank.

The carnage of battle lay all around us. There were personal effects, rifle ammunition, twenty millimeter flak gun ammunition, grenades and German helmets. The grenades caught our interest. We found three boxes of the potato masher type and a case of the concussion type. I looked at the open box of the potato masher type before I picked one out of the case, unscrewed the metal cap from the end of the handle, pulled on the round plastic ball attached to a nylon cord that extended inside the wooden handle up into the explosive, then threw it as far as I could and quickly lay down on the ground. A loud explosion was soon heard and I thought, hell, this is as much fun as the 4th of July! We activated and threw the grenades into a depression until all of them were gone. Fogie walked on east down a country lane to where the German tank was located. There he found a case of potato mashers without their detonator fuses. After finding some fuses, he proceeded to insert them into the explosive head, screwed on the hollow wooden handle after threading the nylon cord through same, pulled on the cord, then gave it a mighty heave. I cautioned him, then retired back up the lane about 50 yards. Fogie assembled two or three more, getting big bangs out of all three. Then he also retired back up the lane with me. I soon realized that this was damn foolishness, toying with military armaments. After all, anything we were not particularly well-versed in was certainly hazardous to our health.

One morning when the ceiling was too low to fly, four of us pilots walked over to a small village just east of the runway for the purpose of learning a bit of the French language. We thought we might converse with some French children we had seen there. The little kids spoke French slowly, a lot more slowly than adults.

The four or five stone buildings in this little village were somewhat haphazard as they had received some heavy shelling recently, but there were the French kids, who were about five or six years old. We saw four little girls and a little boy, all scrubbed up and in worn clothes that had been recently laundered. They approached us and soon became our French teachers. I noticed the screen doors of the houses closing as we came onto the street. I'm sure the French mothers were quite attentive. Out came the pocket size French-English dictionaries issued to us and we quickly looked up a few of the more common phrases. "Bon Jour, mademoiselle et monsieur." At that the children would reply, "Bon Jour." Some further close study and a bit of mumbling finally resulted in the question, "Comme allez vous?" At that, the little boy replied, "Ca Va," then left the immediate area as the little girls replied, "tres bien," while they continued with their play. We tried a few more phrases on them but our pronunciation was so raunchy that they simply couldn't understand us. We quietly watched them play and converse amongst themselves, then just before we left, a tall veteran fighter pilot of many missions over Germany said, "Just listen to those little kids speak French, and I don't know a damned word."

After noon chow we strolled to the channel waters just off the west end of our landing strip. One of the pilots had noticed the French gals swimming there while on a landing approach after a mission. The reputed reputation of the French women fascinated me as we made ourselves comfortable on the rocks along the shore. A nice-looking French gal sat down within six feet of me with a one piece bathing suit in hand. I decided that I might as well view fair womanhood without dress as she made the change while sitting down. First she put her slim legs into the swimming suit, then raised her rump a bit, and pulled the suit up over her hips, wiggling her hips a bit to help the process along. At this point I thought for sure I would see a bosom, as did my fellow pilots, and while we were very attentive, this little gal was well aware of it. Thus far, we hadn't seen as much as a thigh. To complete her change, the gal pulled her left arm out of the short sleeve of the dress. With her right hand she slipped the left shoulder strap over her shoulder, repeated the move with the right shoulder strap, then pulled the dress up over her head. After standing up, she gave us oglers a long, circling look then gave us a rear view of an undulating walk down to the water. We watched until her hips were covered with water then looked at one another with "I'll be damned" expressions on our faces.

Our flight surgeon, Doc Foster, was a friendly man and an excellent doctor. He was bespectacled and most generally wore his helmet liner. He took good care of his pilots. Everyone called him "Doc". One of the pilots was giving Doc flying lessons in a J-3 CUB that was on the field. One day Doc and his instructor gave the field a buzz-job at 100 miles an hour. That evening Doc was asking everyone if they had seen his buzz job. Doc also dug up and identified German war dead graves for the purposes of identification and personal effects which the Red Cross transmitted to the Germans. He asked and I agreed to accompany him some day to assist him. I was talking to one of the veteran pilots who had assisted Doc on one of his digs. Doc was plying the shovel to a grave with gusto when the spade came up with the German's head on it. The pilot wasn't used to such things but Doc proceeded with the uncovering, found the identification, a gold pocket watch, wallet with family pictures, and other personal items. They recovered the grave, marked it, then returned to the field. As a consequence, a German family would know for certain the fate of a loved one.

Fogie latched on to the J3 CUB one afternoon for a flying tour of Omaha Beach. I knew nothing about light aircraft but Fogie had flown a CUB in the army before entering the cadets as a pilot trainee. He knew his way around the aircraft. I entered the back seat, held the stick back and applied the small heel brakes as Fogie propped the engine. It started right off. I was amazed how quickly the little plane got off the runway. We cruised at 80 miles per hour over Omaha Beach then back to our air strip. By then, most of the carnage from D-Day had been removed. The height advantage and fields of fire the enemy enjoyed were appalling. One could see it took tenacity and great courage for the infantry to battle its way inland from the beach. After viewing this battleground, I was glad Dad had steered me away from the Infantry.

Our Fighter Group shared the air strip with a squadron of P-61 night fighters painted black as midnight. I watched them take off just before nightfall. The P-61 was a twin engine aircraft of great horsepower. They set up a helluva roar when they checked the magnetos of the radial engines before take-off. I didn't realize the speed and maneuverability of the P-61 until one morning when I heard aircraft approaching the air strip at great speeds. A British Mosquito twin-engine aircraft came over the field on the deck with a P-61 right on its tail. The Mosquito pulled up, doing evasive maneuvers but couldn't lose the P-61 as he stuck close on his tail. The Mosquito was fabricated from wood products powered by in-line Rolls Royce Merlin engines. It was the hottest twin-engine aircraft going, I thought. The P-61 pilots weren't patsies either. I heard stories about them from some of the older pilots who had seen them engaged in fisticuffs at the officer's club. They wrenched the leg and hip of one of our pilots so badly that he was hospitalized. He'd made an ass of himself from too much booze. He called and got hauled. I never did attend this officer's club for it sounded a little too tough for this lad.

 I was assigned a P-51 D model Mustang for my third mission. The D Model had a teardrop canopy. One could see all around, especially behind. Our briefing officer told our flight of four that our mission was aerial support for our armored column on the Brest peninsula. I was our flight leader's wing-man on this particular mission and felt honored as Jim Brink was one of the original pilots of the squadron and an old hand at this game. We took off by two aircraft elements, found our armored column, checked in, and were directed on to a German supply column. Most of the transport was horse drawn. The German supply column was approximately one-half mile long. The flight leader led the strafing attack from west to east, strafing the entire column with the remainder of the flight doing the same. The flight leader told me to space myself farther back as some of my bullets were ricocheting too close to his aircraft. The typical way to strafe a supply column is to strafe the roadway first, then hit the ditches. I didn't want to hit the horses but there was no other way. The Germans hustled what was left of the column into a tree-covered lane going north off the road. We then strafed this position until fires were observed. When we first started the attack I noticed a horse-drawn wagon a couple miles east of us. The team of horses was driven by a French girl. She didn't hesitate in the least but kept on plodding in our direction. Every pilot in the flight noticed her but paid her no mind. We returned to our landing strip after a two hour mission. While being debriefed, one of the pilots in our flight asked me if I had noticed the German with a machine gun out in the field taking shots at us as we made our strafing runs. I hadn't noticed. He said that he didn't notice the German either after the third pass. Someone must have kicked a rudder over his way.

 Some of the older veteran pilots sometimes drank too much booze the night before flying a mission. I asked how they managed to be sober enough to fly and learned that the secret was to turn the oxygen supply to full on after hooking up the mask. When they did that, they sobered up in a hurry. A reaction took place later on, however, and then one vomited into the oxygen mask which necessitated pulling out of formation, unhooking the mask so that it could be cleaned. The oxygen intake aperture and transmitting mike were directly in front of the mouth when the mask was hooked up to the flying helmet.

A group mission that required a 250 pound bomb under each wing saw me scheduled but I had to abort. As my element leader and I took the runway for take-off, I had a flat tail-wheel. The spare aircraft took my place as I pulled off the runway, shut off the engine, then watched the group take off without me.

August 10. I was scheduled for a group fighter sweep—my fourth mission—sixteen Mustangs from each of the three squadrons. This brought a feeling of great excitement as I had hoped for some aerial combat. At eight o'clock in the morning pilots flying the mission showed at the artillery razed Group headquarters building. I looked around at the old veteran fighter pilots and saw that this was old hat to them. Still, I very much felt that I belonged.

The Colonel stated that the Group would do a fighter sweep southeast of Paris. Then he covered the different squadron altitudes to be flown, and urged us to keep good formations, eyes alert, then synchronize our watches and the start engines or press time. My squadron checked out our equipment, piled into a couple of Jeeps which let off the pilots as the driver drove around our dispersal area, finally my element leader said, "Come on, Brooksie, here's our aircraft." The aircraft were well camouflaged as I could see only my element leader's Mustang. I buckled in with the help of the crew chief. There was about a five minute wait until press time of ten o'clock. There wasn't a sound except for a bird's song here and there, which I enjoyed. A ten o'clock, the Mustangs were starting up around the landing strip. I followed my element leader to our correct position in line, noticing other Mustangs emerging from their camouflaged positions as we taxiied past. My squadron was the second group to get airborne. The group operations officer was standing at the west end of the landing strip with a black and white checkered flag mounted on a three foot long handle, the first squadron to take off with two Mustangs in take-off positions ready for the flag drop as the Ops. officer looked at a timer's watch. He dropped the flag, two Mustangs roared down the landing strip, the next two Mustangs were already in take-off positions by then. As the tail surfaces of the two Mustangs roaring down the runway lifted, the flag was dropped for the next two to take off, and so on until 48 aircraft were airborne, formed up into three squadrons flying east in less than five minutes.

The Colonel situated the positions of the three squadrons on the way to the patrol area southeast of Paris. There were about 2,000 feet separating the squadrons. Flying in a squadron formation didn't leave any time to rubber-neck around. Just flying close formation required much attention, plus sweeping the instrument panel and changing gas tanks. As we flew approximately four miles south of Paris I saw the Eiffel Tower and the Seine River out of the corner of my eye. It was hard to realize that this great city was occupied by the Germans. We continued our patrol as the Colonel continued to place his squadrons, looking for the German fighters to come up or come down if already aloft. Nothing eventful happened on this Group fighter sweep. We landed back at the strip after two hours and forty minutes, coming over the strip in four aircraft flights, peeling off, then landing. Seeing four aircraft on the strip at one time wasn't uncommon. That was considered good spacing. Since we hadn't sighted any enemy aircraft, I was inclined to think that there weren't any left but I felt that I belonged to this Fighter Squadron now in a way that was really special. All the crew chiefs were anxiously waiting for their aircraft and pilots as we taxiied to our original parking spots, and I told my crew chief that we hadn't seen a thing.

    The day after the fighter sweep I boarded a deuce and a half truck with five other pilots to motor up the channel coast to A-7 air strip. Six of our Mustangs had landed there because of bad weather the evening before. During the two hour ride I asked the veteran pilots the odds of finishing a tour alive and the critical point in flying the tour. They agreed it was the fifth mission. My fifth mission was coming up.

    The truck pulled off the bumpy road into a stand of very tall fir trees. I thought the driver was lost but he continued on until he came to an air strip cut out of the fir trees. There were tall trees on both sides of the strip and at both ends, just waiting to grasp an aircraft. The six of us left the truck with our chutes and flying helmets, buckled ourselves into the cockpits, started up, taxiied out to the north east end of the runway. I thought to myself, What a place for a landing strip. On second thought, liberated French land was at a premium when the air strip was urgently constructed by the engineers.

    My turn came to take off, the three that proceeded me had no difficulties but the trees at the far end of the runway grew taller. After a good magneto check, I took the runway, dropped ten degrees of flaps, pulled the stick back, eased the throttle forward. When the aircraft started to creep forward against the brakes, I released same, steadily fire-walled the throttle and watched the trees approach. When the Mustang felt like flying, I gently came back on the stick, the Mustang leaped into the air clearing the trees by beau coup altitude. We arrived back at our landing strip in time for noon chow. I sauntered over to squadron operations afterwards to check the mission schedule; as yet none had been posted.

    Major McWherter was looking for a fourth player for a game of horseshoes. I was asked but tried to beg off as I didn't know the game although I had watched my Grandfather Brooks play

The Major insisted I play so play I did with Chester Rice and myself as partners. Chester was an old farm-oriented boy like I was. Chester had played the game before. As for me, I copied my Grandpa Brooks' form as I remembered it and damn, if those horseshoes didn't start to fall on the peg and around it. Chester carried us by doing most of the point scoring. I backed him up well and we beat the Major and his partner. He asked and we agreed to play again in the near future.

After the game I checked the mission schedule for the next day. I was scheduled on the dawn patrol—my fifth mission. Chester was scheduled for a mission later the same morning, August 13.

Recit du Combat de 13 aout 1944

Vers huit heures alors que nous contemplions l'espace aèrier chasseurs bombardiers Allemands se dirigent vers LeMans au-dessus de la Nationale 23.
A huit heures dix minutes, ils reviennent à toute allure on suivant la 928. Quatre chasseurs Americains les ont pris en chasse.
Les Allemands volent tres bas, Les Americains volent bien au-dessus et piquent sur eux en les mitrailleurs. Les premiers tombent chacun leur tour.
Le premier vers Les Gaudinieres en Margon.
Le deuxième au Bois Tailles à Coulonges Les Sablons.
Le troisième au Val à Coulonges Les Sablons.
Le pilote est sauf et recueilli chez Messieurs et Madames Decraemere au Testres.
Le quatrième à la Chardronnie're. Le pilote est mort.
Un cinquième est tombé règion de Fretigny Saint Victor de Buthon.
L'après midi, vers 14 heures, deux civils français qui ètàient venu voir l'avion ont remassé un petit engin fais ètàit un explosif. Ils ont été tuè et leurs enfants blessés.

Le 3 septembre 1991
G. Dorchene

Account of the combat on August 13, 1944.

Around 8:00, as we were watching the skies, twelve German bomber planes were going in the direction of Le Mans, above the National 23.

At 8:10, they came back at great speed, following the 928. Four American fighters were chasing them.

The Germans flew very low. The Americans flew above them and the machine gunners shot at them. They began to fall, each in their turn.

The first fell near Les Gaudinieres in Margon.
The second fell near Forest Tailles at Coulonges Les Sablons.
The third fell at Valley Coulonges Les Sablons.
The pilot is safe and welcomed at the house of Mrs. and Mrs. Decraemere at Testres.
The fourth fell at La Chardronnie're. The pilot was dead.
A fifth fell in the region of Fretigny Saint Victor de Buthon.
In the afternoon, around 2:00, two civilian Frenchmen who had come to see the plane, picked up a little instrument that was an explosive. They were killed and their children were injured.

Gabriel Dorchene

Statement of Hans Kukla (German Fighter Pilot)

"I saw service as a pilot in the 4th Staffel (First Gruppe) of JG26 from 20 July, 1944, to 17 April, 1945. 'I was no ace.' I was very lucky to have survived the war. I flew about 20 combat sorties . . . My rank was Unteroffizier and I was one of the pilots who was sent to the front after very little training. Only the circumstance that I was shot down twice and wounded permitted me to survive.

"On 13 August, 1944, on my third sortie, I was shot down by a Mustang at very low altitude over no-man's land and landed by parachute. Twelve aircraft from my Gruppe were armed with two Nebelwerfer under the wings and sent out to attack armor. We flew at ground level and had as escorts some Me 109s, who were flying some 6000 feet above us. After we had attacked some tanks between Chartres and Le Mans we flew back toward our base. I flew with three other aircraft of the 4th Staffel in the last flight, which consisted of Fw. Hager, Uffz. Richter, Uffz. von Osterczecha, and myself. We made a fatal error. We saw the Me 109s above us and felt secure. Only when the so-called "109s" dove on our tails did we see that they were Mustangs. Since we were at ground level, there was no possibility of defense. I was first to be hit; my plane took strikes, a Tracer went between my hand and left leg right into the motor and immediately burst into flames. I pulled the nose up and bailed out. My chute opened at twenty meters, and I landed in the garden of a farm. I learned later that my three comrades were all shot down and killed. My position was about 10km south of La Lupe. After I had learned from the farmer's wife that I was in no-man's land, I gave her my parachute and headed north on foot."

Author in front of his kite, "Kansas Aggie."

Lee E. Webster from Wheaton, Illinois. Lee and I took on 24 enemy aircraft ourselves, our top cover flew off and our second element failed us.

Hans Kukla, the first to fall, Hans and I consider August 13, 1944 as our second birthday. Hans had to use his parachute two more times before the war ended, the last after being wounded while in a dogfight with a Spitfire.

Robert Hager with his dog, German fighter pilot who was Han. Kukla's flight leader, he perished in the air battle.

Left: Xaver Ellenrieder
Right: His crew chief
Xaver clobbered Lee Webster's Mustang

Msr. Emile Sorel, he took me in when I was feeling a bit weary.

Msr. Maire Gabriel Dorchene of Coulonges Les Sablons, he witnessed our air battle August 13, 1944. Some of you old Calvados drinkers might be interested to know that the Maire is one of the last Frenchmen licensed to make his very own Calvados. Gabriel was given a commendation for his work with the Resistance during the war.

Jean Sorel, nephew of Emile Sorel. As an early teens lad he visited his uncle Emile's peasant home while I was in residence the afternoon of August 13, 1944. Even at this early age Jean was active in the French Resistance, he received a commendation from the U.S. government. Jean is also a veteran of France's Viet-Nam war. Jean Sorel now resides in Bagneux, France in Saumur.

Standing left: Michel's good friend
Standing right: Michel Laine
Seated: Their French Priest, the parish is in Silli en Gouffern.

Dr. Guy Picot and Mme. Picot with their current bird dog, photo taken during 1942. Dr. Picot was a physician in the French army and was taken prisoner after France capitulated. Mme. Picot lost her father in World War I and could have lost Dr. Picot also, she suffered very much as a non-combatant.

Msr. Roger Benance and Mme. Benance with a young French lady.

Capt. James Ray, later died in combat near Soissons, France. The Captain is buried at Epinal, France.

Three American soldiers present at the disabled Sherman tank the night of August 13, 1944.
Seated: Cpl. Henry A. Peterson of Holdrege, Nebraska.
Standing left: T/sgt. George Banovich of Lorain, Ohio.
Standing right: Maldwyn M. Closs of Wymore, Nebraska.
The two Sgts. were helping with repair of the tank, Henry was close by with his Thompson .45 caliber sub machine-gun.

Chester Rice from Frederick, Oklahoma, my horse-shoe pitching partner who fell a few miles from me at about 11:15 a.m., August 13, 1944.

Dell Hudson from California and Chester Rice's element leader August 13, 1944. Dell is still officially listed as missing in action.

Photo of my Mustang crash and author in Silli en Gouffern during October, 1944.

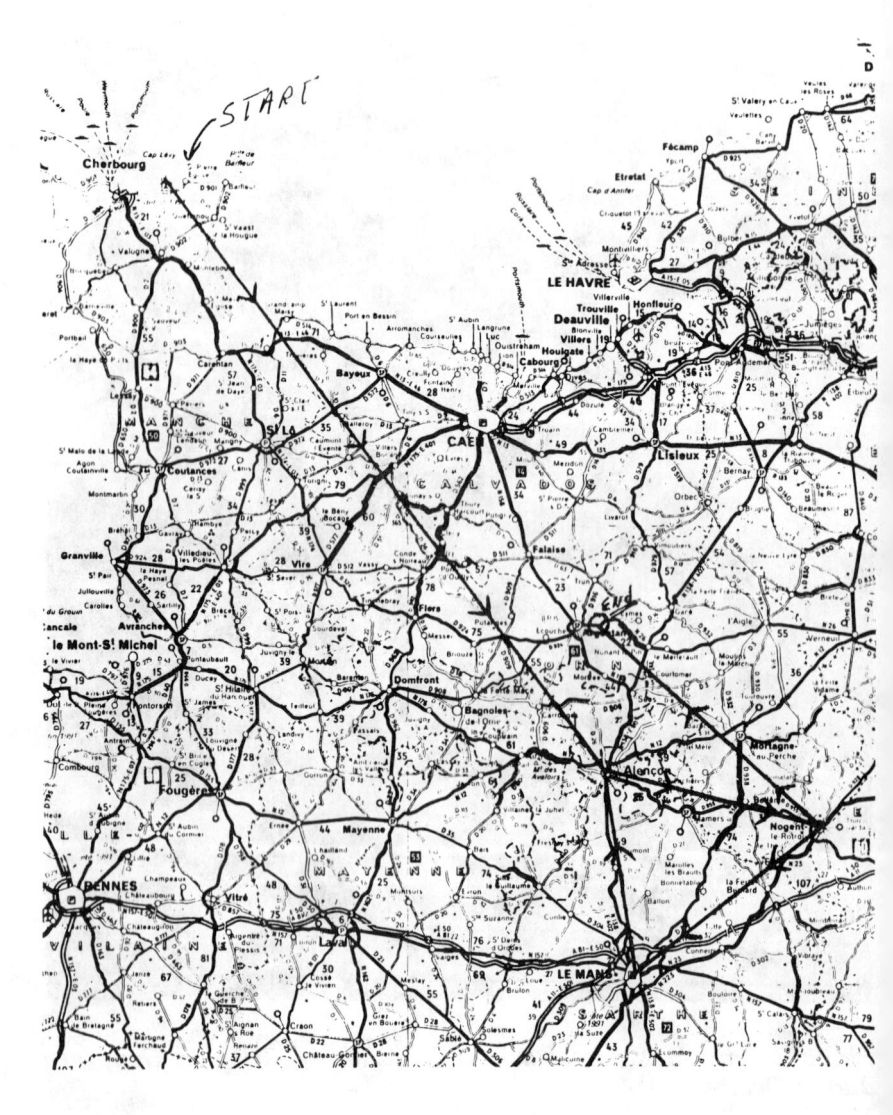

This map shows our take-off origin located near Cherbourg then proceeding to Alencon, Nogent le Rotrou, Le Mans then repeating the diamond patrol area for about two hours. The arrowed lines from Nogent le Rotrou to east of Argentan is my flight path after the air battle and eventual descent to earth.

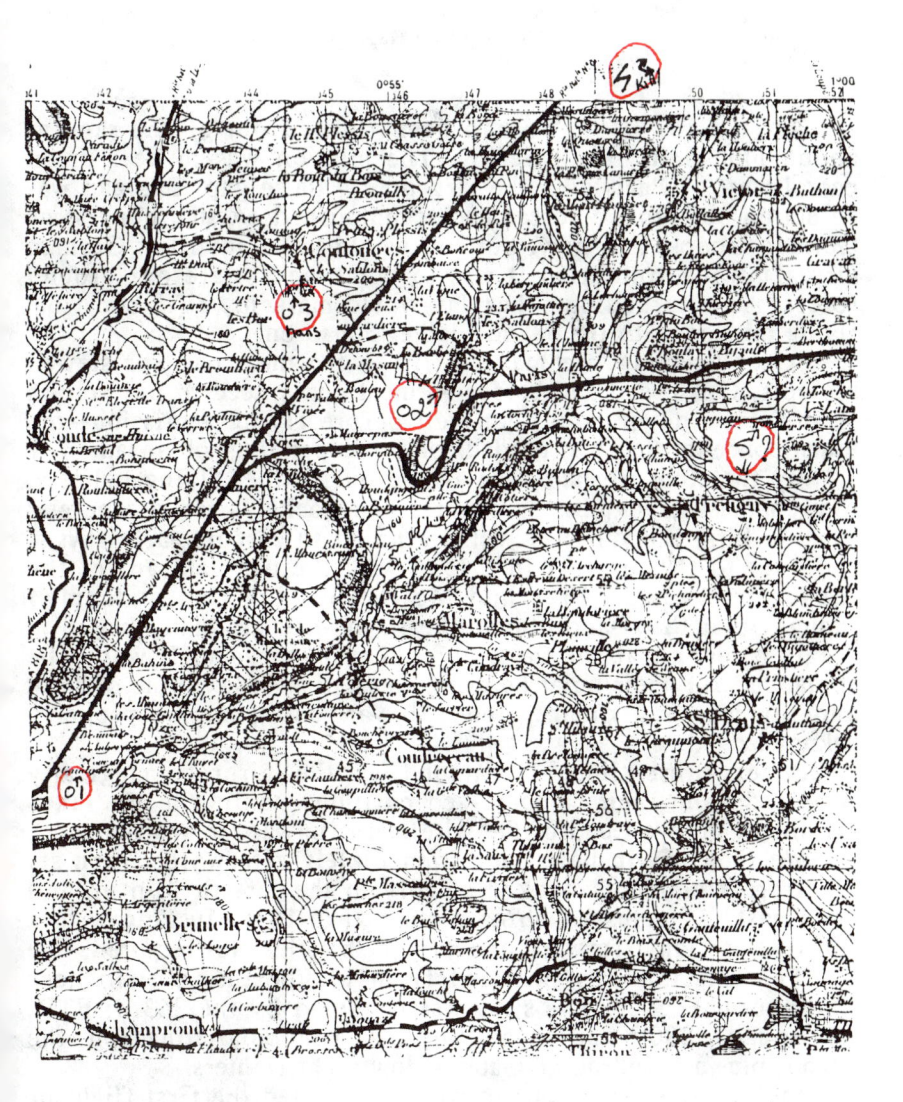

The Nogent le Rotrou area, northeast find the locations of the German aircraft as they fell in turn 1-5.

Chapter Five

The Fifth Mission

August 13, 1944. We had been rousted out of the sack at about 0400 hours for briefing. The mission was to be a dawn patrol west of Paris over the Argentan-Falaise gap. The gap was an action our ground forces had accomplished by encircling some German troops, and now, our job would be to interdict German aircraft whose intention it was to bomb and strafe our ground forces. As it turned out, that day would mark my fifth and final flying mission with the 382nd Fighter Squadron.

After briefing, we made a trip to the mess hall for stewed apricots, G.I. bread and coffee—a meal guaranteed to put you on your feet. I never could eat well before flying a mission—too much concentration was needed for the impending job ahead.

By the time we had been issued our leather flying helmets, oxygen masks, goggles, parachutes and pocket-sized escape and evasion kits, the sun was just beginning to cast its early rays. I rode out to the aircraft in a Jeep with the old veterans of the squadron: Webster, Frey and McWherter. Looking at them, I thought that they—and others like them—had gradually begun to create a legend about themselves. Later, these men would be applauded for their quiet heroism, for setting an example of faith and service that, during times of war, could not be properly acknowledged.

After press-time, I watched as the aircraft magically appeared from their camouflaged positions, taxiing to the take-off site at the west end of the wire mesh runway. It was time.

We took off in pairs, and immediately afterwards, each set of aircraft elements banked steeply to the left to join up and head east. After establishing a steep turn in a Mustang with a full fuselage tank, forward pressure on the stick was required.

The mission was initiated from Maupertus, a strip near Cherbourg, France. The strip was occupied by the 363rd, FTR. GP. squads, 380th, 381st, and my own particular squadron, the 382nd, plus a squadron of black widow night fighters.

Major McWherter, our mission leader, led the first flight of four as top cover. In our patrol, consisting of eight P-51 Mustangs, my position was flying on the wing of Lt. Lee Webster, leader of the second flight of four who flew at 9,000 feet. Lt. Don Frye led the second element of our flight, with Lt. Littlefield as his wing-man. As Webster's wing-man, it was my job to cover him while he was shooting, and to keep his tail clear.

Heading in a westerly direction, we were about to be relieved of our patrol when I looked below and saw six Me 109s and six Fw 190s approximately 1,000 feet below, heading in the opposite direction. Lt. Webster executed a 180 degree diving turn to the left, then added another 90 degrees to the left on the way down, shooting the tail off a tail-end Charlie Me 109. Then he executed another 90 degree turn to the right and came out on some Fw 190s. As he fired on a tail-end Charlie, I fired on another slightly to the right, and saw that I'd hit him good. After watching him execute a dead-man turn to the left, I looked to my right and observed below a Fw 190 making a firing pass on us. I pulled up into an off vertical loop to the right (immelman-turn) and attacked the Jerry on the way down. My first burst was behind his wings, and after correcting my aim, I was about to touch the trigger again as I realized a mid-air collision was imminent. I blinked as his tail surfaces went above my canopy and came out of my dive on the tail of another Fw 190, firing short bursts and scoring some good hits. As bits and pieces broke off his plane, he leveled out somewhat, jettisoned his canopy, then bailed out the right side going by my right wing tip as I broke left. His flight suit was dark tan and I did not discern a parachute.

As I broke left, I felt some hits to my aircraft and dove for the deck, doing a number of slips and uncoordinated turns. When at last I leveled out on the deck, ready for a reefing turn, I noticed a French farmer standing on a haystack with a pitchfork. As I watched, he waved to me with his free hand.

At this time I heard our homing station say, "White Three, where are you?" The reply was, "I'm on the God-damn deck and I'm going to stay here!"

Assuming I'd lost the Jerry, I executed a steep turn to the left, then noticed a Fw 190 tooling on towards the east. The Fw 190 I almost collided with had dropped onto my tail. Knowing my aircraft had been hit, I turned into him, and after clearing my tail, began a climb to find Webster. I found a Mustang heading west and proceeded to close up when he suddenly went into a steep turn to the left.

Webster called in on the radio with a cracked voice, "P-51 on my tail, this is a 51. Who are you? Identify yourself!"

"This is Brooks, your wing-man," I weakly responded. At that, he allowed me to join up and we proceeded to climb towards the west. I noticed that Webster's brand-new Mustang was considerably the worse for wear. Part of his canopy was gone. His tail surfaces were shot up and he'd taken some hits on his right wing.

We were about 7,000 feet when I noticed the oil temperature gauge registering very hot. Putting the selector on manual—full open—only momentarily alleviated the problem. Soon the engine was running rough, and then it quit, as smoke streamed out of the exhaust stacks. As the plane caught fire, I informed Webster of my plight and set up a glide to the west. I readied myself to hit the silk, but the emergency canopy release was jammed. My heart pounded as I sat in my firery coffin. I had to get out!

I put my right foot on the instrument panel and pulled, but to no avail. I put both feet on the panel—still no canopy release. About then, the fire and smoke started coming up from under the instrument panel, and knowing that drastic action was required, I unfastened my seatbelt and shoulder straps, lowered the seat, got my feet on the seat under me and tried to buck the canopy off with my shoulders and neck. No results! I sat back in the seat and stuck my feet back on the rudder pedals which were now engulfed in flames coming through the fire wall. My good ol' G.I. shoes somehow survived the scalding heat, but my knee-length wool socks were burned away below my shoe tops. At this time, I did fleetingly think of my girl back home, my parents, brothers and sisters. As death drew near, every human instinct in my body was reduced to a frenzied urged to escape. Yet I knew it couldn't always be someone else who went into that 100 mph death glide.

The last thing I said to Webster was, "Web, I got two of them."

WEBSTER

"That August 13th was one of those days that a fighter pilot dreams of. I knocked down three Fw 190s and one Me 109 between sunrise and sunset—and almost had my own plane shot out from under me. As a matter of fact, when I went over to look at it, they had taken it apart for salvage. The fellows that were working on it gave me a handful of bullets and various pieces that they retrieved from the fuselage and wings and one 13 mm from the cockpit that very faintly had my name written on it. That baby came through the canopy from the rear, banged into the front of the canopy and exploded. It was a fairly well spent bullet, though, by the time it got there, it just tumbled back into the cockpit with me in several pieces. I just missed a Purple Heart by a few inches."

"It all started with a routine eight-ship patrol of the front lines somewhere west of Paris—the dawn patrol, in fact. We were just about to be relieved and return to base when I sighted some bogies down below. We were flying west at about 9,000 feet and the bogies heading east at about 4,000 feet. I was leading the second of the two flights (about the third time I had been leading), so called in the bogies to the leader as I turned and dived to investigate. Unfortunately, he had just switched to another channel and did not get my call. By this time I was down on the planes and had identified them as Me 109s; I also counted some 12 others on the deck that I hadn't seen when I started down. The 109s turned into me and I followed four of them into a turn. Made a 270-degree turn with them and got the number four man lined up for a deflection shot. Took a squirt at him and hit him the first crack. Strikes all over him in the fuselage and wing roots. Saw him salvo his canopy and bail out. Turned 90 degrees and went down on the planes below, leaving my number 3 and 4 men to take care of the ones that were turning up there. They got a destroyed, a probably destroyed, and a damaged out of the three I left them and two more that had joined in the fight. The Number Four man, Lt. Littlefield, was on the tail of one and all set to let him have it when he looked out the side and discovered himself flying formation with another. He cut his throttle just as the second one saw him and made a diving turn. Followed him down and without firing a shot, chased him into the ground and saw him explode."

"By this time I was on the tail end of a formation of about ten Fw 190s that were on the tree tops headed for home. I hurried them up a bit by taking a squirt at one. Missed him but saw the tracers go under him. Raised the bead a little and saw the strikes play all over the fuselage in little spurts of fire. The pilot pulled the nose up and bailed out. The plane crashed in a beautiful orange-black explosion just off my left wing as I pulled the trigger on another 190. This time there was no playing around and there were hits all over the fuselage. I saw that this plane was done for as I saw him crash and burn, so I started a left turn to clear my tail. That turn saved my life. I had banked the plane about 15 degrees when the right side of the canopy fell in my lap. There were pieces falling off the plane in front of me and I figured I had run unto a hunk of metal from the last 190 when I heard something that sounded like hailstones hitting a tin roof. I reefed that gentle turn in so tight that I nearly blacked out. I twisted my neck off to see what was shooting at me, but all I could see behind me was who I thought was my wingman, following me in trail. I called in on the radio and asked him to identify himself. His weak response confirmed my suspicion. It was Brooks indeed. I stopped my acrobatics and let him pull alongside of me. What a wonderful sight he was!"

"My plane was just barely flying. The only thing whole when I got back to base was the engine. I had no airspeed indicator and from the feel of the controls I was barely mushing along, but if I went any faster the whole ship felt like it was going to fall apart."

"One of the boys in the flight called in without identifying himself and said that his coolant was shot out. Gave a 'Roger' and told him to set course for home. Called the squadron leader and told him that White One and Two were setting course from such and such an area. That I was shot up. Called White Three to see if he was OK and he answered, 'There are about 15 190s around me.' A few minutes later he said that he was clear and headed for home. White Four had already called and said he was headed home and I assumed he was the one that had the coolant shot out from under him."

"About this time, my wingman's plane started giving off smoke and I called him and told him to leave me and asked what the trouble was. He answered that his coolant was gone and his oil pressure dropping. We had been flying for some time and were in the vicinity of our own lines but there was a fog laying on the ground and we could not see where we were. I told him to keep it flying as long as he could—but a few moments later, he said that it was cutting out and that he was leaving it. Called him back to get him to stay as long as he could, but he had already bailed out. Just a few minutes later we broke out into clear ground and behind our lines. Just another minute of flying and he would have been among our troops. He was a new fellow with the outfit—just had a few missions in and was depending on me. He stuck with me like a veteran, but I let him down by allowing someone to get on our tail. The rest of the fellows caught up to me and escorted me the rest of the way home."

GOING DOWN

While agonizing in a peril with depths I could not measure, I fought to calm myself and to think. What had the flight instructor at that Florida Air Base advised us to do in this situation? ". . . TO RELEASE THE BIRD-CAGE TYPE CANOPY OF THE MUSTANG . . . SLIDE BACK THE AIRVENT LOCATED ON THE RIGHT FORWARD PART OF THE CANOPY . . ."

As quickly as I did this, the canopy went spinning away, and so did I. The horizontal stabilizer passed me, I pulled the D-ring, the chute popped and I hit the ground immediately, coming down through the branches of an apple tree in a small orchard. My Mustang was approximately 30 yards away, burning fiercely as its ammunition exploded. Just before I bailed out, I remember entering a blanket of smoke drifting in from the northwest, from the battle of the Argentan-Falaise gap.

After unhitching my chute and Mae West, I noticed two Frenchmen about 30 yards away. They were standing at the back door of a church, totally awe-struck by all the action taking place around them. One was a French priest, and the other a young man about my age. The village in which my Mustang had landed was Silli en Gouffern, three kilometers east of Argentan.

Approaching the two men, I identified myself and asked for help. My right hand was badly burned and my legs were almost numb.

While the Frenchmens' first inclination was to hide me in the church, the approach of German troops with their dogs soon changed all that. Noticing that they were coming down the main street of Silli, less than a block away, the Frenchmen pointed in the opposite direction and frantically urged me to flee.

And flee I did—over a broken rock wall, through the village's open air sewage moat, shoving my flying helmet into same, and over a steel rod fence. The only hold I could get to scale the fence was about 12 feet from the ground, but the need and desire were there, so I succeeded. Upon landing, I scrambled to my feet and stood silent for a moment, listening. I could still hear the baying of the German's dogs, trying to track me. There was a small stream flowing from the sewage moat, so I hurriedly proceeded down the middle of it a ways, hoping to throw the dogs off my scent. Then I crossed an open, dry tan-colored meadow, always crouching low, until at last I reached a road that bordered the meadow, and a forest. Noticing a truckload of German troops approaching, I fell flat upon the ground and lay still until they had passed. I entered the forest, but soon changed my direction and exited, as it looked too foreboding and dark. I later learned that it was a German supply dump heavily guarded.

Emerging from this dark, wooded area, I moved toward the sound of guns, thinking that these must be American weapons taking part in an offensive.

My right hand was throbbing. A ray of sunshine made it feel as if I'd thrust it back into the fire, and my legs were almost without feeling. Proceeding in a southwesterly direction, I was ever mindful of land mines and German troops.

Startled by a sudden commotion, I saw that I had flushed out a covey of partridge. It was an incredibly laughable incident—had there only been time to laugh. As I continued on, I came across somebody's garden. Standing alone in the middle of the garden, I saw a life-size scarecrow. I walked up to him and plucked the old felt hat from his head and placed it on my own. My summer sun-tan uniform was punctured with small burn holes and was now extremely soiled. Earlier, I had turned my collar under, taken off my pilot's wings, and had pulled out the front of my shirt to hide the brass buckle on my belt. My hair was also long and full, as instructed by Army Intelligence. My newly acquired felt hat topped off my disguise.

While in the garden, I felt in need of spiritual help, so I dropped to one knee, removed the scarecrow hat and hastily said the following prayer: "Dear God, Sir, I am in need of help today and I promise to be a better man from here on out. Amen."

While this prayer did sustain me, I also knew that God helps those who help themselves.

Two P-51 Mustangs flying in close formation gave me a buzz job soon after I finished my prayer. I saw them coming and threw up some dirt clods, but they continued on their way heading south southwest—my heart with them.

Lt. Dell Hudson and Lt. Chester Rice were also shot down this day while strafing German armor and troops, they were last heard from at about 11:10 A.M. I firmly believe the two Mustangs were them as our squadron letter "C" was clearly visible on the rear fuselage of the wingman's aircraft, who was flying the leader's right wing. The leader's aircraft was aluminum colored, the wingman's olive drab. Chester Rice flew a perfect-tight-wing position at all times. They both crashed at St. Martin des Champs—8 kilometers south-west from my crash site and were 2 kilometers west of the place where the 5th armored division took me in. It was definitely no man's land.

I cautiously moved on and had been walking for a while when I unexpectedly came across a shocking scene—a German SS trooper and a young German soldier, lying in a prone position. The soldier was the typical Hitler youth, blonde hair and blue eyes; he couldn't have been any older than I was. I stood close enough to see a scar on the right cheek of the older SS trooper. They turned and looked up at me, and my first thought was to give myself up since there seemed nothing else to do. But in the course of raising my arms in the usual gesture of surrender, I suddenly thought better of it. Rather than surrender, I merely yawned and stretched, then walked off in the opposite direction. A quick look over my shoulder told me I was beyond their view, so I ran and leaped over a 15 foot wide ditch, with my leg collapsing beneath me as I hit the other side. I thought to myself what good luck it was for me that the German SS troops had some perverts in their ranks. The two of them had been so engrossed in one another, it evidently hadn't registered in their minds that I could have been an enemy American. Standing up, I found my leg still serviceable and proceeded at a moderate walk to a peasant's hut up ahead where I saw a Frenchman standing by the hut.

Explaining that I was an American, I began to ask for help, but the need was already obvious. The man quickly took me inside his home, a modest one-room structure with a thatched roof, dirt floor and a makeshift fireplace for cooking and warmth. There I met an older woman, and a younger one, and while their relationship to the Frenchman remained unclear, their kindness and concern for me were equal to his.

As the Frenchman clarified our location on my escape and evasion map, the older woman peeled and scraped a raw potato which she then applied to my burned hand, wrapping both in a sheet of cellophane. It had a most soothing affect and I thanked her as I ate a tasty meal of boiled chicken, bread and milk. While these wonderful people were helping me, German troops in trucks were going along a road less than 30 yards from the hut and incoming artillery fire was directed on them.

As I was finishing my meal, I looked up and saw that another woman had entered the hut. She too was French, and extremely charming and attractive. She offered her charms to me, but since I was an upstanding man closer to my teen years than of legal age, I politely declined. She accepted this in a good-natured way, remarking that I was much too young anyway. True I had not eaten the apple as yet and I wasn't about to get caught with my pants down—at this time.

A short while later, they showed me the ladder to a loft and a mattress where I immediately fell into a fitful sleep. In time, several bursts of artillery fire, extremely close to the hut, lifted me off the mattress, much as an earthquake tremor might have done.

I was told recently by Jean Sorel, a small boy at that time and nephew of Emile Sorel, that German soldiers stopped by the little hut and demanded food at gun point, especially butter. The Germans were retreating and under great stress.

Jean Sorel also related to me that a British soldier was hidden in a cellar underneath the hut's dirt floor. I was up in the loft asleep on a mattress oblivious to it all.

During my sleep in Emile Sorel's loft, he proceeded into Sai to arrange a possible contact with the resistance people. On his way back, he came upon a German truck that had broken down. Emile fired it with a match struck from his pants' leg. Upon his return, I was awakened and told that an American ambulance would be waiting for me in Sai. I understand now that Emile's son was a resistance fighter taken prisoner by the Gestapo, and with this hanging over his head, he still endeavored to help me.

Toward evening, Emile and I walked into the village of Sai, about a mile away, where people, mostly women and children, lined the walled streets with flowers in their hands for me and watched as we passed. I think I must have been the first American to come through there. As we turned into a courtyard, I noticed that my legs were becoming weaker and that my hand had swollen to a point where I could no longer flex my fingers. I was assisted into a small room off a main house where other Frenchmen came to my aid. Repeating the word BOCHE, they urged me to be silent. This was the last I would see of Emile and his family. The other French people hid me, fed me, and took me to safety. I have never forgotten the kindness of these people, since to them I was only a stranger, and someone who also endangered their lives. With the language barrier, it was difficult to fully express my gratitude for everything they were doing for me. I knew they had to be concerned for their own safety; the war was here on their own soil, in their own country—and they themselves did not know who was a friend or enemy. Even so, they risked their own lives to help me. No more could have been done for one human being by another.

In a small room off the main house was Dr. Guy Picot and his wife, Marie Louise, who was a nurse. These people applied vaseline gauze bandages to my hand. The medical attention provided by the French people was instrumental in saving it for me. While I was in that small back room receiving medical attention, the owner of the house, Roger Benance, was at the other end of his house observing a platoon of German SS troops bivouacked about 25 yards away. A shot rang out, he came hurrying into the room laughing; the shot had been meant for him. We didn't stay too long in this little room. I was led and half-carried to a small barn across the street from Roger Benance's house, where I was placed in a two-wheeled horse-drawn cart and covered with stalks of corn. Once again, I was warned to be quiet. The cart was then led into a small village square, about 30 yards opposite the German SS headquarters, and on down the street to the outskirts of town, where an automobile was waiting. Roger Benance was at the wheel, and Dr. Picot sat in front beside him, while I rode in the back. As we sped along country roads, throwing gravel every which way, without the benefit of headlights, I felt myself being rocked about, and experienced again some measure of the concern that had overpowered me when my emergency canopy release jammed. Clearly, it was not a great deal safer on the ground, at least not in the situations in which I frequently found myself.

As we approached a forty-five degree turn, Roger Benance hit the brakes and I could hear American voices saying, "Shoot-shoot!" An authoritative voice, quiet, but firm, replied, "Hold your fire." Peering anxiously over the front seat, I saw a Sherman tank with its cannon bore-sighted on us. The business end of the gun looked to be a foot across. Realizing that we had stumbled upon a night reconnaissance patrol, I opened the rear door and fell to the ground with my hands in the air.

"Don't shoot!" I yelled.

An American soldier approached me with a leveled pistol and asked me to identify myself.

"I'm from Silver Lake, Kansas, near Topeka, and I was shot down!"

After my dog tags were checked, I was allowed to walk over to their side. Meanwhile, Dr. Picot and Roger Benance had been pulled from the automobile and were pinned to the ground under the soldier's feet. I saw that rifles were being held to their heads.

Even though I was physically and emotionally exhausted from the constant pain and struggle of survival, I was overwhelmed by a feeling of helplessness and deep concern for these people to whom I owed my life.

I prayed that there would not be a lengthy interrogation by the American Intelligence and that my French friends would be among the survivors of this war.

As I was ushered to a Jeep, the last thing I heard the Frenchmen say was, "Give us guns."

Riding along in the Jeep on the way back to the bivouac, we stopped to pick up a German prisoner. An American soldier with a tommy-gun brought him out from behind a clump of trees. I got in the back seat of the Jeep so the soldier could watch the prisoner from the front seat. The prisoner was told to sit on the hood of the Jeep, feet on the front bumper, with each hand grasping a fender. He did this without having to bend his back or reach while doing so. He was the biggest man I had ever seen; the wary soldier made me feel better.

After reaching the night patrol's bivouac, I was taken to the armored outfit's OPS tent to see if I could supply them with any information. Once they saw I could not, I was given a blanket, taken outside, and found a spot under a tree where I lay down and slept the sleep of the dead.

The next morning I was driven to an American hospital in France. I was taken to an operating room where a surgeon clipped the dead skin hanging from my right hand. When a two-star General suddenly walked in, I immediately tried to jump from the operating table and come to attention but he was quick to restrain me.

For a moment or two, the General watched the surgeon, then told me that the army ground force's job had been made so much easier because young men like me cleared the skies.

The two-star General was Maj. Gen. Lunsford E. Oliver, commander of the 5th armored division, and Gen. George Patton considered the 5th Armored Division as his secret weapon.

After extensive research and help from former veterans of the 80th and 90th infantry divisions I was referred to the 5th Armored Division. One of their units was in that area the night of August 13, 1944. The Armored School Library at Ft. Knox, Kentucky listed for me the units of combat command "A". Col. (Ret.) James McDonough, lately deceased, pinpointed "Charlie" company-34th Tank Battalion of the 5th Armored Division as the likely unit we damn near run into.

After considerable searching, I located Henry A. Peterson of Holdrege, Nebraska. Henry was the driver of the Jeep that carried me back from that almost deadly forty-five degree curve. Captain James Ray, from Tennessee, was the commanding officer of "Charlie" company and in charge when the event took place.

When I recently visited Henry and his wife, Grace, he said I was most concerned about the filthy stinking pants I was wearing. The Sherman tank we almost ran into had broken down and was being repaired when the Americans heard us coming from far away like a bat out of hell. The remainder of "Charlie" company shermans had proceeded on to a point east of Argentan to interdict the Germans retreating east from Argentan. Henry related that the two Frenchmen and I were very lucky we weren't killed that night.

Captain James Ray was killed in combat near Soissons, France north of Paris the latter part of August, 1944. I will forever be beholden to him for being there to say, "Hold your fire."

Chapter Six

After the General left the operating room, the surgeon treated my hand, using first the Vaseline impregnated bandages, then a white outer wrap. I thought about telling him of the difficulty I'd encountered in attaining an upright standing position when I awoke a couple hours earlier. I could not have made it to my feet without the help of a small tree that stood nearby. I was stiff and sore from head to toe, and my right leg was functional but dragging a bit. Slowing down the pace of my walk helped to cover the limp. Had someone noticed me balancing myself against a tree, they'd have thought I'd taken on too much Calvados the previous night.

I saw no other patients at this hospital. The fighting for Normandy had started to wind down a bit, at least in this particular sector.

A pretty little buxom nurse with brunette hair took charge of me, and together, we walked over to a field kitchen set up in back of the hospital for a meal of stew, bread and coffee. The bread and coffee went down well enough, but I was still wound up pretty tight, which gave me a limited appetite.

The nurse showed me around the deserted hospital which had formerly been used by the Germans. It was obvious that they had evacuated in a hurry as many personal items had been left behind. I picked up a cane and put it to good use, along with my scarecrow hat, which I'd managed to keep. Although I fully expected the military to take exception to my unusual attire, no one ever pressed me about it.

When I was ready to leave, I thanked the little nurse and said goodbye as I boarded an ambulance for a ride to the beach air strip for evacuation by C-47 aircraft. Knowing that the German fighters frequently strafed such vehicles—just as we did—I took a seat near the rear doors. The other patients aboard were all ambulatory, but that was all I noticed about them. Just then, my mind was on other things—specifically, my family and Donna. I wondered if my Mom and Dad had been notified of my actual status, or if they'd been told something else. I'd asked the doctor at the military hospital at Tercy to let both my parents and my squadron know that I was all right. Notifying my squadron was of paramount importance, and the military generally did a good job of such things.

A soldier sitting next to me in the ambulance suddenly pulled up the bandage on his left leg and asked for my medical opinion about a rash on the member. I couldn't understand his language so I just shook my head and said, "No compri."

Mid-afternoon saw us pulling into a small field hospital situated on a slight incline that overlooked the waters of the

Channel. Hospital personnel told us to line up in front of the diagnosis tent, which we did. I was relieved to see a long wooden bench close by for every bone in my body had begun to ache.

As I became better acquainted with the other soldiers sitting and standing about, questions started flying back and forth. "Where are you hit?" "What kind of action?" "Where are you from?"

Only eight feet away I noticed another line of soldiers which at first I took to be Americans, but then I saw that they were actually German wounded. I was somewhat startled by this and immediately reacted as an adversary until I realized that the time for such behavior had clearly passed. Upon closer inspection I saw that except for their uniforms, the Germans were quite similar in appearance. There were more blonde heads among their group but that was the only noticeable difference. One of their wounded, a young blonde-headed boy, had splints on both legs from his feet to his hips. As he moaned with pain, I remarked that something should be done for this kid. Another soldier, hearing my statement, was quick to respond: "That little Hitler Youth sonofabitch killed three of my buddies and wounded me. Someone stitched him across the legs to put him out of action. If it had been me, I'd have killed him."

My compassion for the enemy wounded was somewhat curtailed by this remark although it was impossible to ignore the manner in which they sat or lay on the ground, most of them badly wounded.

After fifteen or twenty minutes of waiting, I stood up to stretch a bit, then walked through the German's waiting line to get a better view of the Channel. A German officer approached me, after noticing the gold bar on my collar. He didn't look like the typical German officer to me—ramrod straight and all spit and polish. I inquired as to his military profession and he told me, in good English, that he was a physician, his specialty involving the chest. He wanted me to intercede for him with the American doctors concerning treatment for his most badly wounded men. I told him I was a walking wounded myself and a fighter pilot, and that I had no authority around there. Actually I considered myself no more than a private, the only difference being that I flew a P-51 Mustang.

Soon after the German doctor entered the diagnostic tent, the American doctor hurried out, with the German right behind him. At first I thought the German had managed to make his point but the expression on the American doctor's face told me otherwise. He summoned two of his orderlies and said: "Get this sonofabitch out of here."

The treatment line moved slowly and I was glad when my turn finally came. My hand was badly swollen and I could no longer flex my fingers. After the doctor had snipped off the old bandage, he could see what a mess it really was and quickly rebandaged it, adding a sling to help alleviate the swelling.

Before entering the diagnostic tent, I had left my hat and cane by the wooden bench so as not to appear to be a fun-seeking blade just back from a merry adventure in the Normandy skies. Actually, I had devised a plan. I wanted to return to my squadron just a few miles southwest of our present location, or go to the hospital in Cherbourg only a couple miles from my fighter strip. I asked the doctor if I might do this and he sternly responded that I was to be evacuated to England and that I stood a good chance of losing my right hand if they didn't manage to control the infection.

I left the diagnostic tent looking off toward the southwest with tears streaming down my cheeks. My home was only a few miles away and it seemed to me that the squadron flight surgeon could surely attend to my hand and that I could return to flying once the swelling went down.

Approaching the gate that led to the main road, I saw that it was manned by two military police. The doctor had apparently alerted them as they watched me closely. I'm sure that if those guards hadn't been stationed there, that I would have walked through the gate and back to the fighter strip which would inevitably have led to my being court-martialed for disobeying a direct order.

The field hospital Army nurses were always dressed in fatigues but even so, were extremely feminine and had a highly soothing effect upon the wounded. I couldn't help but address them as Lieutenant Ma'am or Captain Ma'am, and I'm surprised they didn't get military with me. Enough good things cannot be said about the field hospital nurses for their lot was a tough one, which was also the case with the physicians. I remember that the one who redressed my hand had not slept for two days and that his face clearly reflected the extent of his fatigue.

The patients I'd ridden to the airstrip with where all ambulatory, like myself. Beyond that, we were just a walking bunch of zombies—dirty, disheveled, and very quiet. An unshaven infantryman, who still had his M1 rifle and camouflage webbing on his helmet, sat beside me in the ambulance, staring off at nothing. When I inquired as to how he was doing, he said he'd had too many close calls too often, and that he'd lost many of his buddies since coming ashore on D-Day. All this was said as he fixedly stared off into space and his body shook with a series of spasmodic tremors.

The hedge-rows of Normandy were killers for the infantry and excellent defensive positions for the Germans. The enemy knew exactly how to defend in them.

As we slowly went up the steps into the C-47 transport, some of the men were forced to make several attempts before they succeeded in climbing the short ladder. Two tiers of stretchers lined the walls of the transport, all occupied, with many of the men experiencing intense pain. We walking wounded sat wherever we could find the room.

The C-47 crew cranked up the aircraft's two engines, then took off to the northwest. No sooner had we broken ground than I noticed steep cliffs down to the channel waters. Hell, this was the same airstrip where we had landed less than three weeks earlier. Our rangers had paid one helluva price for the ground we'd just taken off from.

After we arrived in England, a ramp was placed against the open door of the C-47 in order to make the unloading process easier. Hospital personnel swarmed around the aircraft and most of the walking wounded were carried off on stretchers. As for me, I walked down the aisle of the aircraft with some difficulty, but when a stretcher was offered, I politely declined. I was determined to walk the rest of the way on my own, which I somehow managed to do.

After disembarking, we were quickly diagnosed again and the disposition tags tied to our shirts helped to expedite this procedure.

I was put in a room where cots were lined up foot to head—there were about three rows of them, and every one was occupied. My khaki pants and shirt were taken from me, but I was allowed to keep my military insignia and good ol' G.I. shoes. I'd wanted to keep the pants and shirt as well, but the orderlies felt these so-called 'souvenirs' were only worthy of being burned since they were horribly soiled and reeked of the muddy sewer lagoon of Silli En Gouffern.

When I first bent over to untie my shoes, I wondered what happened to my socks for these knee-length woolies were now merely anklets. But then I remembered the cockpit fire and how it had sheared them down to their present size.

I literally fell into the cot that had been assigned to me for I was bone-weary, and no sooner had I drifted off than a nurse appeared with her needles, penicillin and sleep inducers. She made rounds every three to four hours, and a time or two I awoke with a start, wondering where I was and how I had gotten there. The room was kept in semi-darkness and now and again, a few moans and groans could be heard as a man rolled over onto his wound. Each time this happened, a nurse immediately rushed to his side to assist him into a more comfortable position.

After about twenty-four hours, I was taken out of this room an issued pajamas, a robe and slip-on slippers. After that, I was taken to a convalescent ward. I still felt that Doc, our flight surgeon, could have effectively treated my hand.

My assigned cot was next to a man whose plaster cast covered him from his armpits to his feet, with openings provided for bodily functions. Upon becoming better acquainted with him, I learned he had recently graduated from West Point and that he was a paratrooper. He related some of his experiences from the time he parachuted into Normandy early D-Day up until the time he'd gotten hit. I soon realized from the things he said that he was one tough dude although his personality gave no outward indication of this. His platoon had held a section of hedge-row in Normandy as the enemy positioned itself opposite them in another hedge-row close by. The hedge-rows of Normandy were mounded rows of earth with hedge trees growing on them. They provided an excellent means of concealment and were difficult to attack and overcome. It had been the lieutenant paratrooper's job to check his platoon's positions along the hedge-row, which had a gap through which the French farmer could drive his horses from one field to another. The paratrooper had to cross this gap, and in order to do it quickly, he'd accelerated into a crouching run so that he might remain concealed behind the hedge-row. As he threw himself across the gap to the cover of the hedge-row on the opposite side, a German machine gun caught him with a burst, stitching him in the pelvic area and legs. The paratrooper said they'd shot him as though he were a game bird on the wing. Nonetheless, he'd managed to gain the shelter of the hedge-row on the other side of the gap where his medic gave him emergency treatment, then put him in the pipeline to evacuation. He remarked that he had hated to leave his men. When I asked how he was doing now, he said that his skin itched like hell under the cast, and that defecation had become a troublesome problem as well. He said it was a helluva feeling, while taking a good healthy shit, to feel it forcing itself out between the cheeks of his ass. He was looking forward to a time when he could sit on a toilet seat again and enjoy his daily constitutional.

 I was told by a nurse to take a shower "immediately, if not sooner" for I hadn't had a bath since leaving England some three weeks earlier. There had been no available facilities for purposes of personal hygiene where I had been stationed in France. I could certainly appreciate that I had grown somewhat offensive to others since my run through the open air sewer lagoon in Silli En Gouffern.

 The nurse looked at my bandaged hand and told me to prepare myself as she or some other ward personnel would be giving me a bath. Well, no one had bathed me since I was a lad on my Mama's knee and I was determined to keep it that way. I asked the nurse if she couldn't tape something around my hand to keep water from getting to it and she finally gave me a woman's shower cap, which worked perfectly. I had a difficult time lathering up the wash cloth but managed to give myself a good scrub, and the toweling down was much easier. While taking this shower, I noticed quarter-sized burns on my legs and buttocks. Molten metal coming out of the right engine exhausts had apparently caught me as I left the cockpit on the right side. I didn't call the physician's attention to this for I thought the penicillin would help to heal the burns. My right leg was somewhat lame but I compensated for this by walking slowly. When the physician asked about my mental health, owing to the fact that I had a rather somber expression on my face, I assured him that I was fine and ready to rejoin my squadron. By then, the bandage on my hand had started to smell like decaying flesh, so the doctor carefully snipped the wrapping off to reveal a hand that was now dark brown in color. Although the swelling was down, the member was extremely stiff. Even so, the doctor assured me that the hand was on the mend, and applied a looser bandage without an arm sling.

  The day after I was brought into the hospital ward, a Red Cross lady stopped by to visit and asked if she could assist me in writing a letter home. While I was not permitted to divulge the nature of my injuries, I said I was anxious to convey that I was in one piece and not seriously hurt. Although I believed the Red Cross lady and I effectively drafted such a message, my mother immediately wrote back, demanding to know the truth about my injuries. She also said she had awakened during the early hours on the day I was shot down with the premonition that I had encountered some difficult or dangerous circumstance. A mother's intuition where her children are concerned is truly mind-boggling, particularly since it is often right on target.

  As soon as I was able to manage it, I wrote to the family for I thought that a letter in my own hand would prove reassuring. I mentioned, among other things, that I would soon be rejoining my squadron.

  I'd also gotten a letter off to Fogie shortly after arriving in England. It was the first word he'd received concerning my survival and it came as welcome news, as the entire squadron had long since written me off as buying the farm.

  The patients in the ward were mostly lieutenants, shavetails and first lieutenants. For the most part they were badly wounded, having lost limbs or in some cases, their eyesight, which made me feel quite fortunate by comparison. I was more determined than ever to reek havoc upon the enemy as quickly as I had the chance.

  I felt extremely privileged to be in a ward with these men, and heard no moaning or groaning throughout the night or day. Two fighter pilots who had flown the P-47 Thunderbolt were on the ward. One was a tall young man who'd been hit in the engine by an Me-109. When his plane caught fire, he managed to bail out but his face was badly burned. The other P-47 fighter pilot was in a private room with a broken leg. I stopped in for a visit one day and learned that his flight had been on a close support mission, working with ground forces. German flak had hit his aircraft which necessitated a quick bail out, and he broke his leg on landing. Crawling along a hedge-row in order to conceal himself, he had had the good fortune to run into American infantry troops. I couldn't help but wonder how he'd managed to rate himself a private room but then I noticed a pretty blonde nurse taking care of him and suspected they were in love. Although I knew how combat in the air went, concerning combat on the ground, I knew very little.

A tank destroyer lieutenant on the ward told me of some of the experiences he had shared with his men. Once in the hedgerows of Normandy, his destroyer was in a night ambush position because of German tanks that were in the area. The lieutenant had had his tank destroyer parked on one side of a hedge row in a field and there was a country lane on the other side; enemy tanks would use that lane for night reconnaissance or penetration. The lieutenant and his crew remained absolutely quiet, their eyes and ears finely tuned for the enemy. Soon they heard a large enemy tank approaching cautiously. Every now and then, it would stop to look and listen, then continue its approach. The lieutenant admitted that waiting for the enemy to appear was a nerve-wracking experience for him and his crew. When at last the enemy tank was silhouetted against the star-lit sky, the tank destroyer fired, hitting the monster tank broadside from very close range, destroying the vehicle and its crew. The lieutenant and his crew had seen much action in Normandy. One afternoon they were attacked by an Me-109, the pilot making several strafing passes at them, wounding the lieutenant in the lower legs. His crew shot down the Me-109 during one of these strafing runs and the enemy pilot landed in his parachute close to their position. The lieutenant's men were irate when they saw that he was wounded and as the Me-109 pilot landed, they put a burst of fifty caliber machine gun fire across his legs to square accounts.

Another lieutenant on the ward narrated his experiences while commanding a platoon of Sherman tanks in Normandy. Advancing in his lead tank through the narrow streets of a small French village, he negotiated a turn and ran directly into a large German tank. The lieutenant's only alternative at that point was to close with the German tank, thereby pinning it against the stone building directly in front of his Sherman tank, and at point-blank range. The German tank tried to traverse its long cannon but kept hitting the lieutenant's tank on the turret. The lieutenant told me this was frightening as hell, but his driver kept the enemy tank pinned in the corner as the Sherman gun crew pumped shell after shell into them and finally destroyed them.

Also on our ward was an infantry platoon leader from the

midwest. When I introduced myself to him, he told me his name was Jack Frost. I asked if he was kidding but he assured me that he wasn't. Jack's appearance belied the fact that he was a killing machine for he had a slender build and there was a constant expression of merriment on his face. How Jack was wounded very nearly defies description. His patrol had been surrounded by the enemy and pinned down to whatever concealment Mother Earth could offer. For close-in encirclement, the Germans had a wooden bullet of about thirty caliber size which was quite accurate at short range but would lose its velocity over longer distances. I had seen these wooden bullets back in Normandy, in rifle clips that lay around the scenes of previous battles. As it was, Jack was concealed by Mother Earth, with the exception of his ass, and this proved to be an irresistible target for the Germans. The wooden bullets splintered after penetrating the skin which necessitated Jack's evacuation to England after the encirclement had been broken. The way Jack put it was: "I'm in the hospital to have splinters taken out of my ass."

After our ward doctor had made his rounds, those of us who could manage it would line up at attention to receive the purple heart by the ward doctor who took this ceremony quite seriously. A lieutenant across the aisle from me by the name of Smith had lost his eyesight in a huge explosion and at first declined to receive the purple heart, but with a little persuasion from the rest of us, eventually changed his mind. Smith had been in combat when the explosion occurred.

When Jack Frost received orders to return to his infantry unit, he gave me his address, then said, "George, you write me a letter and I'll send you the ears of the next German I kill." Jack told me he enjoyed going on patrols, especially night patrols. He enjoyed getting into the enemy's foxholes and for some hand-to-hand combat with a knife. I never did write Jack as I knew he would do exactly as he'd promised.

After lights out the standard operational procedure was story telling for thirty minutes or so, I heard many that were very clever and non obscene. When I was asked for a joke I told them about the guy who had acquired a bad case of trouser bunnies while sowing his wild oats. He went to the drug store to secure some blue ointment, the standard medication in those days to treat such infestations. He stated his problem to the druggist who asked him what size jar of blue ointment he desired, the guy pointed to the largest size to which the druggist replied, "hell that will kill all the crabs in the county," to which the guy replied, "I gott'em." I also told another joke about the carnival wrestler and a strong farm boy who wrestled him when the carnival came through their small town, but it is a bit raunchy to repeat.

After ten days the doctor removed the dressings from my

hand, the burned skin was a very dark brown which had started to peel in spots. I had lost a lot of strength in it and stiffness was experienced but in due time without the dressing it would loosen up. I soon peeled the dark skin from my hand to reveal a healthy pink color. My right leg was still somewhat stiff but improving, the tall P-47 pilot and myself checked out a couple of bicycles from the physical training building. We cycled a short distance to the near-by village to view the local English gals, they were willing enough to attend a movie with us but neither of us had a dime, riding the bicycle did help loosen up my right leg considerably.

The doctor deemed me recovered for return to my squadron, clothing was issued, orders were cut, I cleared the hospital, leaving with my G.I. shoes, insignia, and issue wrist watch. I took a train to the nearest American airfield flying transport aircraft to France, an over-night lay over was required before I could catch a flight. I had a few dollars in my pocket due to a partial payment drawn at the hospital, with money in my pocket I bused to a near-by small city to kill a little time. I managed to engage a young lady clerk working in a small shop in conversation for awhile, her brother was in the Royal Air Force as a ground crew member. She seemed very interested in the United States as she queried me of my home state and family. Of course, Donna's name came into the conversation. This was the first time I had engaged a strange gal in conversation with self confidence, I felt I had accomplished something as I left her small shop to search out a restaurant. My uniform was such that I looked as though I belonged on a work detail instead of entering this fine restaurant for a meal but enter I did. I had in mind fish and chips for supper but such wasn't listed on the menu, nor was there meat plates entered, I ended up ordering a lettuce and radish sandwich, the slices of bread were very thin. The tea was excellent even though this was the first time I drank it with a dash of milk in it. I hadn't realized how rationed the English people were.

I rode a C-47 transport across the channel again to an air strip farther in land this time as the German front lines had collapsed during my two weeks absence. I went to the makeshift operations building to bum a ride to the 363rd Fighter Group, giving the officer the airstrip number. A major and a first lieutenant were standing nearby listening to our conversation and volunteered to fly me to my group but the latest information had it that the group had moved. As we approached a B-26 medium bomber the major explained to me that the lieutenant was going to check him out in the aircraft. The B-26 was a hot twin-engine aircraft and was known as the widow maker but the pilots who flew them swore by them. The major buckled into the left seat and started the engines under the watchful eyes of the lieutenant in the right seat. The major was an excellent student as he wasn't one of the know-it-all types. The major checked the magnetos at the end of the run-way then took the runway advancing both throttles smoothly, the B-26 took to the air with authority being minus its bomb load. After take-off I went forward into the plexiglass nose section where the bombardier usually set, I immediately noticed my eyes were very sensitive to sunlight, my issue sunglasses would have been welcome. The major shot a landing at an airstrip where they thought my Group was now located, he bounced the B-26 a bit but did a decent job of it. We landed and took off from four or five other air-strips searching for the 363rd Fighter Group to no avail, the major was flying the B-26 with assurance by now. While at the last air-strip, the major was told the 363rd Fighter Group had been converted to a tactical reconnaissance group and was still located at my old air-strip so off we go again. Fogie and Ott were still located at the strip, I was damn glad to see them again. Carlton Palmer was also with them, he had joined the 382nd squadron two or three weeks before we joined, our threesome was now a foursome. Carl's home state was Indiana, his father a school teacher.

    The commanding colonel of the Tactical Reconnaissance Group asked us personally to join his group, I was all for it if they let me fly armed while doing recon flying but Fogie, Ott, and Palmer were dubious. I didn't want to break up our foursome, I also declined the invitation. All the other pilots of the group rotated home with tours completed as did Webster or transferred to the hot 354TH Fighter Group who flew Mustangs, the remainder joined P-47 Thunderbolt Fighter Groups. Palmer told me the bad news that Chester Rice had been shot down and killed with his element leader the same day I had went down, our horse-shoe itinerary was shot to hell. When Carl told me this bad news items I couldn't help but think back of the two Mustangs in close formation who buzzed me while I was on the ground southwest of Silli En Gouffern. Chester was a very conscientious fighter pilot, flying almost perfect tight formation at all times. The last they heard from Chester and his element leader was they had sighted an enemy supply column and were attacking same.

    I went by the supply tent to collect what was left of my gear, a few comfort items were missing such as sheets, blankets and pillows, the supply sergeant handed me an Itemized list of the remainder under the headline, "EFFECTS OF LT. GEORGE J. BROOKS". I thanked him and thought the bastards had jumped to a too rapid conclusion. Going down to see the grizzled parachute sergeant was a must, I thanked him profusely. He looked at me with his steely gray eyes and said, "son, you aren't the first to do so, glad to see you back."

    The abolishment of the 363RD Fighter Group never did

make sense to me, of course my judgment is based on flying only five missions with my squadron. Guys like Webster, Heberlin, Pawlak, Jabara, Littlefield, or any of our foursome would have made good flight leaders. Webster would have made an excellent squadron commanding officer. Not counting my two claimed kills my squadron had sixteen or seventeen confirmed kills August 13, 1944. I didn't realize it at the time that there was a lot of politics in the military.

However, somewhere Fogie and Ott had met and talked with a Lieutenant Colonel Barnum who vowed he could use four experienced pilots as liaison officers. These jobs were located in the Cherbourg port area, one of our main ports supplying the war effort. I didn't relish the thought of being on the ground in a rear-echelon area, the sooner I got back to flying missions in a fighter again the better. I had been knocked on my ass before and had always gotten up to do battle again, I also realized I was badly sprung in mind, body, and soul, a little time was needed to mend myself. I think Fogie, Ott, and Carl arranged these liaison jobs to do just that for me, they all could have transferred to other Fighter Groups while I was hospitalized. There are buddies and there are friends, one vast difference. I also realized I hadn't experienced the glories and favors of fair womanhood, almost buying the farm in Normandy without doing so put one helluva fright in me. Norman Ott was in the same boat and vowed to stay there until married, I believed him.

Lt. Col. Barnum took us to a building near the airfield in Cherbourg, our duties were that of booking passage for the Air Transport Command at the airfield. The other rooms in the building were occupied by Colonels, Majors, Captains, Lieutenants on down the line to the lower ranks who did all the work. The lady soldiers were also in abundance, first I had seen since advanced flight. Norman Ott flew Col. Barnum and other colonels and majors around to various airfields surveying this and that in a single-engine Norseman aircraft. Ott and I took some of the WAC's up for a ride in the Norseman, they confided to us that their G.I. boyfriends had went French since they landed in France.

Col. Barnum wasn't on flying status, but during his flying days he had flown the China Clipper, the large four engined flying boat. He related to us that during one landing on rough seas some windows in the passenger compartment had broken, the Col. went back to see to his passengers and there sat Dorothy Lamour soaking wet, that really emphasized her excellent figure.

The four of us were quartered in a hotel overlooking the harbor, this hotel was the headquarters of a Counter Intelligence Corp. unit in charge of the security of the harbor. They assigned the four of us to a large room with a harbor view. We were told to observe strict security on whatever we happened to see or hear of the activities in the building. They had a French chef to cook their meals, the chef did wonders with the powdered eggs and potatoes which were staples of Army chow. All the agents were former law enforcement officers in civilian life, men fluent in French and other languages were available, plus some very intelligent college graduates who could discuss Shelley and Keats extensively.

There were a lot of mysterious comings and goings in that hotel that I didn't want to know about. There were two young French maids who made up all the beds in the entire hotel, one average looking, the other black headed and damn good looking. I made a couple of passes at each of them but their jobs depended on no fraternization. About a month after getting acquainted a bit with them the good looking one come up missing, I asked the other one of her where abouts, she merely shrugged her shoulders and continued with her maid duties. That evening at supper chow I asked one of the agents what happened to the black-headed maid, he replied that she had been and was a German spy, the French secret service had taken her away, case closed.

Orders came through for me to report to an intelligence unit in Paris for debriefing of my evasion experiences. I gave the debriefing officer the pertinent information but when it came to how I actually evaded I didn't want to talk about it and couldn't. I told him after I hit the ground in my chute, I unbuckled same, mae west next, ditched my leather helmet, goggles, oxygen mask and ran for the woods. He must have realized what I was experiencing as he didn't press but did ask if I knew or remembered any resistance people of the Argentan area, which I didn't, end of debriefing.

After supper chow in a transient mess hall in downtown Paris I strolled up the Champs Elysees to the Arc d'Triumphe, strolled up a wide street half a block where I entered a large room utilized as a bar. A lieutenant colonel was at a table by himself, I asked if I could join him, he was only too glad to oblige. I ordered champagne, the first I had drank, it went down very easy, I was drinking my third champagne glass when I noticed the Col. eye-balling two good-looking French gals across the dance floor at another table, they also showed interest in us. When I came to Paris to be debriefed I also vowed to get laid for the first time also. The Col. was an educated man with a knowledge of the French language and proceeded to teach me the ageless question from man to woman, "Voulez Vous Coucher Avec Moi." He rehearsed me for fifteen or twenty minutes for me to get the question down pat as I sit drinking champagne, I was feeling very well up to the situation but my stomach full of supper food plus the champagne rebelled to alcohol again at a very critical time, I told the Col. of my distress, excused myself, picked up my cap and walked by the French gals through the door into the street where I lost my supper and felt all the better for it. I didn't return to the bar as I had an early flight to catch for Cherbourg, I hoped the Col. was successful.

My job with A.T.C. was very boring but talking to the various C.I.C. Agents in the evenings helped a lot. Staying at the hotel were three refugees from Holland, a father, mother and fifteen year old daughter. Their last name was KOHLER, all musicians, father with the accordion, mother on the violin, and daughter also on the violin. They played once in awhile after supper, mostly waltzes and tangoes. I often went to their quarters in the evenings, I tried to play Mme. Kohler's violin but my right shoulder, hand, and wrist were still stiff, I would start a piece of music on the violin, falter a bit and Mme. Kohler would finish it. They were quite accomplished on their instruments and I suspect they were hot intelligence subjects to be staying in our counter intelligence corps headquarters guarded day and night.

The C.I.C. had plenty of booze floating around the hotel, no drinking to excess, our four drank scotch and unsweetened grapefruit juice, nine times out of ten I would lose everything, supper, scotch and the mix. A scotch connoisseur would have shot the four of us.

The C.I.C. agents secured the four of us an invitation to a cargo ship anchored dockside in Cherbourg harbor. We boarded ship at the appointed time, a crew member presented us to a Captain Smith from the Lake Tahoe area of California. He made us feel at ease immediately as he escorted us to the ship's mess. The ship's mess was a long low ceilinged room with a stoutly built wooden table and captain chairs for seating, the decor was such that I had a feeling of well being as one should have contemplating a good meal in the correct surroundings. Army chow was good chow but the Captain's cook's announcement after we had seated ourselves amazed me, almost unbelievable, we would be served fried chicken, real potatoes mashed, gravy, peas, a salad made from fresh lettuce, radishes, diced tomatoes and apple pie for dessert. The four of us relished this meal much to the Captain's and cook's delight, good conversation intermingled while the meal was eaten. After the cook cleared the heavy china plates and eating utensils away the fresh baked apple pie still warm was served, I was enjoying the aroma when the cook appeared at my elbow with a round one gallon container of vanilla ice cream asking, "how many scoops, lieutenant?" Apple pie alamode at home was a delicacy but under war circumstances it was phenomenal. After dessert freshly brewed percolated coffee was served, this meal was the best and most enjoyed of my life, Fogie, Ott and Palmer were of the same feeling. The Captain then took the four of us to the ship's store where he gave us each a carton of Lucky Strike cigarettes of the original green color packaging. We then left the ship thanking the Captain and cook profusely for the excellent meal and pleasant evening. Captain Smith, his crew, and their ship had made many a perilous voyage.

One Sunday with no work to be done for the Air Transport Command Fogie dressed up in a German officer's uniform he talked a C.I.C. agent out of, to complete his disguise he wedged a pop bottle cap in one of his eye sockets, put a cigarette holder between his teeth, then put on the cap. He also put on a pair of black shiny boots, he looked very authentic. The four of us proceeded outside to the front of the hotel to snap a few pictures, we were taking pictures of Fogie in different poses such as the Heil Hitler salute, knocking on a door, enjoying ourselves in general when we noticed a crowd of French people gathering, the looks on their faces told us they were not enjoying Fogie's antics in the least, we retired to the inside of the hotel in a hurry. The French knew the function of the hotel's occupants, and Fogie's disguise was very convincing.

A jeep with driver was dispatched each morning to our hotel to take us to our office jobs and likewise back home in the evening. The driver was Buck O'Farrel from Holister, California, we all became good friends immediately as Buck catered to us by driving us on side trips whenever asked. I asked Buck if it would be possible to check out a jeep to drive to Silli en Gouffern. I didn't exactly know where the village was but I wanted to see the place I almost bought August 13. Buck was on good terms with the motor-pool Sergeant, getting a trip ticket for a day's driving of the jeep was no problem. We started early driving in an easterly direction towards Argentan over gravel roads, almost like driving the country roads of Kansas. The terrain of France also resembled eastern Kansas except most of the building structures were of stone. The few automobiles we saw were of the charcoal burning type putting out the black exhaust smoke as they slowly drove along the road ways. Most would stall when going up a steep hill, the French driver merely set the brakes, dismounted, walked to the rear of the automobile, opened up the charcoal burning stove door, stirred up the charcoal or added to it if needed, then continued the climb up the hill very slowly. Most of the drivers of such vehicles had a dusky appearance to their clothes and faces. Most of the ravages of war had been removed as this was October of 1944 but villages bore bullet marks on their stone houses and stone walled gardens, some buildings blown up by artillery, and every where the killer hedge rows. Upon arriving in Argentan one could see only rubble. Argentan had been a strong point of the German defense on the southern flank holding the Argentan-Falaise gap open for some of the German forces to escape. I knew Silli en Gouffern was east of Argentan about three kilometers, a sign pointed east with

Paris on it was the one Buck took, sure enough the direction sign of Silli appeared indicating a turn right and south into the one block long village. At first I didn't recognize anything as Buck crawled the jeep down the slight inclined graveled main street until I saw the back of the church. I alighted from the jeep, proceeding to the rear of the church, also seeing the apple orchard and there the remains of my Mustang. I was standing there reliving my last presence in this bit of Normandy, Buck at my elbow, remembering the shouts in the German language, the fifty caliber ammunition exploding from the burning Mustang, and feeling like a hunted animal when the rear side door opened, there appeared the same young Frenchman I first saw the day I was shot down. He took a few steps toward me, stopped caught his breath, then fled back into the church, reappearing with the priest, still looking as if he had seen a ghost. I approached both for the handshake, also getting the standard French greeting. The priest offered Buck and I a drink of calvados with coffee, I declined. I had a six twenty film size French camera to take a few pictures, I noticed my Mustang had impacted the ground upside down, my left foot must have kicked the stick in my haste to leave the airplane, the engine was almost buried, every part of the aircraft was burned rubble except the tail section which somewhat resembled that of an aircraft. The young Frenchman, Michel Laine, took me to a dug pit a hundred yards from the airplane where the Germans had buried my parachute, the French had retrieved the chute and put it to good use I am sure. At this time I still didn't know the name of the Frenchman who took me into his peasant hut, his name was Emil Sorel, or the name of Dr. Picot and his wife the nurse who treated my right hand, or Roger Benance' whose home the treatment was accomplished at. These people I wanted to see again but I didn't know where to look for them, the language barrier prevented inquiries, I was a bit disjointed still and was satisfied we had found the village and my aircraft.

Buck and I took our leave of the priest and Michel Laine' to join a few of the citizens of Silli En Gouffern, they offered me a drink of booze, again I declined, Buck took a short one. We were sitting in a small building on the main street of the village communicating a bit when the subject of staying the night came up. A little French gal had found Buck's lap which added to his pleasure to that of being a liberator. It was mid-afternoon, Buck said the motor-pool sergeant would understand an overnight stay, but some of the French people would steal the jeep or strip it which concerned me, they had done without for so long they couldn't help themselves. I vetoed the suggestion reluctantly, we started back west for Cherbourg planning to visit the ground between Argentan and Falaise where the Germans were literally slaughtered. We slowly drove along a road littered with military vehicles shoved aside into the ditch, allied aircraft and artillery had done a tremendous job. Buck and I walked in a field bordering the road to look closer at some of the destroyed vehicles, I saw a steel German helmet lying on the ground top up, without thinking I flipped it over with the toe of my shoe. A German soldier's head sill remained in it, the portion from the upper teeth on up. He must have been a young soldier as the upper teeth were perfect. Buck and I agreed we had seen enough of this slaughter ground as we journeyed back to Cherbourg. Buck O'Farrel was sent up front with an infantry unit at the turn of the year where he did well for himself and others. I felt better about myself and the world in general after the visit to Silli en Gouffern.

Our foursome sometimes walked the streets around the harbor area, most of the buildings were occupied by bars, French accordion music blasted from the bars, I would have entered to listen awhile but knew it was too damn tough for me. One evening while walking down the street I noticed my issue wrist watch was missing. I immediately looked behind in the street just in time to see a Frenchman following us finishing straightening up, at the same time his hand just slipping into his coat pocket. I didn't say anything, I thought for sure I could draw another. The pin holding the wrist strap to the watch must have been bent when I hit the ground August 13.

One evening our foursome attended a U.S.O. show at a cold theatre in Cherbourg, five very pretty and very talented young women performed, an old gentleman, Al K. Hall was their master of ceremonies. We sat in the audience remarking among the four of us such as, "look at that gal, she's for me, damn I'd like to meet her." I jokingly chose the little black-haired pianist with the low voice, then forgot all about the stage performance. The following evening we became aware they were billeted at the hotel next to the C.I.C. hotel. Fogie allowed he was going over and get acquainted with the whole troupe, put on his cap and left our room with a purposeful look on his face. I thought to myself he would be back in a couple of minutes with his tail between his legs, with all the American men available what chance had our foursome of meeting them. Ten minutes went by and no Fogie. Ott stated he was going over to check on Fogie, ten or fifteen minutes went by with no return of Fogie or Ott. Palmer of the astute nature finally stood up from his bed saying he was going to get to the bottom of what was detaining them and left our room. Another ten minutes went by with no return of my buddies, I knew damn well they had the whole troupe cornered and all to themselves, I might as well get in on the action. I left the room without bothering to put on my cap, walked the few steps next door, inquired at the desk of the troupe's room, went up a flight of stairs to that number, hesitated at a door to knock from which emitted conversation and laughter, knocked then entered the room. My three buddies were paired off in conversation with the gals they had picked out during the show the previous evening. I was glad to see the little black-headed gal unoccupied. I was introduced to the five of them, Fogie was in deep conversation with Lee Sullivan, a blond girl with an excellent voice whom he had known back in Spokane, Washington. Fogie had recognized her from the previous evening, he knew what he was doing when he initiated this little meeting. Palmer was in conversation with Gina Lotito from the west coast, a pretty brunette with a beautiful soprano voice. Ott was talking to Ginger Wallace, a gal good looking enough to be a Power's model, a modeling agency second to none. Upon being introduced to Herbie Herblin, the little one-hundred pound black-haired pianist I realized she had been in the entertainment world for a few years. After high school in Wichita Falls, Texas she had studied piano at the famed Julliard School of Music, only the talented did so. The other gal of the troupe wasn't too sociable, we were satisfied with the four we were acquainted with. It was getting late as we reluctantly left the troupe, they would see us again next morning before they packed up to go on the road to entertain the troops again but would keep in touch with us, perhaps our foursome would meet them in Paris when they had a short vacation from their tour. Our foursome leaned on every word.

    Fogie and Ott took a short leave to London, they went to a bar frequented by our Air Forces personnel. They met some of the other pilots from various Fighter Groups in the 8TH Air Force whom we had trained with at Bartow, Florida. The loses from our training group was very high. Fogie run into his advanced flight instructor who was flying with the 20TH F.T.R. G.P., they had a good visit. Fogie told his old instructor that we were without a Fighter Group and would like a transfer from the 9TH Air Force to the 20TH F.T.R.G.P. in the 8TH Air Force. Fogie's previous instructor would submit our foursome's names and expect to hear from the 20TH F.T.R.G.P. in a week or so. A week after Fogie and Ott arrived back from London we heard from the 20TH F.T.R.G.P., it was impossible to transfer from one Air Force to another. Although we dearly loved the P-51 Mustang, it looked as though we would be flying the P-47 Thunderbolt. It was said it would take a beating and still bring you home. I was ready to return to combat flying the P-47, my self esteem was back up after analyzing the events of August 13. Fogie and Ott also came back with the latest class A uniform dress fad, fighter pilots left the top button undone on the blouse to denote one was a fighter pilot.

    A C.I.C. agent from southeast Kansas by the name of Dan took me under his wing as one would a kid brother. He was ordered to Paris for three days on official business, he would include my name on the official orders. I was only too glad to oblige as Dan was an old hand with the ladies. We arrived in Paris by jeep, a good journey from Cherbourg to Paris over unimproved roads. Dan accomplished his official business in a couple of hours, leaving almost three days to spend some time with the French women. C.I.C. Headquarters in Paris was located on a street off the Arc D'Triumphe, from there Dan and I sauntered back to the circle street around the Arc then sauntered down another off the Arc which had more pedestrian traffic. In Paris there were no cats or dogs but many young French gals came pedaling by on their bicycles, hem of their skirts up over their thighs held there by the forward motion against the air or wind. The women all had good figures as there was an acute shortage of food in Paris, and they didn't mind showing off their legs. I was a willing and intensely interested observer. Dan and I took up an observation stand against a building, several women came by walking who looked interesting to me but Dan was leading the mission and would call the bounce. We stood at our spot for fifteen or twenty minutes when a woman in her late twenties approached down the street. She was dressed in a tailored coat and skirt which emphasized her beautifully proportioned buxom figure, hair done up in a neat bun, adorned with a dark colored brimed woman's hat. She looked like a good looking school teacher to me but Dan was away from our standing spot to intercept her, in decent conversational French he introduced himself then ascertained she was not married, and would she accompany him and his friend for a few drinks this evening. She accepted and asked us to accompany her to her residence which was shared by her elderly mother. We were introduced then left the very small ground floor apartment after setting the definite time we would call for her. Dan and I proceeded to our quarters in the C.I.C. Headquarters where Dan shaved and spruced up in general. Shaving regularly was a foreign task to me, I couldn't even grow a mustache which I coveted so much. Dan wore combat boots which he bloused his trouser legs to about half-way up the boot tops, I asked him where he got the strong rubber bands for this mode of dress, the last I heard there was an extreme shortage of rubber back home. Dan replied they come from condoms, the country was full of them. Now I knew how the paratroopers bloused their trousers.

We called for the French lady at the appointed time, we bid her mother good-night, the walk up to the Champs Elysses was pleasant as nightfall began. Crossing a wide boulevard was no problem, civilian automobiles were rare, but the jeeps and staff cars of the rear echelon were in abundance. We entered a nightclub on the Champs that wasn't too crowded, secured a large table and began sipping champagne, I had eaten a good supper and felt confident about drinking if I did it slowly. A lady at the adjoining table struck up a conversation with Dan's lady friend, she was an American married to a Frenchman before the war, no husband was in evidence. She joined our threesome as the stage show began and helped with our French and English interpretations. Much was said about life during the German occupation, it was like being under the heel of someone's boot. One act of the stage show was a gal dancer, her dance was of the exotic nature, for an ending the tear away briefs and bra went flying as she rapidly twirled across the stage to the band's crescendo. This was the first French stage show I had seen, an eyeful to a hayseed from Kansas. The evening was late as the four of us left the night-club for the American lady's apartment she shared with her teenage son, Dan purchased a bottle of white wine for a night cap at the apartment. The apartment had three bedrooms with a large dining room which served for dining and parlor also. We seated ourselves as the American lady fetched the wine glasses. The white wine looked like champagne to me but upon drinking some of it I thought it was sour as hell, it was actually an excellent dry wine, I just didn't know any better.

Dan and his date were doing great together, I knew they would sleep together this night. Realizing this I asked the American lady to sleep with me, she abruptly said she was too old for me. Good thing as my wine and champagne mix rebelled and off to the bathroom I fled, now I was ready for a good night's sleep as she led me to a small bedroom adjoining Dan's and his girlfriend. Three hours later the bedroom door opened, Dan's voice told me in a commanding voice he needed some help. He stood outlined in the partially opened door with his right combat boot still on, thick wavy hair well mussed up, and his olive drab undershirt holding up a limber hard-on. To be sure his attire was correct for sacrobatics. I started to complain about him needing help as did the French gal's voice from their bedroom. Dan left the partially open doorway, I could hear them arguing a bit, but Dan returned to the doorway and said, "get in here." I had secured a rubber from my dress green blouse pocket, unwrapped it as I entered their bedroom, getting up for the occasion was no problem. The woman lying on her back smiling at me as I approached her side of the bed, still covered with the bedsheet which showed her figure full and mature. As I dropped my shorts to roll on the rubber she flipped the sheet aside and held her arms up for me. As I had visualized her she had a buxom well proportioned body, lily white and flawless skin, her long hair was let down from the bun which revved me up all the more. As she helped me get started Dan turned his back to us, propped his tousled head up on his hand, looked at his wrist-watch, by then I had forgotten he ever existed. When we had finished the French woman gave me a big hug and kiss, Dan looked at his wrist-watch and said, "fifteen minutes, George, that's damn good for the first time." I returned to my bedroom with a satisfied feeling I had never experienced before, flying fighters would now be second on my list of life's enjoyments.

We arose the next morning, I was somewhat concerned what the French woman's attitude would be, she merely smiled at me and said, "good morning." She related to Dan that he was the first American she had slept with. I thought to myself she had been my first even though I was second.

The French lady had a job to observe and left for work with the promise to meet us again at the American lady's apartment for supper, I accompanied Dan to his Paris C.I.C. Headquarters, enjoying the gals cycling down the boulevards even more. Somehow, somewhere Dan appropriated army rations of canned beef, carrots, peas, and some powdered potatoes for supper at the American lady's apartment. These people hadn't eaten good food and plenty of it for two or three years, they enjoyed it immensely to Dan's and my pleasure. We passed the evening conversing and sipping a little dry white wine. The American lady's son came in for awhile to visit, he was delighted when I gave him a package of cigarettes, which he converted to pipe tobacco. Bedtime came, I in my small bedroom adjoining Dan and his gal's bedroom. About three A.M. I awoke with alarm and a start as the hallway door to my room was noisily opened. Almost immediately Dan flung his bedroom door open asking, "what's the matter, George?" The light from his room caught the American lady in her housecoat, she replied she only wanted to check on how I was doing, the spell was broken. If she had entered quietly and had awakened me properly I would have followed her as a wingman follows his flight leader. The French lady must have passed a good word about me to the American lady. Dan and I left them that morning for our journey back to Cherbourg and duty.

We soon got a letter from the U.S.O troupe, they would be in Paris for a week of rest and recuperation, our foursome managed to get orders cut for some reason or another to legitimately join them. What a week, seeing Paris with five American gals, attended two operas, the Bal Tabrin night club, strolled the wide boulevards and Seine river bridges. While attending the large opera house our group was broken up into two different groups, our seating accommodations were two loges next to each other. After getting settled in I heard Fogie in the adjoining loge softly saying, "peacorn and popnuts," as if he were vending them. I could hear Lee Sullivan shushing him up. Herbie was by my side explaining the opera to me, her knowledge of classical music was immense. The opera house was without heat, so cold our lined trench coats were comfortable, but the performance was excellent. We attended the Bal Tabrin night club for an evening of dancing and an excellent floor show. The dance period was between the acts of the stage show, a man with an accordion played the dance music, all French flavored. The push-button accordion has a sound all of its own. The final act of the stage show was astounding to me, a circular stage ascended revolving up from the dance floor, adorned with beautiful French gals, dressed in scanty briefs and bare from the waist up. Herbie told me later that the expressions on my face was almost as good as the show. The gals in the troupe had evening gown fitting appointments plus settings with the best photographers in Paris, our foursome visited the Arc De Triumphe with its flame again burning, the four of us threw a salute as we passed through the arch, to me it was very impressive. We also visited the Cathedral of Notre Dame, largest church I had ever entered. As we went down one aisle to some seats to sit awhile I noticed the darkness of the cathedral and remembered a short story Dad told me when I was in high school. During World War I before going up to the front Dad and some of his buddies visited the famous cathedral. They were slowly walking along the very dark aisles, Dad looking around, up and down as his oldest son, George was doing now when he stumbled over his buddy in front of him who had knelt to cross himself before entering the seats. Dad told me, "I didn't know he was Catholic," the intonation in Dad's voice told me he was very sorry about the incident.

We were billeted at the same hotel as the U.S.O. troupe, our last night there Herbie and I sat together the night talking about the present, music, and what the future held for us. She told me she was a married woman as I had suspected, her husband a fighter pilot of fame in the 8TH Air Force by the name of Howard, she used his name in her stage name, Mary Lou Howard. We didn't see the U.S.O. troupe gals again but I would never forget them for taking our foursome into their small family.

After returning to Cherbourg a couple of C.I. agents took Ott to Paris to indoctrinate him to the charms of the Parisian women, I knew they would have their work cut out for them as Ott was a celibate and would remain so until married to the woman of his choice. As the episode was related to me they managed to get Ott well inebriated, a beautiful young blond French gal was enlisted and awaited them in her room. The agents managed to get him to her room, out of his uniform, into her bed then out of the room the agents went, out to the street walking away from the good deed they had initiated. They had walked about one-half a block when they heard shouting behind them, upon turning around they could see Ott coming, uniform was on but not yet buttoned up or his shoes tied. As he drew abreast of them he told them, "YEAH, you sons-of-bitches thought I'd lose my cherry, didn't you?"

Early December saw us leave the A.T.C. and C.I.C. personnel. They treated us very good indeed, our close friends we made among them didn't want us to go back to combat, Buck O'Farrell especially, we were his little brothers.

We reported to a P-47 Thunderbolt Fighter Group located at Dijon, France, one could see the French Alps. Dijon had suffered from the war also, many a block of buildings were flattened. We were billeted with a French family, their home standing alone amidst ruin. They had a young buxom live-in-maid who took a shine to Fogie but Fogie paid her no mind, as a matter of fact he got damn irate when I teased him about her. I thought her to be pretty but she paid Palmer and I no mind. Our foursome reported to the flight-line to check out in the P-47, a lieutenant colonel, the group commander was present clueing us in on the Thunderbolt. We watched the fighters take-off and land for about twenty minutes, there was no joy in our eyes as we did so. It was unanimous we dearly loved our Mustangs. Fogie realized this and as a committee of one he stepped up to the Colonel and point-blank told him, "Colonel, we don't want to fly your god-damned airplane!" The Colonel replied good naturedly, "That's alright boys, I'll see what I can do for you." We four thanked him, saluted and returned to our billets. The next day we had orders to report to the 9TH Weather Reconnaissance Squadron. We had left our Air Transport Command connections, it was a long train journey to Laon, France on devastated railroad equipment and right-of-way.

Chapter Seven

Ninth Weather Reconnaissance Squadron

During the latter part of November, 1944, I reported to the 9th Weather Reconnaissance Squadron along with Norman Ott, Carlton Palmer and Elmer W. Fogelquist. The field was just east of Laon, in northern France, and had an east-west runway. We shared the field with a B-26 medium bomber group that later converted to the A-26. I remember one day when I counted five A-26's wrecked around the field. It took them awhile but they finally worked the bugs out. It was our duty to survey flying conditions in enemy territory before the bomber squadrons took off on their missions. This might have been a simple and routine chore had the weather over the European continent not been so dangerously unpredictable. The bomber squadrons had not anticipated that the weather might prove to be a formidable enemy, but it was. Even if they managed to avoid a mid-air collision, enemy aircraft or flak, they could still reach their designated target only to find it totally obscured by clouds. The fact was, the success or failure of a mission and the lives of the crew depended to a large extent upon weather conditions.

Daylight missions were flown with two aircraft flights, the lead pilot navigating and reporting on the weather, with the second pilot flying cover. Night missions were solo flights and were timed so that the pilot would encounter friendly territory by sun-up.

We flew erratic courses, covering several target areas in order to disguise the exact location of an upcoming bombing mission. The 9th W.R.S. call sign was Low Gear, and if I remember correctly, mine was Low Gear 32. The information requested was understandably varied since the bombers, fighters and transport units all had their own standards for Go/No Go minimums.

The 9th W.R.S. reported all types of weather information including the height and positions of clouds, haze and smoke layers, turbulence, ground cover and, of course, visibility. No routine flights were ever scheduled. Reconnaissance missions were flown according to the schedules of missions flown by the bomber and fighter squadrons. Two pilots were always on 15-minute stand-by, two for one hour, and another two the next. Ideally, a period of some 40 minutes was needed and requested for a pilot and weather officer to properly plan a mission.

We checked into our squadron area southwest of the runway, where a collection of squad tents and a weather trailer were located. Carpenters were building a headquarters building to house our briefing room and parachute room. Just east of this building stood a 2-room prefab shack of German design. We promptly latched onto it, secured a potbelly stove and Carlton Palmer installed a sink. Our beds were the German double-bunk type which we nailed to the partition wall in order to hold them steady. Having lost all of my issue equipment when I was shot down, I slept on the steel webbing with my trench coat rolled up for a pillow.

Norman Ott made a nameplate for our new home on which was featured an empty Scotch bottle with the slogan: Ye Olde Standee. Norman had been an English major in college.

We felt fortunate to have this prefab shack as we were then experiencing record cold temperatures. Others less fortunate were trying their best to stay warm inside flimsy tents.

I paid a visit to the squadron supply officer to replace my lost equipment and was issued a British flying helmet and goggles which were much better than our American helmet and goggles. Gloves were important to me now; a pair of British flying gauntlet type gloves were issued also. An issue wristwatch was unheard of but a letter home to Dad solved that problem in two weeks time. He took one hundred thirty-eight dollars out of my savings account, then had Mom sent me a watch via registered air-mail.

The only type of bedding I could secure was an olive drab cocoon shell, and its outer weatherized covering was damned thin for winter sleeping, and there was no air mattresses. A scarf was made from a strip of orange nylon parachute. Watching Mom with a needle and thread while at home now came in handy. The scarf was long enough so that I could put it around my neck front to back, bring it around both sides, then tie a loose knot in front with the ends tucked down in my shirt front. Carlton Palmer came up with some genuine white silk for his scarf; he was a very efficient scrounger.

We met our squadron mates; there weren't too many of them at that time and most had about completed their flying tours. One memorable older type was Alberto Nido from Puerto Rico, with a prevalent Spanish accent. An old Royal Air Force tradition was to wear one's pajamas under your flying clothes for good luck, which is what Alberto did. When he came out of the briefing shack, it was easy to discern his pajama top collar under his flying attire. Just before Nido was scheduled to go home he came into the mess tent one evening, took a helping of the diced beets, carrots, powdered potatoes and a canteen of coffee, then set them down on the table. Then he did a soft shoe dance in place, singing a little sing-song about the Army chow. I started to laugh until I saw the expression in Nido's eyes. He had flown his share of trips. He was truly ready to go home.

Late in December our command was taken over by Captain Stewart Mims. Captain Mims was an ex-R.A.F. pilot who had participated in our Naval fight program. Upon receiving his wings, he was assigned to a destroyer to fly the launched biplane scout plane. He later resigned his Naval commission and joined the R.A.F., then went on to the Army Air Corps. He brought with him a certain R.A.F. flavor. His billed cap was stiff with the groument and he had a handle-bar mustache so long that he had to take care to tuck it in when he hooked up his oxygen mask. Such was Captain Mims influence upon our squadron that we frequently found ourselves singing songs like: "The Bloody Great Wheel" and "Friggin' in the Riggin". The words to these songs are too gross to be repeated, unlike a song about a brave group leader that was sung to the tune of McNamara's Band. The lyrics are as follows:

>My name is Captain Mims
>I'm the leader of the group,
>Gather round me, fighter boys
>And I'll give you all the poop.
>I'll tell you where the fighters are,
>And all about the FLAK.
>I'm the last one to take off
>And the first one to get back.
>Early aborts—avoid the rush,
>Early aborts—avoid the rush.

Some special R.A.F. language was used. Missions were referred to as "trips". Character was "type" (he's a good type). Women or mademoiselles were "baby dolls". The possessive word "my" was "me", such as "me arse, me shoes, me friggin' sack". Aircraft were called "kites", a mission in the offing was a "due" and a reconnaissance was a "recce."

One night we all went to Captain Mims' tent to get better acquainted. The standard drink was one part Scotch to three parts water served up in a canteen cup two-thirds full. This proved plenty for an entire evening of drinking. I didn't drink much in those days and remember sitting on an old kitchen-type chair, balancing on its two back legs. When I hoisted my canteen up to drain the last of my drink, I suddenly toppled over backwards.

Captain Mims hit the Scotch pretty heavily, but always managed to pull himself together, downing a hearty breakfast the following day.

Not having flown since being shot down in August of 1944, I had to check out in the Mustang again. I flew a kite belonging to Captain Warren Harding as he stood on the ground observing me. I flew for an hour and forty-five minutes and managed a decent approach despite a somewhat "rusty" performance. But then, when I broke my glide about thirty feet above ground, the left wing fell off in a stall. Instinctively, I applied full right rudder with the stick back and a little right aileron, coming down on three points. I apologized to Warren, allowing that I'd had plenty of flying speed. At that, he informed me that the P-51 kite had been previously bellied in and was a bit out of line anyway.

After checking out again, I went up the next day on a local flight to shake the rust off. When I could do a good steep reefin' turn again, my confidence began to come back. And my landings weren't too bad either. Bill Budge took me up for some close formation and a good rat race. A test hop or two gave me the much needed time in the Mustang before flying trips again.

December 15, 1944. I was ordered to fly a replacement kite back from Paris. They'd ordered the right pilot as I hadn't been to Paris since the previous fall when Dan finally got me enthused about the French gals. A helmet bath was taken after our potbelly stove warmed up our shack, a Class-A uniform and trench coat were donned, along with my parachute, helmet and goggles. A shack-bag completed my plans for a three day pass in Paris while waiting to fly the replacement kite back to Airfield A-69 at Laon, France. I now looked upon my parachute as a dear friend and took special care of it.

I was flown to Paris in our twin-engine transport kite, left it at Villacoubly Airfield, where I made arrangements to later pick up the Mustang. At the same time I checked in my chute and flying helmet for safe keeping at the operations building.

It was no problem securing a ride to the outskirts of Paris. Once there, one could ride the underground into the city, the pleasant smell of garlic and perfume was evident on the metro. With my shack bag in tow, I rode to the Pigalle district of Paris where the French baby-dolls were numerous.

It was getting on toward late evening in Pigalle as I entered the Moulin Rouge nightclub. Upon entering, I could feel the history and closeness of the place. I asked and received permission to sit at a table with three paratroopers. The place looked tough and had a reputation for being tough. The paratroopers' presence was comforting to a small town boy in such a large city. Over a few drinks of cognac we got pretty well acquainted as the evening wore on. We watched the floor show taking place in the center of the room with great interest. These paratroopers were from the divisions that fought in the Battle of the Bulge. They were young, like myself, and were due back to their units the next day. I've often wondered how they fared.

The Moulin Rouge closed shortly after midnight. Upon regaining the street, I was met by many French baby-dolls. One had only to choose, then depart with one. My choice was a little brunette gal whose room was just across the street, which insured that we wouldn't have to walk down any darkened areas. Many a soldier had been way-laid and robbed while walking down dark Paris streets, even if he walked straight down the middle of the street.

I was somewhat bashful about disrobing, but the pleasure in the offing helped me to overcome this small problem. The petite French brunette had a beautiful figure and only wanted to please. A night of pent-up lust was soon taken care of in a good bed with a naked woman. Some of my high school buddies had bragged about their "back seat" conquests but I knew those experiences could never compare to mine.

The next morning, six or seven of the gals in the hotel met in a large room on the ground floor to compare notes about the night before. They even bragged to one another about the number of times they had made love with their man. When my little gal bashfully proclaimed six times, I corrected her by holding up seven fingers. Everyone thought that seven times was excellent. What they didn't realize was that I had a lot of catching up to do.

I took leave of the hotel about mid-morning and ate dinner chow at a consolidated mess a few blocks away from Pigalle. I entered the mess hall located on the second floor of an old French building with beautiful architecture. The steps leading up spanned the entire front of the building and were constructed from stone. The mess hall was immense with large support columns of beautiful architecture. As I stood around waiting for the chow line to form, I started looking for a familiar face and damn if I didn't see little Red Carlson only a few feet away. I approached him, shook his hand, and noticed his pilot wings and shavetail bars, all similar to mine. We compared experiences and I learned that Red was flying the P-47 Thunderbolt. He still wore his standard worried expression but it had become more intense. He told me he wished he had washed out in basic flight and I said I knew what he meant. We both had caught hell in pre-flight from our upper-classmen but they hadn't broken us. We would do our job now even if it killed us. As the chow line formed up, Red went back to his squadron buddies. I knew he would continue on in spite of anything.

The food was served on china plates and the coffee in real cups. It was good to be able to take a sip of coffee without burning the hell out of my lips on a canteen cup.

The entertainment provided was an instrumental group that I took to be from Rumania as they were dressed in below-the-knee shiny black boots, silk-like breech pants, shirts with bloused sleeves, and brightly colored vests. Their instruments consisted of violins, an accordion, and a mallet-played zither. Their waltzes and polka had a gypsy flavor that was not familiar to me although it seemed I had been listening to such music all my life. After finishing my meal, I hung around just to hear this group. I suspect they were all refugees since Paris had many such displaced people of talent.

Late that evening, a P-47 pilot and I went back to the

Moulin Rouge. We took a table to ourselves, sipped two or three cognacs, enjoyed the show, and looked over the available baby-dolls. Once the P-47 pilot had found the girl for him, he left me alone while he approached the table where she was sitting along with three other gals. He talked to her a minute or two, then returned to our table with the girl on his arm. I had to hand it to him for he was certainly an operator. Either it was love at first sight, or the price was right. When they asked if I would like a girl of my own, I admitted I would. With that, the P-47 pilot's baby-doll returned to her table and selected a short blonde girl for me. Her hair was long and straight and she was seven or eight years older than I, but had a mischevious smile I liked very much. As she stood in front of our table, I looked her over as one might do if they were buying a horse. Then I came to my senses, stood up, grabbed my trench coat and the girl's arm, and led her out of the Moulin Rouge. Along with the P-47 pilot and his girl, we went to the Hotel a couple blocks away. My buddy and his date were in the room next to ours.

I asked my baby-doll what her name was, after telling her mine. She said, "Martine Claire," and added that she was a very expensive girl. I counted out the invasion money, then proceeded to undress down to my O.D. shorts. Damn, but I was getting bold, and enjoying every minute of it! Earlier, as we were leaving the Moulin Rouge, the little brunette of the night before grabbed my arm to take me back to her hotel room. All the while, she totally ignored Martine. I remained aloof, as if I couldn't remember who she was, and finally she left. When Martine questioned me about the girl, I found myself lying like hell. It was great to be in demand!

After that, I would see Martine Claire whenever I could get into Paris. We also wrote letters. Hers were in French and mine were in English. The small issue English-French dictionary was put to good use once gain. At the start of the war, Martine had been studying physiology at a university in France. She also had an excellent contralto voice. She taught me in many ways—and I was her apt pupil.

The next morning I picked up the replacement D model Mustang and flew it back to A-69 airstrip at Laon, France. It was the first time I had ever flown in a Class-A uniform.

Captain Harding had devised a specific let-down procedure for the squadron at Laon. The field was located one mile east of Laon, which was situated on a pile of rock approximately 400 feet high. A cathedral had been built at its highest point with a spire that extended another 300 feet in the air. There were hills to the south and east, and north of the field were a stretch of plains. Making an instrument let-down—with no visibility—was an extremely hazardous undertaking. Harding's procedure for the let-down was for the pilot to call the direction finding station, get a steer and position himself north of the field so that he could approach going 180 degrees south. After getting a reciprocal heading from the direction finding station, you timed yourself a minute or so at cruise speed and 1,000 feet altitude, then took a heading of 90 degrees east, holding it for a period of 15 or 20 seconds. Then you would take a heading of about 340 degrees, making a let-down as you turned. Captain Harding's procedure allowed you to safely let down in a valley to the southeast as you approached the field. I practiced this approach several times during clear weather which was fortunate since I was forced to use it on three separate occasions when the chips were down.

Captain Harding took me on some of my first trips. In one instance, we were up less than a thousand feet with only a blank wall ahead of us, closing down to nothing. Warren instructed me to climb through and steer five degrees right of our present heading. I suffered a siege of vertigo on the way up, but stayed with my instruments, even though I felt I was in a dive. I popped out on top in a steep climb angle and probably would have spun-in had I not popped out when I did. After that, I was more inclined to believe what those instruments told me, having learned that my personal judgment could not always be relied upon.

Captain Harding was killed during the Korean War, flying an F-82, the twin Mustang. I was told that he took off one morning with frost on his wings.

Most of the types I flew with were trained fighter pilots who'd come from every corner of the U.S. The squadron flew Mustangs with built-in armaments of four .50 caliber wing guns and later, another model sporting six .50 caliber machine guns, which could only be used in defensive action since offensive action was prohibited.

Trained as we were, we seldom passed up an opportunity to shoot at a Nazi target. Fighter pilots instinctively fight rather than tucking tail and running. We all enjoyed the dogfights, and when no enemy planes were encountered, we concentrated on other Nazi targets. Everyone had their favorites: trains, military convoys, even Nazis on bicycles.

A fuss was made over all our unauthorized offensive actions and there were even threats of fines and court martials. But finally our tactics were reluctantly approved, and so, we continued on as usual.

December 18, 1944 saw me flying my first combat mission as a member of the 9th W.R.S. I flew the wing position to Killingsworth on a trip to the Ardennes where the Battle of the Bulge was in progress. As we neared our target area near St. Vith, I had the feeling of flying into a very large box, with clouds on all sides and the terrain completely covered. Killy and

I flew thirty minutes of actual instruments to break clear of the weather-front as we tooled south towards home base. For now the poor ground units had to fight the battle without air support. Captain Mims gave the pilots a situational weather briefing every morning. The Battle of the Bulge wasn't going our way as our ground forces were falling back to avoid encirclement and to shorten our lines. We flew several missions at this time, leaving our B-4 bags packed in case the Germans broke through to force the squadron to evacuate.

When we first joined the weather squadron, I was surprised to see Tom Heine, we had trained at Bartow, Florida together. He had originally been assigned to the 354th FTR. GP., a crack outfit, but had transferred to the 9th W.R.S. January 5th 1945 they asked Tom and I if we would fly two war weary Mustangs to an airfield near Paris, our eyes lit up as we agreed. The old Mustangs were old B models with the bird-cage canopy, I felt extremely restricted in vision after flying the D model Mustang and they flew as if war weary, sick engine and all. Tom led the way to Paris thirty minutes south, had a helluva time finding Villacouby airport as the weather was closing in and down very fast. We landed then checked our chutes and helmets into operations for safe keeping, by then the weather was almost down to the ground. A war weary P-47 Thunderbolt was attempting to land but had difficulty lining up with the runway due to the weather. Tom and I walked out to the end of the runway as the P-47 pilot made another approach, he still couldn't get lined up correctly, as he applied the throttle to pull up and make another circuit he flew just in front of us, damned if he didn't have a pipe in his mouth. When he circled to the left to set up another blind approach he disappeared completely from our view, he did this five or six times before getting the approach right and finally making a landing, the pipe still in his mouth.

Tom and I looked like a couple of raunches as we bummed a ride into Paris, we went to a section of the city where military personnel were few and far between, secured a couple of rooms at a small but clean hotel then walked and looked around. We entered a small bar that evening for a drink or two then back to the hotel for a night's rest in a comfortable bed. I secured my room key from a pretty brunette working the reception counter, I was starting up the stair way when I heard Tom say, "It's going to be cold sleeping alone tonight," the brunette's reply was, "I will sleep with you." The big city boy from Detroit was an operator. I rose the next morning at sunup to check the weather and secure a breakfast. After doing so I was walking back to the hotel when an M.P. approached me and told me silkscarves were forbidden in Paris, my general appearance was the same as if I had just come back from a rough trip over Germany. He realized this and went on his way. I wasn't about to receive any state side bull-shit as I had on the railroad train a year prior.

I woke Tom up from a sound sleep, his brunette French gal had taken her leave. We hitched a ride out to Villacoubly to pick up the replacement kites, only one was available. Tom flew it back to our air strip leaving me to secure other transportation. With my chute buckled on, helmet under my arm I approached the transportation office for a ride north to my air-strip, as luck would have it a semi-truck was about to leave in that direction, a black soldier as driver. I tried a bit of conversation, but got no reply. I wanted to tell him about the squadron of black fighter pilots down in Italy, but his concentration on driving was such that I hesitated. We joined the procession on the red ball express road which seemed bumper to bumper to me, damn but that black man could drive over that unimproved road. On a curve descending in the road I saw a gray haired old Frenchman standing erect with a crutch under his right arm pit for support as his right leg was missing below the knee. He waved his hat as our convoy went by, no doubt in my mind what the old gentlemen did during World War I, he and Dad might have passed by during that war. The driver turned off towards LAON to the north and skillfully negotiated some treacherous roads through the hills south of Laon, I didn't realize those hills were so damn high.

On the day before Christmas, 1944 I flew a mission with Lt. Clark. He led the mission and as we moved along the Rhine river in a northerly heading at about 11,000 feet, I suddenly called out: "Bandits three o'clock low Me 109's heading south 2,000 feet below." There were seven or eight of them.

Clark waited until they went by, then we attacked in a diving turn to the right. I flipped on the guns and gunsight switch as we went down, putting about 40 yards of maneuvering room between Clark and myself. We were in an excellent position, had the altitude and speed we needed, and were to the right of the whole gaggle. At just about firing range, they all broke right and came up into us in perfect formation. Clark called a break to the right and we immediately climbed away. Although I would have favored a head-on pass and a split-S to come up underneath them, I did as I was told and followed my leader. Climbing to our altitude again, we resumed our original heading for another five minutes, and I called out: "A bandit Me 109 going the same direction as the others, at the same altitude." Clark called an attack, we dived to the right and down, arming as we went. We were 90 degrees to the Me 109 and ready to fire when he broke right into us, his belly tank flipping away. I realized then that we'd tackled a veteran. We maneuvered to the left to get on his tail and ended up in a lufbery to the left. The Me 109 was first, Clark second, and I was third. Clark would raise his nose, then scissor down to the Me 109, getting ever tighter after four or five turns with me flying wing and looking around for the other Me 109's we had seen earlier. The Me 109 was getting on my tail and the centrifugal force was powerful. Another two turns and all I could see was the Me 109's nose and wings, as the malcolm hood on the P-51 was advantageous for looking back and below. The nose and wings of the Me 109 were lighting up every half-turn for about two turns. He would pull his nose in for lead, when he fired his guns, his wing would wobble. I knew he was in a stall, but he managed to catch it and pulled in again. I knew that if I could see the fire from an enemy plane's guns, there was nothing to worry about.

I called to Clark and told him to get the sonofabitch, then let my hand fall from the throttle quadrant to the flap handle, dropping 10 degree flaps and easing back on the stick a bit more. The next time I looked back, there was no Me 109. I called Clark and asked where he'd gone but Clark didn't know. I figured the guy had spun out and probably recovered because he was that damned good. Years later, I'd have been happy to treat him to a fancy supper, had we happened to run into one another.

Clark claimed one Me 109 wing-tip, and I frequently kidded him for not having gotten the plane after I'd gone to all that trouble of setting it up for him.

Clark and I flew quite a few trips together, two of them highly intrepid from a weather standpoint.

At Laon, we had a little dog by the name of Mustang. Captain Bill Budge from Hawaii was his sponsor. In the briefing room there was a pot-bellied stove with a five gallon can of coffee warming on it early every morning. During the day the can was put on the floor with an old board over it. Mustang always hung round that can of coffee. The coffee was never changed, just added to, a canteen cup of it would put you on your feet no matter what. Captain Budge was an ex-B-24 bomber type and also a meteorologist. The briefing room also housed two navigation computers, a R.A.F. type and an E6B A.A.C. type. The R.A.F. type was explained to me and I used it the first time I led a trip. We calculated our courses before we took off and copied them down on a knee-pad. We flew the courses I computed and after flying them we let down supposedly over the home field. When we broke out, all I could see were tulips and big wind-mills. Sgt. Dixon was on the D.F. that day and got us home safely. I can't say enough about Sgt. Dixon and his crew running the D.F. station, many of us owe our lives to him and his crew.

At Laon, coming back from a mission, we needed transportation to come out to the line to pick us up. To make sure they would know we had arrived, we would buzz the weather trailer. I loved to do this after a late night trip when daylight was just coming over the squadron area. When coming in for a landing, we peeled up from the deck into an off-vertical loop, bringing back the throttle and while almost on your back at 150 m.p.h., extend the wheels; by then you were on your approach, dump your flaps full, push the prop-pitch full which acted as an air brake when it flattened out. It worked out well after much practice, I eventually got it down to 18 seconds pulling streamers almost all the way around. An A-20 came in one day and did a flat peel-off for a landing, he pulled streamers all the way around and did the whole thing in 16 seconds from peel-off to touch down, I timed him. Eventually, I was assigned an airplane of my own with my own crew chief and everything. The kite's designation was 80-U, I flew it on a test-hop and I thought it was the sweetest kite I had ever flown so I offered to let Fogelquist (Fogie) fly it. He did and came back and told me there was something wrong with the kite. Not long afterward Lt. Killingsworth flew it on a mission. He took off to the east and entered an over-cast almost immediately, at about a thousand feet, one bank of the engine quite, Killy did a let down turn to the left of 180 degrees and bellied in north of the field, he unbuckled and damn well fled the aircraft, he waited to be sure of no fire and called Sgt. Dixon at the D.F. station, the Sgt. thought he wanted a steer and gave him one of 180 degrees, the second time Killy called him, he still got a 180 degree steer which Sgt. Dixon thought was unusual, so he started pulling wires, thumping tubes and what-not, they finally got together on the message and got some assistance up to Killy, a less experienced pilot would probably have bought the farm in such a predicament.

January 3, 1945, I flew as Clark's wingman on a two hour trip, one hour of solid instrument flying. When we called the directional finding station for a steer we were informed the field was socked in, Clark elected to try once to land. He told me to circle then called for a steer to the field, he let down as much as he dared but to no avail, as he pulled up he gave me a call advising me of conditions and try it if I wanted to, he was going to divert to another field. I positioned myself, called the D.F. station getting a steer of south southeast for an instrument let down, keeping the high hills south of the air-strip in mind. I was lucky, I came out over the air-strip but could only see bomb-craters. There wasn't enough altitude to set up a landing pattern, I too pulled up and asked for an alternate air-strip to land at. I was given a southerly heading as I climbed up above the clouds, air-strip A71 twenty minutes south was open. I flew south a little over fifteen minutes seeing no break in the clouds, all the time thinking of my next alternative if I couldn't find A71 air-strip. I was mentally calculating my fuel supply to England when I looked down and saw a break in the clouds, A71 air-strip was directly below. A fast steep spiral down saw me through the clouds and over the strip, as I called for landing instructions I could see C-47 transports parked all over the field. I did a training command peel-off as I flew over the end of the runway at one thousand feet altitude, completed the landing pattern circle and set down on the strip. I completed my landing roll, turned off the strip run-way where a parked jeep was waiting for me with the large, "FOLLOW ME", sign on the rear of the jeep. Every fighter pilot likes to show off a little bit at a transport aircraft base so I rolled the canopy back, cocked my elbows up on the sides of the fuselage, slowly taxiing by the line of C-47 aircraft with the ground crews and some air crews giving my Mustang and I the once over. The "follow me" parking jeep found a parking space for my kite and I pulled in to the parking spot doing a one hundred and eighty degree turn using a little extra throttle so they could hear the rolls-royce merlin engine. I unbuckled, left the kite and got down and patted old terra firma. I spent two or three hours at the field's operations building, finally my home air-strip cleared enough for me to fly back, the weather was still raunchy but one likes to enjoy familiar surroundings at night such as our shack and my buddies.

During January 1945, the Royal Air Force put many Lancaster four engine bombers into the air on their night bombing raids into Germany, on these occasions one could look to the west and see the Lancs coming in a steady and long stream. The target they were after must have been very important as their altitude was verily high enough to escape their bomb blasts. It was a very impressive sight, one had to realize they had suffered great losses of air crew and still they kept coming. I was on one trip when my course into Germany paralleled the bombing run of a group of our B-17's. Their bombing altitude was at about twelve thousand feet, much lower than usual. The big black bursts of flak came up in heavy concentrations, I pulled off their course and well to one side fascinated by the deadly spectacle, first actual bomb-run I had ever witnessed. One of the B-17 kites took a direct hit in the area of the number four engine in the outer right wing which sent it into a spiral down to the right. Two or three parachutes appeared as the B-17 went down. I said loudly to myself, "come on your guys, get the hell out of there." I then came alert again to my well being knowing FLAK loves big bombers and enemy fighters do too, my head was on a swivel again.

Instead of saying "Roger" over the VHF radio meaning I have received message and understand the squadron pilots now replied, "Aw Oui." Instead of referring to many enemy fighters seen, we now said "Bags of Enemy Fighters Sighted." Capt. Mims brought bags for many from the R.A.F. About this time

German jets were numerous, we referred to them over the radio as blow jobs, a month later a directive from 9th Air Force headquarters came down to all units stating German jets would no longer be called blow-jobs as our W.A.C.'s worked the 9th Air Force radios on the ground. My in-flight weather reports were often received by a W.A.C. January 27, 1945, I was assigned my own kite to fly, I wanted to name it "Donna," but after a week of thought I decided to name it "Aggie" with KANSAS preceding, Aggie was a jazzed up "Agnes," Mom's first name as she was my best girl.

About this time, one of our older pilots by the name of Dutch Holland, an old R.A.F. type, disappeared. He left on a solo night mission and didn't return. Dutch was a good likeable man, a good pilot, and had been raised in Europe so he could speak French like a native. There was an old Frenchman who was employed as a wood-cutter for the squadron and Dutch would interpret for us with the old Frenchman for the purposes of barter; cigarettes for eggs, etc. His disappearance was disturbing, he had disappeared without a trace, but we didn't give up hope for a long time that he was somewhere safe. Captain Bill Budge, who could also speak some French, passed on the news of Dutch's disappearance to the wood-cutter. When the old Frenchman understood that it was Dutch who was missing, he broke down and cried like a man. This incident touched me very deeply.

Our line chief was Sgt. Phillips, he was the only man I have ever witnessed who could run up a Mustang at full power and hold it on the ground with just the brakes applied. I tried it once while checking the engine just before taking off, as I approached full throttle the kite started to creep forward, no way could I hold the Mustang at full power.

Sgt. Phillips also rejuinated a little J3 CUB he had rescued from a junk heap. He did a beautiful job of it, he made the mistake of loaning it to a couple of our pilots, they promptly nosed it over on its back. If I had been him, I would have made them help rebuild it, but rebuild it he did. Sgt. Phillips had bags of flying time in civilian aircraft. I asked him why he didn't take a Mustang around the field a time or two, he allowed he didn't want any part of it.

The crew-chiefs were required to appear before their respective pilot when they desired a three-day pass. Sgt. Nance got my blessings plus a fresh bottle of scotch. He also secured me my infrequent haircuts.

January 29, 1945, Fogie and I were still deep into Germany but on our way out when an English speaking voice came over the radio, "corn beef this is cabbage, over." Neither Fogie or I answered, it had to be the Germans. Ott and his wing-man flew over the same route a couple of hours later getting the same call,

Ott answered, carrying on a conversation for awhile before ignoring the caller. Ott thought the call was from the Germans on the ground. I checked with the intelligence people, "cabbage" was the enemy.

January 18, 1945, I flew a trip flying Lt. Killingworth's wing and everything was socked in on the continent of Europe, so we diverted to Wormingford, England. Everything on the field was spic and span, including the personnel and the kites. As for me, I hadn't had a bath for a month, didn't have to worry about shaving, and had on a pair of O.D. pants with no crease that were baggy at the knees. My flying scarf was of orange nylon, my G.I. shoes were dirty and our kites were a bit dirty. I'm sure we were a sorry looking sight. I visited the supply Sgt. there and talked him out of a pair of sheepskin flying boots, one boot was two sizes larger than the other, but I was tickled to get them. My feet are like a dog's nose, always cold. We spent the night and came back to Laon the next day.

January, 1945, was a cold snowy month, our little shack was warm as long as we kept the fire going in the stove. We ate our chow in a tent of squad size. It was decently warm if one sat near the cook stoves. The cooks put out good chow with the G.I. rations, a lot of the guys bitched a lot but I noticed they always ate. I was always hungry along about eight o'clock every evening, one such evening one of the cooks knocked on the door of our shack and asked that I step outside for a word. He asked me, "Would you like some fresh beef-steak?" I hustled back into our shack for my flight jacket and cap. I thought of some of the round steak suppers I had enjoyed at home as I made my way to the cook tent with my flash light covered with the fingers of my right hand. Black-out conditions were strictly enforced. I made my presence known at the cook shack, was admitted into the back room, seated at the cook's table and served steak and fresh potatoes. It was the best steak and potatoes I have even eaten, I asked no questions and kept my council about the clandestine meal. Later on after a fresh snow the same cook appeared and asked if I would like some ice cream, I love ice-cream and asked him where they had gotten such an unheard item. He replied that it was snow ice-cream which I had never before eaten. I again journeyed down to the cook shack back door to enjoy a large bowl of snow ice-cream. Those cooks were glad I couldn't tell the difference from ice cream parlor vanilla ice-cream.

If I was scheduled for an early mission I still couldn't eat a hearty breakfast before take-off, the cooks would fix me up something after I arrived back from the mission. When the pilots had their egg ration it was a strange sight viewing us going to breakfast chow, mess kit in one hand, two eggs held gently in the other. The cook would fry the eggs for us the way we desired. After coming back from a late afternoon mission, I was hungry as a bear, went through the chow line getting generous portions of food, a steaming canteen cup of coffee then to the mess table where I put three or four teaspoons of sugar in the coffee then stirred well to commence the cooling procedure. After enjoying a few mouthfulls of chow a few sips of coffee was in order. I further cooled the canteen cup by putting the palm of my hand on the canteen cup where my lips would touch it, after going through this procedure, one gingerly touches the canteen cup to one's lips which I did taking two or three long sips. Damn, the sugar can was filled with salt instead of sugar, that was the worst taste mistreat I had ever experienced. I bucked the chow-line for another canteen cup of coffee, this time using the sugar can.

While the snow was on, Carl Palmer and I went rabbit hunting off the east end of the run-way, the rabbits in France were called hares, almost the size of our Kansas jackrabbits. Carl and I walked the fields for awhile spotting several hares which I shot at with the carbine I had borrowed. I would come close to hares but no hits, I became concerned shooting this infantry weapon in open country, the bullet is deadly for a long ways. I elected to return to our shack leaving Carl with his German P-38 pistol, as I walked away I glanced over my shoulder, Carl was stalking a hare that ran into a group of small trees. I thought to myself his chances of bagging a hare with the P-38 pistol as zero. A couple of hours later here comes Carl with a dead hare, he cleaned it, cut it up into fryable pieces then secured a cooker from the cooks along with a large onion and other spices. Carl was an eagle scout, his knowledge of cooking the tough hare amazed me. He built up the fire in our stove, cooker on top full of hare, onion, and spices, there he hovered all afternoon monitoring the stove fire, water in the cooker, and proceeded to tell me the hare would be as tender as butter, not tough like the Kansas jackrabbit. After supper chow, he judged the hare to be tenderized enough for eating, to finish the cooking procedure he browned the hare in his mess kit plate using yellow army axle grease butter as a cooking oil. Carl must have invited half the squadron for some of his hare as men came in for the next two or three hours for a bite or two of it, I admit it was delicious.

The cooks also purchased French bread when they went into Laon. Our foursome often ended up with some of this French bread, we sliced it then spreading the axle grease butter from the tin container on one side and on to the hot stove top butter side down. A two to three foot long loaf of bread lasted our foursome no time at all, it was delicious. If one ate a slice of bread spread with the army butter cold it would coat the inside of your mouth. One of the cooks told me about the time he gave a loaf of army bread to a French family. You might as well have given them an angel food cake he related. Besides being friends with the cooks I also had the 1st Sergeants of the Squadron as friends, securing a three-day pass to Paris to see Martine was no problem.

I was assigned my own Mustang 80-Y. This particular model of aircraft was equipped with six .50 caliber machine guns. Sgt. Nance was my crew chief, he met me at the airplane and briefed me about the kite and damn well told me to understand that this was his also. He said, "I'll do anything to this kite that you want, an ash-tray, a rear-view mirror, anything you want, but don't you mistreat it." I had 'Kansas Aggie' painted on the left side of the kite, Sgt. Nance painted 'Ginny' on the right side. We didn't use external wing tanks, I even had Sgt. Nance take the bomb racks off for more speed. I can't over-emphasize the importance of our crew chiefs and other ground personnel, we pilots' wouldn't have done beans if not for them. I test-hopped the kite immediately, met Carlton Palmer upstairs and a good ratrace ensued. Carlton was trained in the P-47 kite before flying the Mustang with the 363rd Ftr. Gp. He didn't display any fear and was an excellent pilot. While flying with the 363rd, he received the D.F.C. for shooting down a ME-109 during an air battle with only one gun firing. I only flew one trip with him as his wingman, but once on an early trip, flying back to Laon, I heard a voice over the V.H.F. trying to contact any aircraft in the air. I didn't answer as the enemy often called us. As I was coming out of Germany, Carl was going in and he answered the call. It turned out to be an infantry unit being attacked by a ME-109. Carl maneuvered around and got on the ME-109's tail, but just as he was about to touch off his guns, the ground unit shot it down right in front of Carl's nose. As Carl was leaving the area, the unit thanked him for his assistance and apologized for shooting at him. Carl told them they couldn't have hit him anyway and continued on his trip. Carl was from Indiana, and had "Hoosier Honey" painted on his kite. He had two girl friends back home and was in love with both of them.

Norman E. Ott was also an excellent pilot and had the uncanny ability to always get home during intrepid weather while everyone else was being diverted to other fields. Ol' Ott was a sack-rat. I remember one night trip he flew, ground control informed him of the many German night-fighters in his trips' path. He just informed them, "Hell, they can't catch me anyway," and they didn't as he was really tooling along. Norman even lit up a V1 Buzz Bomb, an aircraft with a rocket engine (a flying bomb) on one of his trips. Elmer W. Fogelquist, another excellent pilot, was one of the smoothest I ever flew with. He flew his trips with no complaints. He was full of mischief, as it fairly danced out of his eyes. He used to crack me up murdering the English language by getting his v's and w's mixed up on purpose. His father was from Sweden and had that difficulty with the English language. When available, we would get our egg rations by the dozen. Some of the squadron people would boil the whole dozen at once and with a couple bottles of Belgian beer would have a feast. Once, a weather officer, I forget his name, but he was a big guy, six foot-two, had boiled all of his and was sitting in a wooden arm chair cracking and rolling the eggs on the arm of the chair. All at once, he hit a raw egg and got it all over his pants leg and blouse cuff. He had just gotten all cleaned up as he was ready to go on leave to Paris or London. Elmer Fogelquist fled and hid out most of the night, he had exchanged the one egg. Late night solo missions were flown to report information for early morning bombing missions. The 9th W.R.S. desired minimums for night missions was 1000 ft. ceiling with three mile visibility, but regardless of the weather, daily operations continued for us even if other 9th Air Force activities had been grounded. Weather reconnaissance's were rarely canceled. I flew six night solo trips and every one was eventful. Once, I even popped out over Switzerland by mistake, luckily, it was the only place on the European continent not blacked out.

February 8, 1945, I flew my first night solo trip for the squadron, standard equipment for such a flight consisted of a G.I. flashlight, a flare gun loaded with a cartridge of colors of the day and your night eyes. There were no run-way lights, black-out conditions for the field and aircraft was standard operational procedure. The crew chief helped me buckle in then shone his fingers occluded flash-light beam on the instrument panel and other controls to help me get started up. After attaining the run-way I lined up by the gray color of the cement run-way as compared to the blackness of the ground bordering it, cranked the canopy forward and slowly advanced the throttle. The gray run-way rushed by and I was airborne, wheels up, I was on my way into the black sky. Turning the instrument panel lights to the lowest possible setting was paramount as the German night fighters watched for such clues plus the fire from the kites exhaust stacks. I made my penetration into Germany at about twelve thousand feet to my first weather check point then took up a heading of north for my next point. There were numerous fires on the ground to see when I did take my eyes away from the sky about me. I had been toolin' along for about ten minutes when two search-lights pinned me to the night sky, I immediately dove into them and they soon lost me, I reversed my diving right turn to the left back to my original course and noted a loss of three thousand feet of altitude. While the enemy search-lights had me lit up I was blinded when I dove into them, this blindness lasted for a few seconds after I lost them. One of the old veterans of the squadron now departed for home told me this technique if I were ever caught up in searchlights. The searchlights were used in coordination with the big flak guns and German night fighters. Soon after take-off on a night solo trip I always varied my altitude, airspeed, or direction every five seconds ever so slightly, this to my judgment would screw up the radar tracking of the FLAK guns or the aim of a night fighter. Night-fighters were numerous at this time, ours and the enemy. I attained my last check point then gratefully turned west for the home air-strip, on the way radioing my information to ground control. Approaching the home strip after receiving a steer from our directional finding station posed some hazards also, I always asked the control tower to notify the field FLAK guns I was coming in, also getting the flare gun handy to shoot out the flare gun port in case there was a mix-up. Most generally the air-strip was more visible on return so shooting a landing proved no problem.

The weather was very intrepid over Europe, one would take-off with good visibility, on one's return from a trip the air-strip would be fogged in or the ceiling too low to shoot a landing. One such day about mid-morning I was walking out to the flight-line to shoot the bull with Sgt. Nance and noticed a blanket of fog over the run-way. I knew Carl Palmer and his wing-man to be off on a trip and were due back any time, sure enough two Mustangs came winging over, one could see them circling looking the situation over. Carl's wing man broke off heading for an alternate airstrip, not Carl, he continued to circle getting some familiar landmarks indented in his mind's eye for reference ther set up a rather long approach, wheels down and full flaps. With a little throttle he had a nice slow rate of descent, I could see him and his Mustang disappear into the fog bank then only hear his engine as he descended feeling for the run-way. At last I heard his gear tires contact the run-way, if he could keep his landing roll straight he had pulled it off. I then heard the rolls-Royce Merlin chuckling at idle throttle and emerging from the fog bank came Carl, canopy rolled back, left arm up on the side of the cockpit looking as though he did such a feat every day. Carl possessed great abilities and a damn good fighter pilot, I wouldn' have attempted such a feat unless it was an extreme emergency.

After the snow the run-way became very slippery, somehow the ground people had removed the snow from the run-way pushing it to the sides leaving a four to five foot deep snow bank along the entire run-way. As I was leading a trip during one of those hazardous run-ways days I had a former B-1' Flying Fortress pilot as my wing-man by the name of Hendricks on my right wing. We had attained about eighty miles per hou when I glanced to my right to see if Hendricks was staying in position, my instant of inattention let my left landing gear ente some soft snow which pulled me towards the piled up snow bank, I instantly visualized a viscous ground-loop or a cart-wheel into my wingman. Aggie and I had not attained flying speed ye but back on the stick I came and in went the right rudder and full right aileron to keep the left wing from digging into the snow and turf alongside the runway. It took all my young strength to hold that left wing off until flying speed was attained then ease the throttle and propeller pitch back and finally bringing the gear up. Another brush with buying the farm was narrowly avoided this day, we took off separately from then on until the snow had melted. I shook for twenty minutes after that take-off.

  We were returning to our shack after darkness fell, overhead a kite was toolin' at a judged five thousand feet of altitude, its two engines sounded out of synchronization. I made the remark, "I wish that guy would get his engines in synch." Someone of our foursome said, "That is a Junkers 88, their engines just naturally sound out of synch." I continued to hear the JU 88 for three or four nights but thought nothing of it. The Germans used the JU 88 as a night fighter capable of dropping bombs also. We were all in our sacks sound asleep when the damndest clatter of fifty caliber machine guns woke us up, Fogie was up on the cold floor first. With the arches of his feet bowed up, toes almost straight up, arms reaching for the floor he crow-hopped over to the stove and got behind it. The cone of the convergence of the tracers from the machine guns as they followed the JU 88 across the east end of the air strip from north to south illuminated Fogie's and my room through a small window on the east side of the shack. I bailed out of the upper bunk, Fogie had the only place of refuge so I just hunkered down, at the same time the north door of our shack crashed open as a gray streak went through it. There was a bomb crater not too far from our shack which Ott or Palmer was making for a damn good idea I thought as I took the three steps to the open door. The area was lit up from the umbrella of tracers following the JU 88 flying at about three hundred feet altitude; fifteen feet from our door sat Palmer on his bare ass, legs extended straight out front, arms out behind him propping up his torso, face to the sky watching the tracers follow the JU 88. I knew Carl didn't just rush out of door bare assed with his gym sweater on, set down and watch the fireworks for the hell of it. He told me later he just wanted to get the hell out of our shack, at full speed his toasty warm feet hit the ice and on his bare ass he went sliding. Ott got up last and asked, "What happened?" The next morning the report came in that a JU 88 had crash landed south of the air strip near Rheims.

  I had flown trips the day before Christmas, Christmas Day and New Years Day, my birthday came around, I was now of legal age. A trip up flak valley commonly known as the Ruhr Valley was accomplished on my birthday. This was the only trip I had sweat out the night before, that is, not much sleep. After take-off and under way the anxiety vanished, we didn't draw one burst of flak the entire trip.

February 22, 1945, I led a trip. Take-off was before dawn with Dan Johnson as my wing-man. We were well into Germany under a fifteen hundred foot ceiling. A locomotive with several railroad cars appeared to our left at about a mile distant going in the opposite direction. Dan wanted to strafe the train but I ordered a continuance of our trip as the train had no less than four flat cars loaded with FLAK guns. Dan didn't like my decision worth a damn but our paramount mission was to get weather information, if we had seen the train coming out of Germany we could have worked it over. As we penetrated deeper in Germany the ceiling lifted to allow us more altitude. Dan's engine started to vibrate violently, he turned west calling for information about a possible emergency air-strip. I followed him to make sure he did make the air-strip then continued with the trip alone. Dan Johnson was a free spirit, initially trained and assigned to a P-47 Thunderbolt Group. From the P-47 Group he transferred to a Ferry Command outfit then to the 9th W.R.S. I flew several trips with Danny, once when we were coming out of Germany my attention was to the left of our flight path as I heard the sound of automobile tires sliding on cement. I quickly turned my head to the right to where Johnson should be, he was, in too damn close formation upside down. He stayed in that position until his engine started to cut-out then he rolled right side up again.

He told our foursome one evening in our shack about an incident he experienced while flying with the ferry command. Dan was a tall lanky fighter pilot from Mobile, Alabama with the slow southern drawl in his speech. Dan was flying a violinist from the continent of Europe across the English channel to England in a single engine Norseman kite. The violinist had been on tour entertaining our troops. Dan took off with decent weather but over the channel it got lower and lower with the same closing in behind them, going ahead to England was their only alternative. Dan started to get concerned as the channel waves were close beneath the Norseman's wheels, so concerned that he told the violinist to get his fiddle out and play it as it might be his last chance, the violinist did exactly that. Dan and his passenger did safely land at an English air-field. After the narration I asked Dan the violinist's name, he replied, "Yehudi something or other," I replied, "Menuhin," Dan replied, "Yeah, his name was Yehudi Menuhin." I stated to Dan he was one of the world's greatest violinists and you damn near went down into the channel with him.

A replacement pilot from Iceland or Greenland joined our squadron, the first replacement since our foursome joined. He was a small man and kept to himself at all times, from what I could gather the man had been stationed at one or other of these bases for a long time. One day I stopped by the tent he was quartered in to get acquainted and eventually get him acquainted with the rest of the squadron. When I entered the semi-dark tent I saw him seated on a chair hunched up against the stove in the middle of the tent reading a pocket-size book under the light coming through the tent vent hole. This was normal behavior except there was no fire in the stove. I tried to engage the man in conversation but all I received was a look of disdain so I departed. The next day our operations officer, Lt. Andrew Clark was to check this new replacement pilot out in one of our Mustangs, I related my experience with the man to Clark to help him with a bit of insight. Clark asked him what aircraft he had flown as we approached the Mustangs on the flight line, the small man replied, "I have flown them all." I stood by as Clark helped him get buckled in and started up. He hadn't yet taxiied to the runway when his left main gear tire went flat, he taxiied another ten to fifteen yards before he realized the flat tire. Clark put him into another, he started up, taxiied to the runway, checked the magnetos, closed the canopy, took-off, executed a maximum climb to a thousand feet, leveled out, took a course of east northeast, that was the last we saw or heard of him.

March 23 1945. I was to fly a late night solo mission and was in the briefing room planning the flight. I stepped outside for the usual night mission leak and looked up at the sky—there wasn't any. I thought for sure the trip would be called off. I went ahead and got the check-points of the mission and carefully calculated everything on the E6B computer then jumped into the back-end of the weapons carrier for the ride to the flight line. To this day, I don't know how the driver found his way out there, it was ceiling zero with fog. I buckled in, started up, and had the crew-chief on the left wing directing me to the center of the run-way. I lined up with the magnetic compass, then minutely set the gyro compass to it, went around the cockpit once again, then steadily applied the throttle while not letting that gyro compass vary at all. On lift-off and wheels-up and on my way, I was ordered to call the tower and advise them so. No sooner had I released the mike button, two or three voices rang into my ears saying, "back to the sack," "You said it," and "me too."

On the way to the weather check point I found a cloud layer about five hundred feet thick which I used for concealment from enemy night-fighters even then I varied my direction, speed, and altitude slightly every few seconds. As I was doing one of these slight adjustments I popped out on top of the cloud layer into clear moonlight. I immediately moved the stick forward to regain the cloud's concealment, in so doing the flashlight I had lain against the wind screen on the left side became levitated, slowly moving to the rear of the cockpit past my head, I followed the movement with fascination until it disappeared around the VHF radio. I had calculated my course very carefully while being briefed, time on my wrist watch told me to descend to the target area. The clouds were broken much to my likeness, visibility to the check-point excellent as I could see the Rhine River. Tracer bulefts from each side of the river were close as I descended to get the base of the lowest clouds. I got to the bottoms of the clouds south of Cologne, as I hit that check-point, I was doing 400 m.p.h. The bottom of the clouds were between 600 to 700 feet. By the time I arrived back at the base, the fog was mostly dissipated. Later on that morning, an Armada of C-47's came over our field loaded with a Para-trooper Division to jump across the Rhine River.

    The squadron carpenters built the officers a club furnished with a few old chairs and a make-shift bar serving scotch whiskey and Belgium beer. It adjoined our shack, a pleasant hour or so could be enjoyed every evening after supper chow. Someone of our squadron appropriated a low frequency radio from a B-26 that had bellied in alongside the run-way including the battery. After flying a mission as Fogies wing-man and enjoying a good supper I was listening to a station broadcasting opera arias, an excellent tenor was singing them. I was thoroughly enjoying myself when the radio's battery run low and the station faded. I was attempting to re-tune the station back in without having much success when Captain Tom Harmon, a stoutly built man backed up against the nearest wall of the building and finished the aria with one of the best operatic tenor voices I had ever heard. After he had finished and I had overcome my amazement I asked him how long he had been singing and where. When our country entered the war he was singing at the Metropolitan Opera in New York City, not a top line star but singing a lot of good support parts. Tom Harmon and I were good friends, a friend in the squadron personnel office was a plus. Captain Harmon left the club for his tent, I secured a bottle of Belgium beer to be sociable with a few of the other pilots recently new to the squadron. My flight leader was getting well plastered much to my amazement, he was scheduled to fly a very early night mission in six hours. I finished my bottle of beer, retired to our shack to hit the sack, I had a hunch the night operations clerk would be rousting me out in five or six hours.

    I was sleeping soundly when a hand shook my shoulder, then a voice informed me that my flight leader couldn't fly the mission. I stated I would, slipping out of my warm sack I latched onto my flashlight, lighting same to dress and shoe myself. My wristwatch read 01:30 hours, that meant a night take-off and landing also. The operations coffee was the usual eye-opener as I computed my courses and wrote them on my knee-pad. After securing my chute and leather helmet I boarded the back end of the weapons carrier, after leaving my flight-line transportation I looked to the sky, no stars were shining, no moon to be seen, one of the darkest nights I had ever flown in. The crew-chief helped me buckle in my flight-leader's Mustang. I would have preferred my kite, Kansas Aggie, but this kite had been pre-flighted and deemed ready. I started up, taxied out and took the run-way after getting clearance from the control tower. I lined up the kite with the magnetic compass as I had two nights previously then set the gyro compass to it, no fog this time but still only a gray path I knew to be the run-way. I made my take-off and just before lifting off I felt a whump from my left landing gear, the landing gear retracted without any malfunction. Nevertheless I filed the whump away for future reference when I came back to land. My night mission was the same general area as of two nights previously, after penetrating east into Germany my next weather check point was north. I was tooling along at eleven thousand feet when to my right at three o'clock level a fire ball burst in the sky, it was huge and seem to hang in the night sky with small streams of fire falling from it. I soon left the area thinking it another strange incident of war. I checked my northern most weather check point then turned for my home airstrip. I called the D.F. station for a steer when nearing the air strip, coming over the strip I identified it, called the tower for clearance also had them notify the FLAK crews then set up my landing pattern. The whump on take-off was a foremost consideration in setting up my approach so as to touch down on the right side of the runway. When I touched down the left tire was flat and immediately started pulling the Mustang violently to the left, sparks were flying rearward from under the left wing as I braked hard with the right rudder and brake, at the same time using enough throttle to have some rudder control and hold the tail on the ground as I had the stick back into my gut. When I finally came to a halt, I cranked back the canopy, unbuckled, stepped to the left wing, the left wheel rested on the extreme left side of the runway. In a couple of minutes I heard a jeep motoring up, the crew chief and his assistant approaching the Mustang. I couldn't see them until they were six feet from me. They asked, "Are you all right Lt. Brooks?" I replied, "YEAH, I think I hit something on the left side of the runway when I took off." All the sparks from the wheel rim and grinding metal noise as the left wheel contacted the runway made them think for sure I had made a wheels-up landing. Our operations weapons carrier picked me up, I was back in my sack in no time, it was still dark as ever, I went back to sleep thinking of the two fried eggs, bread, marmalade and coffee I would enjoy at a late breakfast. I always enjoyed a meal after a trip.

  Dad asked me in one of my letters from home if the World War One trenches were still visible from the air. I test-hopped a kite for one of my buddies shortly thereafter and sure enough the old trenches were clearly visible to the southeast as far as the eye could see and also the northwest.

Someone received the news of a promotion which called for a celebration at the club after supper chow. I got caught up in a chug-a-lug affair, after three down the hatch drinks I got away to our shack, I had a dawn trip to fly. I arose feeling a bit hazy but felt I could fly after drinking a cup of operations coffee. The runway and surrounding country had a thin layer of hazy fog over it, I was leading the trip, taking off was no problem but while climbing out my wing-man on my left wing called out a wind-mill at three o'clock level. I looked right and sure enough there was a wind-mill disappearing behind us. A re-check of my altimeter showed us at one hundred feet instead of the one thousand feet I thought we were flying at. I watched my intake of scotch thereon the evening before flying the next day.

After being assigned the Mustang 80Y as my kite I didn't think the engine had enough power, I talked to Sgt. Nance about the possibility of getting a new engine. He said the engine was border-line as to the flying hours on it, however he would attend to the matter. In two weeks time he was out on that cold-assed ramp installing a new engine, he did the exchange in seven hours by himself. After flying the new engine in for a period of two to three hours I noticed the engine to be a bit rough while taxiing at idle throttle. I asked him if he would smooth it out at idle throttle to sound like my Uncle Vince's Farmall tractor, he did so and made the statement that he was right in thinking I was a farm boy. Also I had one of my buddies check the retraction of my wheels when I took-off, one was coming up quicker than the other, Sgt. Nance adjusted them so they retracted into the wheel-wells in unison.

Bill Budge and I flew a few trips together, I as wingman, as Bill had a degree in meteorology, he led. Bill insisted on a good job of flying wing, especially when flying instruments. On one trip it was necessary to penetrate a weather front, I was ordered to tuck in tight to climb through the weather, the turbulence was rough and bouncy, for instants I lost sight of Bill and his kite but he was steady as a rock flying instruments, staying in tight formation was the only way to come out on top as a team. I monitored my own flight instruments while flying such penetrations, it took great concentration.

On one trip flying Bill's wing we climbed our Mustangs to forty-three thousand feet while over Germany. I looked to the east on this particularly clear day and could actually see the curvature of the earth. Coming out of Germany we dove to the deck for the purpose of checking Bill's guns, he picked out a small shed a little ways from a farm house and hit it with the convergence of his six fifty caliber guns. An old man and a young woman burst out of the farm house as we zoomed over and away. I'm sure Bill had strafed their out-house, the ventilation of it much improved.

When Bill reported his weather findings back to headquarters, it was like attending a clinic, I'm sure their forecasting was made easier.

While our foursome was at Cherbourg, France we were told a transfer between the 8th and 9th Air Forces was impossible but around the middle of March, 1945 six or seven 8th Air Force fighter pilots came to our squadron. After being around them for a few days I soon realized they hadn't transferred to our squadron, they had been booted out of the 8th Air Force. One of them finally told me why he had been forced out of his 8th Air Force FTR. GP., he was eager to atone for his mistake and applied himself to our squadron's mission. The others didn't show me too damn much, I was reluctant to fly with them, watching them like a hawk.

German night fighters often came over our airstrip at Laon, France. At this time 9th A.F. headquarters must have attained a few radar tracking units set up around northern France. I was asked to go up for a try at them, I stated I would try but the whole action was forgotten, radar was just in the infancy stage.

One day Fogie wasn't scheduled for a trip, being the master manipulator he flew his Mustang to Cherbourg, France to visit with our former friends of the Air Transport Command, when he was checking his instruments before take-off for his return flight his coolant temperature was reading very hot. Fogie being an avid automobile driver knew something about engines with the ability to diagnose operating problems. His clandestine flight put him in a helluva fix as such flights were frowned upon. The coolant pump was inoperative, but Fogie found a wrecked Mustang on the Cherbourg airfield, borrowed the necessary mechanic tools, secured the coolant pump from the wreck then installed it into his Mustang. The exchange worked fine as he flew back to our air-strip without any difficulty. Fogie related the incident to me, he was concerned, but his crew-chief put the kite and whole affair to right. I thought Cherbourg was a better place for the coolant pump to malfunction than over Germany.

On a mid-day trip with Tom Heine as my wing-man we got separated well into Germany while climbing through turbulent weather. Tom was no where to be seen when I broke out on top. I continued on the trip to the appointed check points then hit the deck coming back out of Germany. I was toolin' along with AGGIE at two hundred and fifty miles an hour cruise speed, ever so often turning right or left a bit to get a good look behind and above. My course took me along an autobahn highway when I suddenly found myself approaching a temporary air-strip with a ME-109 fighter taxiing from tree cover to a taxi path through the trees, the pathway led to the autobahn highway which served as their run-way. The twenty millimeter FLAK guns saw me as soon as I saw the air-strip, I flew over one gun as he chambered a round then over the taxiing ME-109, I was too low to depress my kite's nose for a shot at the ME-109 and more FLAK guns were in evidence along the autobahn highway, I departed the area well below the trees. If there had been two of us we could have worked the area over and perhaps gotten a ground kill or two as more German fighters were sure to have been hidden amongst the trees.

Two of our pilots came back from a trip relating a sight they had witnessed on their trip. They had passed a large German airfield, well out of range and no inclination to attack it. They witnessed two other Mustangs circling the airfield just out of range of the FLAK guns as if attempting to make up their minds to attack or not. Finally they dived and flew balls-out across the enemy airfield, they were two balls of fire before getting half-way across.

While on a three day pass to Paris I was shop-talking with a P-47 fighter pilot, I asked him of their technique attacking an enemy airfield. If the enemy airfield's location was given at briefing he kept his flight out of sight of the airfield just far enough to get it's exact location then turn on his gunsight, lining up on the airfield while diving for the deck with his flight. Keeping the dot in the middle of the lighted gun-sight reticle on the spot he last visualized the airfield plus other points of reference on the horizon assured him of coming over the airfield on the deck balls out with an element of surprise.

On another trip of two hours and five minutes my wing-man aborted with a mal-function, I continued on solo taking advantage of clouds whenever possible. Coming out of Germany the weather cleared, diving to the deck was the safest place. I was toolin' along in a westerly direction hopping over timbered ridgelines then down to the deck in the valleys, ever looking ahead for the cables the Germans strung across the valleys. I just hopped over one ridgeline, coming down the west slope when I came upon a military camp. A game was in progress, the participants were playing a form of softball, but on hearing my approach the German soldiers broke in all directions. As I buzzed over I could see they were young teenage boys, one was Chambering a round into a twenty millimeter FLAK gun. He was a kid in an ill fitting uniform but he sure as hell could shoot his FLAK gun. I waited three or four seconds after flying over them before doing a quick ten degree turn left, to my right were three FLAK bursts where I would have been. A quick turn back to my original course saw me out of range.

My wingman lost me a couple of other times, one such time I was on the deck coming out, flying across an agricultural valley I saw a lone old woman planting her spring garden crop. When she heard me coming the poor gal started digging into the earth with her bare hands like a dog to hide herself as much as possible, as I passed over I could discern she looked much like my grandmother Spacek with her kerchief over her head, tied under her chin. Continuing on down a valley in a westerly direction I tooled by two good looking blonde German gals about my age, when they saw me they waved and smiled. They were definitely in my age group, I wish the war could have ended there and then, it would have been good to land and get acquainted with them. One saw many strange things while on the deck deep into Germany especially when the weather was too raunchy for flying.

9th Air Force gave a call stating there would be no trips for us to fly April fourteenth, nineteen hundred-forty five, we were to stand down. I took this information with a grain of salt as about two-thirds of the pilots headed for the club to enjoy a day of drinking and relaxation. I decided to wait until evening to enjoy my usual beer from Belgium. A group of four or five pilots was gathered near our shack discussing some newly arrived former 8th A.F. fighter pilot, Fogie was in the discussion circle. I had run out of cigarettes, knowing Fogie seldom smoked but always carried a pack I edged up behind him to bum a smoke, after hearing my request he turned around and took a pack of cigarettes from his shirt pocket, the pack was quite flat. I told Fogie it appeared he was out of cigarettes also, he replied, "Yust a minute harr," as he deftly extracted a cigarette from the Old Gold pack. The cigarette was damn near flat and wavy but rolling it between my fingers it took on the shape of a cigarette, it tasted pretty damn good. Fogie returned to the discussion about the hot rock pilot, summarizing his thoughts by doing three things simultaneously. Verbally he said, "that guy is so hot he's got to set torque just to walk straight," while making the statement Fogie's left hand was turning an imaginary rudder trim control located on the left side of the Mustang's cockpit and also jacking his right foot out in front of him in an exaggerated motion as if on the right rudder pedal at the same time making the sound of a ratchet wrench. He wasn't hunting for laughs but he got belly laughs from the gathering.

The pilots had been in the club for a couple of hours when Capt. Mims appeared and ordered our attendance at the operations building. He proceeded to inform us the A-26 bomber group we shared the strip with had received several new pilots from stateside. They were to fly practice formation south of the airstrip, they needed a couple flights of fighters to bounce them. Keeping tight formation while on a bombing raid was most important, our job was to try to break-up their formation. There wasn't much organization of this peaceful flight, I was to fly Capt. Mims wing. After arriving at the flightline I buckled into

Aggie and waited for Capt. Mims to do likewise in the kite next to Aggie. The crew-chief of the Captain's kite was in attendance as he took his time buckling in, first the Capt. fished out a pair of black steel rimmed spectacles, eased them under his flying helmet over his ears, pulled the helmet down snugly over his head then proceeded to hook up his oxygen mask. Capt. Mim's handle-bar mustache was a thing of beauty, he took great care while hooking up the mask, he tucked his mustache under the mask on the leftside first then as the mask covered his chin, mouth and nose he gingerly tucked the right end of the mustache under the mask before making the final hook-up on the right side. Everyone cranked up as our Capt. started up, I S-taxiied immediately behind him as he went to the east-west runway. We took off in two kite elements, the Capt. did one circuit of the strip then started to climb for the bomber formation. I took a quick look behind and below to check on the other Mustangs, hell, it wasn't a formation forming up, it was a gaggle. Capt. Mims climbed his kite one thousand feet above the bomber formation to the right and ahead a bit. The Capt. made a training command pass then pulled up to the left side, I did likewise forming up on his left wing. I had a birds-eye view of the other kites making their passes, the fourth or fifth kite to make a pass from the right side actually dove on the bomber formation with his six fifty calibers blazing way, the damn fool didn't realize the gun switch was wired so the guns would fire whether flipped to guns and camera or just camera. In the heat of combat this was necessary, the toggle switch standing out from the instrument denoted the guns safe, up or down the pilot had guns plus the gun-sight lighting. At this time we had three or four replacement pilots from the states just freshly checked out in the Mustang, they had no fighter training as they had been instructors in the training command. They could take a Mustang off and land her but they sure as hell couldn't fly her with authority. After a pass from the left side I climbed up and away to watch the spectacle, all organization was lost. While watching I noticed two Mustangs simultaneously making passes from each side, as they both pulled up in front of the bombers they damn near collided much to my horror. The bomber formation was strung out all over the sky, a two kite element here and there was to be seen as our gaggle headed back for the air-strip. I landed immediately after the Capt. landed, there was some very raunchy landings that followed. Ed Funk landed, zig-zagged in and out of other Mustangs ahead of him as his brakes mal-functioned, finally did a mild ground-loop to avoid hitting other Mustangs parked at the west end of the run-way.

  I arrived back at our shack before Fogie did so, first thing I asked him if he knew the two pilots who damn near collided. Visibly shaken Fogie related he was one of them, he said everything got very quiet just as he thought the collision was imminent. It must have been damn close as Fogie had experienced aerial combat and close FLAK bursts were no stranger to him.

Chapter Eight

St. Trond

The day after the near disasters with the A-26 bomber formations our squadron was ordered to St. Trond, Belgium. I was scheduled for an afternoon trip, leave Laon, France, fly the trip, land at St. Trond, Belgium. We were to leave our luggage outside our shack's door for early pick-up, it didn't take me long as I was down to my B-4 bag plus my shack-up bag. I hated to leave our little home of a shack as we spent many a happy hour there and also many sweat hours thinking about impending dues.

My trip this day was down by Switzerland with Ed Funk as my wing-man. It was going to be a long one, I had Sgt. Nance top off Aggie's gas tanks by elevating the tail section to level as if in flight, the extra gallons of fuel would come in handy in case of a weather diversion. The trip was uneventful with thirty minutes of actual instrument flying, we had to be careful as Switzerland was a neutral country. Their Air Force flew the ME-109 adorned with Swiss markings, if any aircraft strayed into their airspace a couple of the ME-109's came up to escort you down to one of their air fields. After checking the weather near the Swiss border we took up a northerly heading to another check-point then northwest to St. Trond, Belgium. Sgt. Dixon and his D.F. crew were waiting to take our calls for a steer to our new airfield. Upon arriving over the field and circling before getting landing instructions one could see more than one runway, permanent buildings, and the city of St. Trond close by. After landing and parking Aggie on her new hard stand we were picked up by our operations weapons carrier for transport to our new operations headquarters then on to our new lodgings. A barracks type building housed the Sqd. pilots, tile floors, tiled latrine and showers with lots of cold and hot running water was something to behold. I immediately made good use of the showers, no more helmet baths for me. I took a short walk around the area after my shower, I discovered a swimming pool with water. I was told this airfield was a former Luftwaffe training airfield. We shared the airfield with the same A-26 Bomber Group, their trip flying wasn't as active as ours with the war winding down.

After enjoying a good supper in a spacious dining room I was informed I had a solo night trip down by the Swiss border again. The WHEELS in 9th A.F. Hdqs. were interested in something down that way, I arranged to have Aggie topped off again in case of a bad weather divert. The operations clerk shook me awake at two o'clock in the morning, waiting for me to dress then transported me to our operations building. I computed my various courses with the latest gin on winds aloft, different temperatures at various altitudes, even on a map it looked like a long trip. The first thirty minutes of the trip was smooth flying but penetrating on southeast the weather became violent, scattered broken cloud layers with gusty winds taking me up and down, it was impossible to keep the altimer and heading constant. I thought to myself that it would take a damn good German night fighter pilot to get on my ass in this weather. I flew my allotted time on the southeasterly heading, as I was turning left to take up a northerly heading the clouds broke away beneath me and there lay a lighted city directly beneath me. Hell, I was over Switzerland, my turn to a northerly direction was hastened, I entered a cloud layer also in case the Swiss had night fighters. I would like to have tooled around the skies over that lighted city but it was the wrong place at the wrong time. I flew north for my next weather check point, the weather clearing and smoothing out as I progressed. With the help of Sgt. Dixon's D.F. crew I found St. Trond and landed at day break. After a good breakfast I journeyed down to operations, it was a nice walk with permanent buildings around and trees which were well along with their foliage. I was scheduled for an afternoon trip to a point south of Berlin with Lt. Wood as my wingman. The weather was clear, I wanted to see Berlin, we flew south of the city at fifteen thousand feet. Berlin was utterly devastated, the allied bombers had done one helluva job at a great cost.

Our foursome walked back to our quarters from operations that day, it was warm enough that we carried our flying jackets over our shoulders. On the way from our quarters to our operations building earlier in the day I noticed a small cemetery of about twenty graves. As we walked by I noticed a civilian feeling around in a body bag lying next to an open grave, body juices were leaking from the bag upon the ground, I damn near stepped in it. The Belgian civilian proceeded with his task trying to locate dog tags as we passed on by. The Germans had built up a nice little cemetery with their FLAK guns around the field, it was organized and well cared for. Officer John Burgeimer particularly enjoyed strafing trains, but ran into a bit more than expected once as he later recounted: "I was returning from a weather reconnaissance mission one day when I noticed a particularly inviting train traveling along below us. I came down on the deck with my Mustang and started shooting up the engine, cars and everything in sight. On my second pass, I got into trouble. The Germans had armed everyone on the train with a weapon and they started shooting as I whizzed past. 'Whang.' I caught one right in the engine. I gained altitude while I could and headed back to the Rhine River. Once across I knew I'd be safe. The engine got worse. It sputtered, coughed constantly, and I was starting to lose altitude gradually. I was ready to bail out at the time, but decided to nurse it home. I called a 'May Day' and was picked up by a radar outfit. They led me into an emergency strip across the Rhine."

April 23, 1945. I flew Lt. Lang's wing on a 3 hour mission, Lt. Lang was a ferry pilot with lots of experience. We were toolin' in a north-easterly direction, about half-finished with our trip, with me flying wing. Off to our right also toolin' along under the 1000 ft. overcast was a JU-52. As I was starting to call it out, Lang cut in front of me and attacked the three engine transport going in the opposite direction. I followed him and stayed off to the side to cover him, keeping a sharp eye out for fighter cover. Lang made three passes and didn't' even light the JU-52 up, it cruises just under 100 m.p.h., so I called in to Lang and told him to give me a shot at it. I made a training command gunnery pass and lit him up, then throttled back and sat on his tail firing on one wing engine then the other. They both caught fire and the pilot was forced to crash land. He did a good job of crash landing, so I circled to look-out for fighters, found none in evidence, then made another pass at the downed JU-52 for conformation of the crash site. I fired above the crash site a little as people were coming out of the fuselage door. As I was sitting on that JU-52's tail I had to actually do rudder-exercise stall recoveries as I was going so slow and with the recoil of six 50 caliber guns going off stall speed was close. As we cleared the area to finish our trip, we saw a large formation of allied P.O.W.'s who were waving and had seen the whole show. We picked up a little flak then and hastened our departure. We approached the runway on the deck in tight formation and on the peel-up, Lang did a roll, I went around and did likewise. The control tower enjoyed the show.

Carlton Palmer had completed his one hundred trips tour but elected to stick around until Fogie, Ott and I completed ours. He continued to fly a trip now and then in order to feel useful, and also, to prove to himself that he could still fly combat. Carl and I at times discussed fear. I readily admitted that fear was always with me while on a trip. Carl, on the other hand, admitted nothing. He continued to accomplish feats in a Mustang, proving himself over and over again. Toward the end of the war, Carl became rather distant from Fogie, Ott and I. The three of us sometimes discussed this, but attributed Carl's behavior to combat fatigue.

The 9th Air Force headquarters got word to our squadron about an A-26 bomber that had gone down while on a mission. It had some highly secret equipment on it that had to be located. Carl immediately volunteered to lead a flight of four to attempt to locate the twin-engine bomber. After obtaining an approximate location, he started asking for volunteers. I was asked to lead the second element of the flight but politely declined. Carl didn't appreciate this, but the way I saw it, my talents had already been volunteered too many times in the past.

Carl took his flight of four to the approximate location of the downed bomber, circling at a low altitude while searching the area which was infested with German troops and their motor transport and tanks. The Germans made no effort to shoot at them as they circled the area until one of Carl's flight started strafing. Then the Germans opened fire and one kite was hit, causing a bad oil leak. Carl related this incident to me when they returned. The entire trip had been screwed up by one green pilot strafing while on a search mission. After that trip, I told Carl to hang it up since by then, he had flown one hundred and four trips. He took my advise and spent most of his time on the flight line working with our engineering officer and the crew chiefs.

One evening, during the latter part of April 1945, I asked Carl what he was doing the next morning. He informed me that he was flying to another airfield to pick up a part for our AT-6 kite. It was a nice day, and since Ott, Fogie and I weren't on the schedule, we walked to operations to see Carl off. He strapped himself into an old Mustang bordering on being war-weary, cranked up, and taxiied out to the active runway. He was followed by four P-47 Thunderbolts who had landed at our field the previous night because of bad weather at their home airstrip.

Carl did a normal take-off and started to initiate a climb-out away from the field, at which point my attention was diverted by the P-47's taking off. The flight of four were forming up as they circled left around the field at about one thousand feet when a Mustang made a pass at them. The P-47's went in all directions. Carl would get on one P-47's tail, then break off to get on another's. He was on the tail of the third P-47 when he lost the Mustang in a high speed stall caused by a full fuselage tank and the added complication of having his maneuvering speed drop to one hundred and fifty miles per hour. Carl's Mustang headed straight down for the earth, rotating as it did so. He managed to get it out of the rotation after turning one hundred and eighty degrees and went into a recovery dive to gain flying speed. I could see the nose of his Mustang coming up as he passed from view behind some trees. I fully expected to see him and the Mustang zoom back up into the sky, but instead, we heard a 'whump', then a large ball of fire and black smoke erupted into the sky.

We all started to run in the direction of the crash but then slowed down to a walk and finally stopped, just looking at that pillar of smoke. The whole incident seemed impossible to me. Carl was the epitome of a fighter pilot. When he'd first jumped the P-47's, I'd said out loud, "Get the hell outta there, Carl!" Bent over with hands on knees, I waited for the tears to start, but none came. After a while, I straightened up, then slammed my right fist into my left palm and muttered, "Son-of-a-bitch. God damn it anyhow, Carl!"

Our threesome were extremely subdued for the balance of the day and that evening, the squadron arranged for Carl's burial at a military cemetery east of Liege, Belgium.

Immediately after Carl's crash, the four P-47's had landed, all expressing their sorrow at what had happened. We didn't blame them for it hadn't been their fault. Whenever a fighter pilot is attacked, it is up to him to take evasive action, whether the attacker is a friend or foe.

That evening, I was asked if I would accompany Carl's body to the military cemetery the following morning. I deemed it an honor to do so. When I asked Fogie and Ott if they would come along and give moral support, they respectfully declined. I then asked Ed Funk who said he would be only too glad to go along.

The next morning we reported to the Bomber's Group flight surgeon's building where an ambulance was waiting. Carl's body was on a stretcher nearby, covered with a sheet. I noticed that the sheet had a tent-like shape and asked the ambulance driver if I could view my ol' buddy. As he pulled back the sheet, I was surprised to view his body whole and it was charred black. An aircraft fire is intensely hot and all of his clothes had been burned away. His right leg was fully extended, as though it were still on the right rudder pedal, his left hand was extended as if on the throttle, and his right was positioned as if it were on the stick. There could be no doubt that Carl had been flying that Mustang right up to the time it mushed into the ground. Incredibly, the fire hadn't burned Carl's silk flying scarf. It was only slightly signed and was still carefully wrapped around his neck, just as he'd always worn it. The driver, along with Ed and I, loaded Carl's body into the ambulance and then we began our journey to the cemetery. It was an exceptionally beautiful day. I thought about Carl's body in the back of the ambulance. We'd made plans for after the war, plans about going home, marrying our gals, then enrolling at a good university to further our education. Carl was interested in mechanical or electrical engineering while I was more interested in petroleum engineering. Carl had always been a hard driver. He would have tutored and made me study extensively to attain a degree.

We arrived at the cemetery located among tall fir-like trees. It was beautifully landscaped and many who were interred there were victims of the Battle of the Bulge. We were told to unload Carl's body into a squad-size tent which served as a mortuary. After the ambulance driver had arranged for a replacement stretcher, we started out on our return journey to St. Trond. As quickly as the ambulance doors were closed and we'd started on our way, we began to smell the unmistakable stench of death. The replacement stretcher had borne an American soldier who had lain for some time after falling in combat. All the windows of the ambulance were quickly rolled down to keep the odor under control.

As we passed through Liege, I spotted an ice cream parlor, and after the driver had parked nearby, the three of us ran inside like three eager children. We hadn't eaten fresh ice cream in nearly a year.

The next morning saw every pilot not scheduled to fly at the cemetery in Class A uniform. We formed a single line at the head of Carl's yet uncovered grave, and I remember leaning over for one last look. Carl's body was still in the same position as it had been on the stretcher. It was now encased in a blue and white narrow-striped bed tick. After the chaplain had said a few words, taps were sounded, which immediately brought us all to attention. After the last notes of taps had faded, we left the grave site, even as we heard the clods of earth hitting Carl's chest as the grave diggers shoveled it on top of him. Damn, but I felt sad! Carl and I had been like brothers, adversaries in a healthy sense, but also confidantes. I knew I was going to miss him very much.

While still in the cemetery, some of us had looked around and stumbled upon a cross with Dutch Holland's name on it. Sometime later, the story of his disappearance came out. After being shot down by a German night fighter, his body had been found close to his kite with the parachute deployed, it was assumed that he hadn't had enough altitude to properly utilize it. Dutch wouldn't be going home either.

My last trip of the war was that of a wingman to one of the 8th Air Force rejects. It was a clear day and staying at altitude was important.

An ME-262 German jet shadowed us for fifteen or twenty minutes but never showed any inclination to attack. I changed my position several times to keep him from gaining any advantage. I never did sweat the German jets for a Mustang could out-turn them; they were also handicapped by their short fuel supply. One simply had to keep one's head on a swivel in order to see them first.

After flying my last trip in May 1945, I had some time on my hands. One evening, while enjoying a drink at the club bar, a familiar voice behind me said, "Pop to, mister." I jumped off the bar stool and was damned near at attention when the grinning face of a former pre-flight upper-classman appeared before me. He told me to stay put, that he had someone else with him that he wanted me to meet. In a few minutes he came back with Larry Darst from St. Louis, Missouri. Larry and I had been under-classmen together during pre-flight in the same flight. Two years earlier, we had all been in pre-flight but now we were veteran combat pilots.

One evening, in this same bar, a couple of bomber pilots cornered Captain Mims and threatened to cut off his mustache. Finding an empty bottle, Captain Mims broke it against the bar's edge and stood poised and ready as the other men executed a hasty retreat. Suffice to say Captain Mims was extremely proud of his mustache.

The commander of the field announced that a victory celebration would be held at the club. All the local gals of St. Trond would be allowed on the field for the dance but were instructed to leave by noon of the following day. Toward evening, the procession of baby dolls began to arrive. I had never seen anything like it. Most of them were decent-looking, and of those who came to our barracks, I was most interested in a small brunette, but a Major of the Bomber Group soon spirited her away. Two Belgian Red Cross women in their early thirties thought I was much too young when I put in my bid for an evening's date. One was a large woman, and the other a small blonde. Eventually, they paired off with other men in the barracks.

On the way from the barracks to the club dance, I turned to see Norman Ott walking behind me. He was dressed in his summer tans, sporting a yellow tie that wasn't tucked into his shirt. He was definitely out of uniform and I immediately questioned him about the yellow tie.

"I'm a member of the Babylonian Air Force," he said. The wheels, who were in an unusually magnanimous mood that evening, never made an issue of the matter.

I left the dance around one a.m., hoping to get a decent night's rest, which wasn't all that easy to do with everyone raising hell most of the night. Late the next morning, one of the men told me that he had gone to the latrine during the night and found the big Belgian Red Cross gal sitting on the floor, stark naked. A nearby wash basin, with its water pipes broken, was spraying water all over. Apparently the girl, while in a state of drunkenness, had attempted to douch by straddling the wash basin, and just the thought of it was enough to give me my first good belly laugh since Carl's death.

A few days after the war had ended, Tom Heine and I flew our Mustangs to Nurnberg, Germany to visit a buddy of his with the 354th Fighter Group. The day before, I had told Sergeant Nance to unload Aggie's six fifty caliber machine guns. On take-off, Aggie literally leaped into the air without the burden of that extra weight. Tom did the navigating while I flew a loose formation, looking at the terrain instead of the surrounding sky. When we were within VHF radio range of the field at Nurnberg, Tom called in for landing instructions. These were promptly received along with a warning to keep a sharp look out for German fighters in the area. I felt like a damned fool, toolin' around with empty ammunition chutes, but Tom thought it was funny as hell and vowed to protect me. Since it was a short field, we touched down at the extreme end of the strip but still had to brake a lot as we rolled out. No sooner had we parked and unbuckled when a P-47 Thunderbolt came over the end of the strip, too damned hot in airspeed, landing too far down the airstrip. Applying his brakes too vigorously, he nosed over and landed upside down. As ground personnel rushed out to aid him, the fighter pilot's anxious words, "Get me outta this son-of-a-bitch!" emanated clearly from the capsized P-47.

While Tom visited with his buddy, a German liaison aircraft landed and a couple of the Group's Mustang pilots picked the German pilot up in a Jeep. Past differences were forgotten as they drove to the club for a couple of drinks, then participated in an ushered inspection of one another's aircraft.

On the flight back to St. Trond, one could clearly see that German towns of any size had been severely clobbered by the war. Even so, the countryside was beautiful with its forests, country lanes and farms, all of which had proven deadly for the combat ground forces.

The following day, Bill Budge and I flew our Mustangs into Paris to see our French baby-dolls, returning the same day. On the return flight, just after take-off I buzzed hell out of Paris, especially the Champs.

The fuselage gas tank was removed from one of our Mustangs to make a piggy-back kite of it. I asked Sergeant Nance if he would like a ride and he declined, although Captain Banks, our chief weather man, agreed to come along. The Captain was somewhat cramped, sitting behind me, but gradually relaxed as I started up. He asked me not to engage in any fancy maneuvers, for on a previous stateside ride, a really hot pilot, performing all sorts of complicated aerobatics, had made the Captain violently ill.

After take-off, we climbed to ten thousand feet over Brussels, Belgium, then gently spiraled down over the city to give the Captain a better view. We gave the country-side a married man's buzz job at one thousand feet, then landed at St. Trond. From what I could tell, Captain Banks seemed to enjoy the forty-five minute flight.

Bill Bulge asked me to accompany him to Paris for the purpose of inspecting an airfield, as per our official orders. I was only too glad to comply since this would be my last opportunity to see Martine. Sergeant Phillips' J3 Cub, which was now back in flying order, had been loaned to Bill for the flight.

Early the next morning, Bill and I walked around the little kite, and while Bill did the inspecting, I quietly observed. Once again, I was in the back seat, holding the stick back and setting the brakes with my heels. The little engine started on the second pull of the prop, and as we taxiied out, I thought we were two of the best-dressed fighter pilots ever to inspect an airfield in Paris, complete with shack bags.

A cross-country flight from St. Trond to Paris in a J3 Cub takes a lot of time. I enjoyed the French country-side as it passed below, and remember thinking that my small contribution to the war effort had been well worth it. We landed at Laon, France for a refill of eighty octane gas. Our old field was deserted, except for a custodial crew. I noticed the spire of the cathedral to the west, which seemed higher than ever. We arrived at a field near Paris a bit before noon, and after setting a time to meet three days later at the little kite, proceeded on to see our French baby-dolls.

I spent a memorable three days with Martine, visiting a few night clubs, walking and conversing in what English and French we each knew. I wanted to attend a show at the Moulin Rouge in Pigalle, but it had been placed off limits.

At the appointed time I met Bill at the little J3 Cub for our return flight. We took off at mid-morning for St. Trond, and gassed up again at Laon. The weather looked a bit stormy off to the northwest, and fifteen or twenty minutes later, the storm actually hit. Bill immediately took the Cub down to the deck to maintain visibility of Mother Earth. The forty-five mile an hour wind coming from the west brought with it sheets of rain that obscured the ground below. It would have been tough to fly a Mustang through such weather with all of its flight instruments. But I didn't sweat our immediate situation for I'd flown Bill's wing many times through bad weather. Even so, he had quite a time keeping us upright and on course with just a needle-ball, airspeed and compass to work with. But in another fifteen minutes the storm was no longer a threat for we'd managed to fly out of it.

Orders came through for me to return to the Zone of the Interior, which meant going home. I vowed to have one more "farewell" flight in Aggie, for the many trips we'd shared had made us one. Over a period of time, we'd been in every possible situation together.

Three other pilots and I took off for a mild rat race and a bit of formation flying. After an hour of toolin' around, I led them in on the deck, echelon right for a peel-up and landing. As I turned off the active runway, I glanced back and saw that the flight had all landed. They were doing their roll-outs and staggered right and left, as per training. It really brought a lump to my throat.

Carl and I had often discussed our feelings awhile flying a fighter. He'd often said that he felt as if he were buckling the fighter plane to him whenever he buckled into the cockpit. As for me, I thought that flying a fighter took the greatest concentration of mind, body and soul that any young man could ever experience.

While I was flying with the 9th W.R.S., two Distinguished Unit Citations were awarded to us. We flew a lot of trips that we weren't really supposed to return from. When the war ended, I felt as if I'd lost a close friend. I wasn't the best fighter pilot in the European Theatre of Operations, but I could turn and I could shoot and I had courage. With difficulty I admit at that time I was callused and a bit agnostic.

GOING HOME

The last part of May, 1945 saw us placed on orders for home. By now, Fogie, Tom Heine, Ott and I were the old timers of the squadron, we packed our B-4 bags and proceeded to the flight line to board a B-26 twin engine bomber for the first leg of our home-bound journey. After take-off and climb out from St. Trond airfield four Mustangs pulled up alongside us, they were from our squadron, Kansas Aggie being one of them. I managed to snap a few pictures before we reached the English Channel where they peeled off for return to base.

We made land-fall into England at about two thousand feet, looking out the tail gunner's plexiglass tail cone I noticed four or five bursts of flak at three o'clock level about two hundred yards off our right wing. The Captain flying the B-26 tooled straight ahead, hell, FLAK wasn't anything new to him or his passengers, we had seen FLAK thick enough that one could walk on it. We circled a field near Liverpool, England, entered the traffic pattern and the Captain set up to fly the pattern. When he came back on the throttles and lowered the landing gear I thought his airspeed was low, as he turned on the approach to landing then lowered flaps I knew he was too slow. A fighter pilot can feel a stall in his ass and mine told me we were close. I held my breath during the approach and sure enough when he came back all the way on the throttles and breaking his glide at the same time for the landing the left wing fell in a stall at about twenty feet above the run-way. Fortunate enough the left gear contacted the run-way first with a jarring whump. The Captain had beau coup flying time in the B-26, but hadn't flown one for three months, it's stalling speed was higher than the twin-engine A-26 bomber they had converted to at the turn of the year.

We waited in a transit camp near Liverpool for three weeks waiting on a ship for our west crossing of the Atlantic. Blackjack games broke out through the camp, two men ended up with all the camp's gambling money, these two men never did face off in a snow-down game.

Our ship was a new one, the moving of troops was it's primary purpose. Tiered canvas bottom bunks from the deck to the ceiling were the sleeping accommodations. Chow facilities was a stand up proposition, eating from a long waist high steel chrome table supported by steel chrome poles attached from the deck to the ceiling. Two meals a day were served, my experience coming over saw me in line for every meal.

After clearing port I was at the promenade deck rail getting my last look of Europe's shores I saw a familiar face down the rail aways, only he was a Captain now, hell, it was Howard Marks, the Texan from Bartow, Florida training days. Howard and his buddy Jimmy had joined the 363rd FTR.GP. With Ott, Fogie and myself only assigned to another squadron. After shaking hands I inquired of his buddy Jimmy. Howard squarely faced me and said, "Jimmy got hit bad while flying his P-47, as he was going down he kept saying over the VHF radio, mama, mama, mama, until he impacted the ground." Howard had his ever present grin on his face when he related this incident to me but it didn't include his eyes, they were full of very deep hurt. Howard also related that nothing happened to him during the war.

About thirty minutes later I recognized another familiar face from Bartow days standing at the rail gazing out to sea as if lost in deep thought. It was Rhode Island Red, the last time I had seen him was on the train from Boston to our shipping out camp when he had taken a drink from the gallon of whiskey then allowed he was a Rhode Island Red. He now wore the gold leaves of a Major. After shooting the breeze a bit I asked him how he had climbed up to Major in a year's time, he replied, "Brooksie, I just kept on livin'."

Some of the pilots I trained with at Bartow, Florida come to mind as to their eventual fates.

Porky Rheinbolt—badly injured when crash-landing his Mustang.

Norman Dixon—killed in action.

Little Joe—tail came off his Mustang while on a test hop.

Hornickle—missing over the north sea while on a recon. mission.

Chuck Dimmock—killed in action.

Steve Boren—dove into the ground while strafing.

Cooper—killed in action.

Ozzie—killed in action.

Slovak—crashed into tall trees inverted while strafing.

Selby—called Slip, put his affairs in order before we left for overseas, told his family he wasn't coming back, Slip didn't.

After a day out on our homeward bound journey we hit a storm which lasted most of the way over. I heard tell our ship had a sister ship that left port when we did, the two Captains were good friends and had a bet who could cross the quickest. I believed the story as it seemed our ship's screw was out of the water when we topped the huge waves. One meal was navy beans spiced with ketchup, first all navy bean meal I had enjoyed since entering the military. Eating it was an adventure as one's tray slid along the slick chrome table if not held by one hand. I managed to put an arm around one of the vertical table support poles, hold the food tray in position and enjoy my beans. As we left the mess room large delicious red apples were issued one each to us. I hadn't seen such an apple for a year, I enjoyed just looking at it before eating it. Later on I felt the need to pass some of the navy coffee, a journey to the head was an adventure even though my sea legs were good by now. Upon stepping up to the long trough type urinal one could see it was half full of chewed up apple.

    Our ship made a quick crossing, we disembarked, trained to the army camp and were on our way home the next day. Our westward bound train was a long one, a coal-burning steam engine pulled us along. The passenger cars were of a vintage I hadn't rode before, I'm sure they were the first put into service by our railroads. It was hot, the open windows let in the soot and cinders as we tooled along for home. Some train stations we dropped off passenger cars, most of the civilians in trains we passed were in pullman cars, windows down to enjoy their cool comfort, they got a good hazing just from our stares as some of them pulled their window shades down. Hell, we didn't give a damn, we were going home. Our particular car was dropped off at Ft. Leavenworth, Kansas. The very first thing I did after checking in was a shower and change of uniform, the only clean part of us was our faces which we rinsed while on the train. The same day saw me on a train for Topeka, on arrival, Mom, Dad, and my little sister, Marcia were there to meet me. After the greetings I looked around for my girl, Donna,—no Donna. Dad looked as though he had aged fifteen years, gray around the temples, and a bit lighter in weight. Three years of six day weeks, ten to twelve hours a day had taken its toll on him. It was good to be home again, it was good to partake of Mom's cooking again. My little brother, Larry was doing well with his swearing. My old high school coach said one could literally hear Larry for a block as he unbraided his older brother Sammy, who was a number one bugger.

    I had thirty days at home, I borrowed my old bicycle from Larry to see all of my old friends around town. I visited the mother of a former team-mate friend who wasn't home from his infantry unit as yet, she allowed I looked pretty wild.

    I had a problem of sleeping with nothing to do, I missed the excitement of action, there was no place to spend my energy. I did go see Donna a few times, the spark was still there.

    The most enjoyable incident was when Mom, Dad, Donna and I journeyed to western Kansas for Dad's World War One

Company "H" reunion. Dad's old company commander, Captain Atkins was in attendance. Dad proudly escorted me before the Captain who was seated with all his former men around him and introduced me to him. I hit a position of attention and saluted the old Captain as he arose from his chair, he returned the salute, shook my hand and said we had done a good job this time around. It was a proud moment to finally meet my Dad's World War One Commander under these circumstances, I felt like one of them.

Sgt. Nance from North Carolina and my crew-chief when I flew with the 9th Weather Sqd. filling up Kansas Aggie.

*Our Foursome with the 9th Weather Reconn. Sqd.
Left to right: Author, Elmer W. Fogelquist, Norman E. Ott, and Carleton Palmer.*

Carleton E. Palmer, a helluva pilot and a good buddy.

Headquarters
Army Air Forces Pilot School (Advanced—Single Engine)
Office of the Commanding Officer
Foster Field, Texas

January 7, 1944

Mrs. Agnes V. Brooks
Silver Lake, Kansas

Dear Mrs. Brooks:

Your son, George, graduated today at Foster Field as a fighter pilot.

Behind him now are many months of tough, hard training—training so severe that only the best qualified have made the grade. The silver wings he has won are proof that he belongs to the finest group of pilots in the world today, the Army Air Forces.

But he has learned far more than skillful flying. He has a new understanding of the qualities of tolerance, thoroughness and leadership. As an officer he knows the soldier's meaning of loyalty, of honor, and of courage.

What we, at Foster Field, have been able to teach him has been based on what he learned from you. He is a gentleman, as well as a man, and he will be a credit in peacetime as in war to his Country and his parents.

Permit me, then, to add my own congratulations to the many others due you today.

Sincerely yours,

H.H. VAN AUKEN
Colonel, Air Corps
Commanding